SHADOWS OF
RACE AND CLASS

SHADOWS OF
RACE AND CLASS

RAYMOND S. FRANKLIN

University of Minnesota Press
Minneapolis   Oxford

Library of Congress Cataloging-in-Publication Data

Franklin, Raymond S.
  Shadows of race and class / Raymond Franklin.
    p. cm.
  Includes index.
  ISBN 0-8166-1956-5 (alk. paper) :
  1. United States—Race relations.   2. Social classes—United States—History—20th century.   3. Racism—United States—History—20th century.   I. Title.
E185.61.F8   1991
305.896′073—dc20   90-32446
                                                      CIP

A CIP catalog record for this book is available from the British Library

Published by the University of Minnesota Press
2037 University Avenue Southeast, Minneapolis, MN 55414
Printed in the United States of America on acid-free paper

The University of Minnesota
is an equal-opportunity
educator and employer.

To Margery, Ken, and David

CONTENTS

Preface   ix

Acknowledgments   xi

Introduction   xiii

1
From Civil Rights to Civic Disgrace   1

2
American Slavery: Contemporary Meanings and Uses   22

3
Scientific Racism and Social Class   42

4
Economics of Dominant-Subordinate Relations   69

5
White Uses of the Black Underclass   89

6
Race-Class Connections   117

7
City as Promise? Shades and Politics of Race, Class, and Gender   136

Index   179

PREFACE

This book explores race-class relations among African-Americans in the United States from 1950 to the present. The debate about race and class and their ramifications is embedded in the civil rights movement and in the white backlash to it; in the great ongoing debate about slavery; in scientific IQism; in the behavior and status of the black middle class; and in the reality and perceived threat of the black underclass.

The current, pressing, and historically perplexing question of whether race or class determines the African-American population's subordinate position provides a key theme of this book. Answers to this question determine how people and their leaders understand the status of African-Americans and influence policies developed to eliminate racial barriers. The debates occur between whites and blacks; among radical, liberal, and conservative scholars; and among African-Americans themselves. The arguments contribute to a larger agenda of transforming American society and the quest for equality and social justice.

In my endeavor to develop a framework embracing a range of historical, theoretical, and experiential issues that exemplify the interplay between race and class, I became acutely aware of why it was necessary to bypass the major competing perspectives: rational individualism; class reductionism; and non-Eurocentric culturalism. The Introduction suggests the limitations of these major perspectives and proposes an alternative direction.

In place of the main orientations, I emphasize the unique interplay of race and class, and how they are derived from dominant-subordinate relations prevailing in a variety of economic and social contexts. The race-class connections that have developed cast shadows beyond their immediate boundaries. These shadows are manifest in the contemporary meanings and emphases given to slavery and its legacy; in the way the black middle class is perceived in relation to the status of the poorest third of the black population; in the way that the black urban underclass itself is used and perceived; and perhaps most important, in the images that blacks have, and project, of themselves.

Analyses derived from the major perspectives on black-white relations have initiated inappropriate strategies for change, and their sterile ideologies have failed to nurture a sustained dialogue between blacks and whites about America's racially divided society.

My alternative perspective is aimed at integrating analyses, strategies, and public goals. In the final chapter, I delineate the basic conditions that define the black population's present situation and propose an agenda and moral framework focused on the unfulfilled promise of city life. In reconstituting the idea of rebuilding a meaningful city life for all citizens, I simultaneously address the specific material and social needs of African-Americans.

ACKNOWLEDGMENTS

Many people have contributed to my work on this book. A number of friends and colleagues read drafts of chapters or the entire manuscript at various stages and provided important insights. I wish to express my appreciation to Paul Blumberg, Ruth Carr, Robert Factor, Barbara Tischler, Paula Rothenberg, Frank Warren, Marie Winn, and Michael Wreszin. I am particularly grateful to Jeffrey Isaac, the late Robert Lekachman, and Bertram Silverman. Each made invaluable suggestions that clarified some of the ideas developed in the book.

Portions of chapters 1, 4, and 7 appeared in *The Political Economy of Racism*, which I coauthored with Solomon Resnik (1973). I thank Solomon Resnik for his contribution to the included portions of chapters from the earlier work.

Janet Baus and Neil McLaughlin, graduate students of the City University of New York, carried out a number of tasks related to perfecting a manuscript. I appreciate their assistance.

I thank Biodun Iginla, my editor at the University of Minnesota Press, who provided many helpful suggestions for substantive and stylistic changes.

To my wife, Margery, I owe the book's title. Finding the title enabled me to bring together the disparate parts of my argument with a clarity I did not previously possess, and so marked a turning point in my thinking. I am also deeply appreciative of Margery's contribution to organizing the issues of the IQ debate discussed in chapter 3, her forbearance of my preoccupations, and her helping me to understand that a computer is more than a typewriter.

Finally, I am deeply indebted to Hylan G. Lewis, with whom I have been acquainted for many years. After he was chosen as the first occupant of the Michael Harrington Chair of Social Science at Queens College of the City University in 1990–91, our acquaintance was transformed into a working relationship and a friendship. In reading the manuscript of this book in its penultimate version, Hylan examined the substance and organization of each chapter, as well as transitions between chapters. In his characteristically thoughtful way, he pointed out errors, alerted me to nuances, and offered suggestions for changes. Not least, he encouraged me to keep my eye on the metaphor that constitutes the title of this book. I have benefited immeasurably from Hylan's deep knowledge and wisdom about race and class. His encouragement, guidance, warmth, and wit are extraordinary.

Any oversights, errors, or miscast interpretations that remain are my responsibility alone.

INTRODUCTION

Is the subordinate position of the black population ultimately derived from the stigma of color, or is it due to the black population's inferior class or economic position?[1] Even when both the race and class categories are employed, either the question of primacy is raised or class and race are affirmed simultaneously without a coherent statement about their interaction. Race is frequently employed to include unique historical roots and culture; class is often enlarged to embrace a variety of economic characteristics. The choice of category or emphasis forms the basis of arguments about the determinants of black status and the nature of discrimination. It also determines the kinds of policies and strategies advocated to eliminate racial injustices. The race-class arguments take place, moreover, within the African-American community, between whites and blacks, and among radical, liberal, and conservative scholars and leaders. Finally, and most important in my view, the race-class dialogue is transacted daily through the mass media, inside our institutions, and on the streets of our major metropolises. Lurking beneath many individual experiences and incidents, both within the separate communities and between them, are judgments that are linked, knowingly or otherwise, to either class or race logic or some confused combination of both.

When white Americans think about black criminals and hardened youth, about black dope addicts and unwed black teenage parents, about black basketball players and professional black fighters, about black intellectuals who head African-American studies programs in our academies, about the overrepresentation of graduating black seniors majoring in education, about conspicuous consumption patterns among different segments of the black population, what kinds of mind-sets are employed to cast their interpretations? Are they class and economic or race and cultural ones?

Do members of the white professional class interpret the black underclass differently from members of the black professional class? If so, is this difference in interpretation due to race or to class? Why were privileged white radical students who smashed windows on university campuses in the late sixties and early seventies casti-gated as spoiled brats who grew up with too much privilege, while black militants who also smashed windows were often classified as animals?[2] Is looting by blacks seen or remembered differently from that perpetrated by whites? When a black medical intern coming off duty from New York Hospital on the upper East Side spends ten to twenty minutes more per day trying to catch a cab than his white cohort, and when black cab drivers as well as white ones con-sciously avoid the pickup, is this rejection based on race, class, or the assumed ghettoized place of residence where race and class are often fused?

Answering these and similar questions is the task I undertake in this essay. To do so involves the synthesis of a wide range of historically rooted materials and experiences, and the application of theory in a form that captures the texture of black-white contemporary experi-ences in post-World War II American society.

What I find inadequate in most broad historical and theoretical per-spectives is their abstractness or distance from the web of social and economic realities that I observe, encounter, and know exist. Even when statistical data are presented in abundance, they often fail to cap-ture what black-white, subordinate-dominate relations are about and miss much of what we should be trying to understand. Since I pose my own race-class interactionist perspective as an alternative to a number of major contending views, I shall proceed by first depicting those ma-jor perspectives that I reject. There are three: *rational individualism, class determinism*, and *non-Eurocentric culturalism*. All these founda-tion perspectives are implicitly or explicitly in battle with each other; all have a view about the nature of the social science enterprise that is used to explain black-white relations and the overall status of African-Americans.

Rational Individualism

Gary Becker's influential book, *The Economics of Discrimination*, was the first endeavor systematically to use mainstream microeconomic theory to explain income differences between groups associated with discrimination.[3] The book's impact was perhaps related more to this fact than to what Becker actually proved through evidence about discrimination. Economists, not unlike other academic professionals, readily see truth in models they have been trained to use and aesthetically appreciate. Becker starts his argument with a notion he identifies as the "taste for discrimination" (subjective states of mind decision makers employ to guide market choices). Development of tastes is an individual affair and has no explicit source. Beginning on the demand side of the market, employing blacks or working with blacks or living next door to blacks has a disutility (negative feeling) to whites that leads to racial inequalities. In the absence of skill and educational differences (the economist's definition of productivity), additional psychic costs are incurred or experienced by whites when they must relate to blacks on equal terms. Whites, therefore, seek to avoid extra costs or seek compensation when they occur. In Becker's model, racially guided decisions are not fundamentally different from those that determine why some individuals prefer apples to oranges and, thereby, discriminate against orange growers when apples are selected:

> Discrimination and prejudice are not usually said to occur when someone prefers looking at a glamorous Hollywood actress rather than some other woman; yet they are said to occur when he prefers living next to whites rather than next to Negroes. At best calling just one of these actions "discrimination" requires making subtle and rather secondary distinctions.[4]

From this and related kinds of individual choice-theoretic hypotheses, statistical inquiries are made to explain income, wage, employment, or residential location differentials which are unrelated to productivity per se. Whites exclude blacks or demand extra compensation if required to associate with them. Underlying Becker's reasoning is an effort to equate discrimination with tastes that guide choices made by consumers or other economic agents, choices not necessarily related to the absence of knowledge about the products or factors. They are related, as I have emphasized, to individual values or psychic expressions.

The labor market is the pool from which labor is recruited and in which labor is disposed when it is no longer needed. Individuals who recruit and exclude in such markets are assumed to make decisions guided by narrow economic interests. Broader social and political ramifications of individual decisions are ignored, analyzed separately from each other, and viewed to be part of another sphere in the social structure. The differences in economic well-being between the races that cannot be explained by "objective" factors often have been taken to represent discrimination, or the economic costs of being black.[5] If some assumed cultural traits, independent of the conditions that determine the black population's status due to discrimination, are considered, income differences related to race may statistically disappear.[6] If the school system fails to educate blacks and businesses refuse to employ blacks because of their lack of education, economic discrimination does not appear in the equation. Blacks can then be legitimately rejected on the basis of productivity per se.

The sources of individual taste differences are not examined or sought; tastes, at best, are relegated to unexplained vagaries of culture that exist outside the economic order and are taken as given. In this sense there is no account taken of the possible repercussions of a "discriminatory" wage or the exclusion by the dominant group. Motivation and diligence are assumed to remain constant despite the injustices experienced by blacks. The fact that black workers may become less productive as a result of discrimination against them is a dynamic not part of Beckerian reasoning.[7]

Rational individualism avoids tracing the way organizational hierarchies constrain individual action and affect incentives.[8] Deficient educational systems, chronic economic instability, ghettoization, the absence of interclass contacts, and general subordination in the distribution of power produce individual modes of adaptation and lifestyles that are not considered by analysts who simply aggregate outcomes from aggregating individual decisions.

Becker and his numerous followers, in equating "race tastes" with general kinds of "tastes," avoid the question of why they are unable to predict or explain whether one prefers apples to oranges by observing one's skin color, but would not hesitate to predict the color of one's marriage partner through such an observation. The reason is simple: choices guided by race are not trivial, secondary distinctions derived from the vagaries of culture; they are not randomly distributed like other market values in the society, but are already patterned by institutionally determined practices.

difficulties experienced by women, blacks, and other victims of discrimination are, in the last resort, caused by worker exploitation.[17]

Erik Olin Wright, another well-known Marxist and influential scholar, in seeking to avoid class reductionism maintains nevertheless that class structures constitute the central organizing principles of societies; they shape the range of possible variations in race, ethnic, and gender relations.[18] While he finds that black-white returns to education tend to disappear when class is considered,[19] Wright nevertheless seeks to escape, albeit awkwardly, from class reductionism by suggesting that "it would be a mistake to interpret the results . . . as indicating that all racial discrimination is really disguised class oppression. . . . Social processes . . . distribute people into class positions in the first place."[20] This need to maintain a primacy of class, even when social relations appear to be its determinant, stems from a fear that without a class analysis social science is likely to slide into the "multiple oppressions" approach to understanding society. Societies, in this view, are characterized by a plurality of oppressions, each of which is rooted in a different form of domination—sexual, racial, national, economic, and so on—none having any explanatory priority over any other. Class, then, becomes just one of many oppressions, with no particular centrality to social and historical analysis.[21]

There are many unattended questions in the Marxian perspective that will be addressed in subsequent chapters on a different level. Suffice it for now to suggest that racial discord in the nonwork sphere may be more important than that found in the work sphere.[22] What values people bring to work may be as relevant as those determined by work. Furthermore, discordant relations that weaken the collective interests of workers at the firm level may lead to production disruptions and problems that raise costs. It does not follow that "divide and conquer" tactics are axiomatically in the economic interests of capitalists. As a matter of fact, the desire and capacity of white workers to exclude blacks from some industries or occupations may increase white wages more than it lowers black ones and thereby increase the total wage bill. More important, white and ethnic workers did not need capitalists to divide them from black workers; the history of organized labor from its inception to its present struggle against affirmative action has an indigenous voice.[23] White ethnic workers did their excluding job more thoroughly than any capitalist could ever have imagined. Finally, racially oriented thinking may be driven by social, moral, and cultural interests that cannot be subsumed solely under the economic structures related to profit maximization, "objective" material interests, or economic exploitation. They may even have social costs that are not beneficial to the business system as a whole.

Non-Eurocentric Culturalism

In contrast to the above orientations—that racial inequalities are the result of the aggregation of rational, individual decision makers or that they are derived from individual enterprise's objective needs in the work site that are aggregated to serve the general class interests of the whole business system—a cultural and/or non-Eurocentric perspective has also developed.[24] The cultural and non-Eurocentric categories at times overlap. Some, but not all, proponents of this view initiate their position by criticizing Marxism or some variant of class reductionism: "Marxism is inadequate because it fails to probe other spheres of American society where racism plays an integral role—especially the psychological and cultural spheres."[25] Or, in the words of two radical culturalists seeking to break away from Marxism, it is believed by many radicals (Marxists et al.) that "the focus on class . . . could permit communication across the chasms and gulfs that separate minority communities and racial minorities as a whole from the white working class."[26] Radicals, in this critique, "failed to grasp the comprehensive manner by which race is structured into the U.S. social fabric."[27]

The culturalists (race advocates), in the course of rejecting class reductionism, also reject the liberal, pluralistic methodology that emphasizes a multiple number of factors without any one necessarily being central. Like the Marxists, the culturalists, at the extreme, argue for the primacy idea, which, of course, is race rather than class:

> [Race] is a fundamental organizing principle of social relations.
> . . . At the micro-level, race is a matter of individuality, of the
> formation of identity. The ways in which we understand
> ourselves and interact with others; the structuring of our
> practical activity—in work and family, as citizens and as
> thinkers. . . . At the macro-level, race is a matter of collectivity
> of the formation of social structures: economic, political and
> cultural/ideological.[28]

Pushing the argument beyond the boundaries of the United States and the history of capitalism, Cornel West reminds us that racism predates capitalism: "Its roots lie in the earlier encounters of Europe, Africa, Asia and Latin America. . . . Racist folktales, mythologies, legends, and stories that function in the everyday life of common people predate the 17th and 18th centuries."[29] This mode of approaching racism casts a very wide net; it sees racism as part of a Eurocentric civilization that embraces "three discursive logics: Judeo-Christian, scientific, and psycho-sexual discourses [that] . . . have been employed to justify racist practices."[30]

From Eurocentric religion we learn that "black skin is a divine curse."[31] From scientific logic, which promotes, among other things, the "activities of observing, comparing, measuring, and ordering physical characteristics of human bodies," we acquire notions of "black ugliness, cultural deficiency, and intellectual inferiority."[32] From Eurocentric psychosexual discourse, we acquire the view that Africans are imbued "with sexual prowess [and that non-Europeans are] either cruel revengeful fathers, frivolous carefree children, or passive longsuffering mothers. . . . Non-Europeans (especially black people) [are associated] with dirt, odious smell, and feces."[33] The race advocates, when generalized, argue that "racist practices directed against black, brown, yellow and red people are an integral element of U.S. history, including present day American culture and society."[34]

This extreme historicism, with its trans-epocal view of racial categorizing by white Europeans, not only leads to a rejection of many current tenets of Western civilization, but it comes close to suggesting that white supremacy is biosocially determined. Such a pure race emphasis necessarily leads to nationalist exhortations, strategies, and programs. More problematic is the fact that "people of color" are called upon—as if minorities of color had common grievances—to oppose Eurocentric civilization and/or U.S. hegemony. Native Americans, Hispanics, Puerto Ricans, Asian-Americans, and others are thematically clustered and identified as being oppressed and culturally dominated by a common white source.[35]

Each of these foundation approaches is muted in practice and often, depending upon the context, is combined with the others in inconsistent ways; for example, a class emphasis, often used for political reasons, leads to race-specific programs.[36] Nationalist ideologies frequently require polices dependent on white transfers or benign white cooperation.[37] These inconsistencies are not necessarily wrong if they are understood as part of the paradoxes of liberal, democratic social orders. But the advocates of one-dimensionally driven perspectives are not comfortable with such paradoxes or contradictions and rarely respect the social orders in which they articulate their case.

Each of the foundation perspectives is driven by an initial assumption that ultimately derails the perspective from a compelling analysis with appropriate strategies and policies. Rational individualists begin with the axiom Know Thyself and neglect the institutions that determine the self. Class determinists begin with the need to know "thy" economic class and neglect other collectivities that determine conflict and affect change. And non-Eurocentric culturalists affirm the necessity to know "thy" cultural or geographic roots and neglect the need to use existing institutions and circumstances that are unrelated to the historically determined trajectories. Each of these primary launching assumptions is inadequate and tends to take the social science enterprise down a path that makes it less useful than it might otherwise be. They tend to create models or orientations that are removed from the real experience of the subjects whom they are seeking to understand. While each provides partial insights, none generates clear strategies and interventionist policies appropriate to a liberal, democratic market system like our own.

Having eliminated from consideration the three major perspectives—rational individualism, class reductionism, and non-Eurocentric culturalism—it is legitimate to ask what remains. The answer is to focus on the wide repercussions of a chronic condition: consequential portions of the black population have been historically and are at present overrepresented in subordinate economic and social positions. By concentrating on the nature of subordination that defines black-white relations, it becomes possible to integrate history, theory, and experience in ways that address the enduring economic and social injustices inflicted on African-Americans.

Race-Class Interactionism

There is a dynamic and reactive interplay between race and class that is frequently absent in the analysis of black-white relations. Central to my analytical framework is how race relates to class and class to race over time and in varying social and organizational contexts. This book, therefore, is not about a narrow range of economic differences per se, nor about how race and class each separately determine differences in black-white conditions. In this sense my orientation differs from authors whose works either avoid the race-class nexus by focusing on individual-level characteristics or proceed from assumptions that either emphasize class domination in work site relations or race degradation as rooted in Eurocentric history and culture.

My alternative approach is developed in less universal or global terms; its backdrop is specific to the United States. This is not to reject comparative analysis as a matter of principle, but I believe that black-white relations in the United States can be explored more insightfully by emphasizing their unique dimensions. African-American uniqueness, in my judgment, is more profound than similarities employed to demonstrate commonalities.

This more circumscribed focus is justified for a number of reasons. First, the history of African-Americans from enslavement to the present has a presence in the larger drama of American life that makes the historical relevance of black-white relations qualitatively different from that of other racial minorities. As a group in struggle for social justice, African-Americans have induced periodic constitutional and social crises responsible for shifting the whole direction of our national deliberations about ourselves as a nation and a democracy.

Second, whites in all strata of American society manifest perceptions of a distorted and misanthropic nature that have a greater breadth, depth, and durability than those held about other discriminated-against minorities who constitute the American mosaic. African-American biological features, when associated with class and cultural differences, are more indissoluble than ethnic differences in the absence of biological ones. Race ideology as it applies to African-Americans, we are reminded, is ever present and "helps insiders make sense of the things they do and see—ritually, repetitively—on a daily basis."[38] Race thinking and interpretations of events, even when incorrect, provide coherence to both whites and blacks, albeit for different reasons. In other words, race ideology and its everyday uses and validation may be false from a scientific view, but they are socially real and cannot be readily ignored as long as the actual routines and activities of everyday life are maintained. Breaking away from the perennial patterns of activity is a necessary precondition to eliminating the ideological categories that explain and justify the animosities embedded in everyday practices.

Third, while race categorizing is sociohistorically rooted, in the United States it is almost exclusively reserved for African-Americans to signify status and not physical features.[39] Thus, "havin' a little Negra blood in ya'—just one little teeny drop and a person's all Negra."[40] What this means when applied to African-Americans is complex. Physical features are instrumental to status degradation because African-American features have social associations and meaning to both whites and blacks. "Blood" ancestry is also relevant—even without identifiable physical features—if the ancestry is African-American. Yet, the story of one's status changes if one's accent is foreign. Foreign blacks are identified by their national origin. This problem becomes manifest for U.S. census takers when they survey Hispanics. Members of the same family may well fall under three different categories: white, Hispanic, or black.[41]

Finally, the larger arena of oppressed ethnic-racial communities embracing Caribbeaners, Latinos, Asian-Americans, Filipinos, and others, does not constitute a seamless or interrelated web, a cohesive social and political group with shared sentiments toward whites. The system of chauvinism that has affected their respective well-being is not shared with each other or with African-Americans. In many vital respects, a number of these oppressed minorities in fact possess racist sentiments toward African-Americans. Recent slurs by the Japanese and the black conflict with Korean grocery-store owners are just the tip of the iceberg.[42] Just as African-Americans who visit Kenya learn that they are viewed as American tourists, Caribbeaners make distinctions as revealed by a Haitian college student's comment: "When I am with whites, I am black. When I am with blacks [African-Americans], I am Haitian."[43] And, in a pilot survey aimed at measuring race or class reactions to ambiguous situations that involved some form of discrimination, West Indian blacks overwhelmingly interpreted the situation in terms of class bias or as class and a "little" race bias, whereas African-Americans almost uniformly saw race as the only factor in their interpretation.[44] Class as used here, and as I use it throughout this book, perhaps needs to be defined before I proceed to delineate the structure of my framework.

Class is not an a priori abstraction defined by relations in the work sphere independent of its meaning in everyday routines and perceptions. In this sense, airline pilots who sell their labor power to private companies for $40,000 or more per year are not in the same class as those who sell their labor power for much less. Their structural "togetherness" has no social meaning for my purposes here. While I am closer to the Weberian definition of market capacity to command income in the labor market, either as an individual or as an affiliate of an organized group, this definition is also too restricted for my interests.

Class, for the purposes at hand, constitutes the individual's or group's average ability (actual or potential) to communicate command capacity in three spheres: the labor market, the consumer market, and the internal market of enterprises. It should be further noted that actual capacities may be more or less than those communicated, or they may be communicated in ways detrimental to the individual's success. Actual capacities may also be at variance with the way the dominant group evaluates what is communicated by the subordinate one. Black families whose incomes are identical to those of whites may be forced to communicate their consumption capacities in ways that have differential consequences. A big, fancy car driven by a black person is not interpreted by whites in the same way that whites interpret "their own" conspicuous forms of "making it."

While the different spheres of communicating command capacities are related, the attributes that determine the actual or potential communication of command capacity vary and can be known only through empirical investigation. Communicating a command capacity to acquire entry into an enterprise does not mean that the same attributes will work inside the enterprise as one seeks to enhance one's career. Individuals with identical incomes may not have the identical communication capacities to purchase the same bundle of goods related to well-being. The individual's group identity, or its absence, will affect the capacity to communicate command. An aggressive white male inside an enterprise may be seen as having the kind of attributes that are valued; the same attributes for an African-American may serve as a barrier. The inability to buy a home through the capital markets in a desirable location, however adequate the income and secure the employment, could well determine one's accumulation of wealth and thereby eventually affect one's communication of command capacity in other spheres in which individuals or groups must function.

Since the communication of command capacity differs systematically when race becomes one of its determining attributes, race and class are defined in relation to each other. But to understand the dynamic and reactive interplay of the race-class nexus, to view its operation and trace its varying patterns, one needs not only to differentiate among kinds of markets, but also to examine some subtle differences within similar markets.

Shadows of Race and Class

African-Americans themselves—religious and secular leaders, scholars and writers, middle-class professionals, workers, welfare recipients— have a history of engagement and struggle over the meaning of the American experience in its various modes and of the uses to which the social sciences are put in the exploration of issues concerned with family, community, education, intelligence, values, class, and race. This long-standing engagement is unlike that of any other ethnic-racial group. That is why

> in the United States, there are scholars and black scholars,
> women and black women. Saul Bellow and John Updike are
> writers; Ralph Ellison and Toni Morrison are black writers.

George Bush and Michael Dukakis were candidates for president; Jesse Jackson was a black candidate for president.[45]

Or as John Hope Franklin further remarked upon publication of his most recent book, *Race and History: Selected Essays, 1938–1988*, when he was asked what role race has played in determining his specialization as a historian,

> It's often assumed I'm a scholar of Afro-American history, but the fact is I haven't taught a course in Afro-American history in 30-some-odd years. They say I'm the author of 12 books on black history, when several of those books focus mainly on whites. I'm called a leading black historian, never minding the fact that I've served as president of the American Historical Association, the Organization of American Historians, the Southern Historical Association, Phi Beta Kappa, and on and on. The tragedy . . . is that black scholars so often have their specialities forced on them.[46]

However accomplished John Hope Franklin may be — as a historian, as a historian of the whole South or of the whole nation — and whatever division of labor he may wish to project as constituting his identity, he is forced to reflect the shadow cast upon his black self that W. E. B. Du Bois's oft-repeated observation revealed:

> The Negro is . . . born with a veil, and gifted with second sight in this American world — a world which yields him no true self-consciousness, but only lets him see himself through the revelation of the other world. It is a peculiar sensation, this double consciousness, this sense of always looking at one's self through the eyes of others, of measuring oneself by the tape of a world that looks on in amused contempt and pity.[47]

The shadow cast on individual blacks emanates from the group characteristics of "all" blacks. This process has many consequences and a variety of dimensions. It constitutes one of the main dynamics of the race-class nexus that I develop in chapter 6. The race-class connection itself emerges from the aggregation of dominant-subordinate relations in most spheres of American life. This is explored in chapter 4.

The general proposition that I demonstrate involves how the overcrowding of blacks in the lower class — which thoughtful whites often identify as a "pure" class issue derived from the deficiency of skills, education, and so on — casts a shadow on middle-class members of the black population that have credentials but are excluded or discriminated against on racial grounds. Middle-class black reactions to this shadow vary: they have internal and external dimensions. The internal dimension involves examining the intraclass and gender differences in well-being and outlook among blacks themselves. The external dimension requires an examination of the debates between the races. The internal and external debates are not similar. Thus, understanding the race-class nexus requires an examination of race relations between the populations and the interplay of class differences within the separate racial communities. White middle-class responses to upward mobility endeavors by the black middle class are often related to concerns about the black lower class. In a similar vein, the black middle-class outlook is frequently conditioned by the status of the black lower class.

The dynamics of the race-class nexus, it should be further noted, unfold differently in varying contexts. The variations in labor markets, the internal markets of enterprises, and sites in which consumption patterns are communicated limit or extend the impact of the race-class dynamics with regard to the allocation of blacks and whites in the microspheres of society. In these latter spheres, dominant-subordinate rule tends to be followed. But dominant-subordinate patterns vary in subtle ways and depend upon variations in the mechanisms, sources, and forms of discrimination on the one hand, and types of commodities produced or sold and the technologies used in production on the other. The micropatterns established along a dominant-subordinate axis determine and are determined by the interplay between race and class on the more aggregate level; both inform each other in the course of their related movements.

The nature of dominant-subordinate relations and of the race-class connections is embedded in black affirmations, white reactions, and black-white debates over a range of issues that make up the history of the past forty years. These center on the civil rights and black power movements, white backlash, the legacy of slavery, scientific IQism, rules governing black-white economic relations, the status of the black middle class, the rise of the black underclass, the central city/suburban division along racial lines, and a range of issues focused on community, family, and gender.

The concluding arguments of this book extend the implications of my analysis in the context of the central city's decline. I develop an agenda concerned with rescuing our cities from decay, building communities, and restructuring family life in ways that embrace the needs of African-Americans and the larger white society.

FROM CIVIL RIGHTS TO CIVIC DISGRACE

The hopeful changes many expected from the civil rights movement in the sixties proved unwarranted. By the mid-seventies, many liberals and conservatives had come to believe that the civil rights movement had outlived its usefulness.[1] Throughout the first half of the eighties we witnessed a resurgence of racially motivated incidents throughout the country that appeared to signify a hardening of white resistance and a serious interruption in the economic progress and social integration of blacks. These developments constitute the "disgrace" that informs the title of this chapter.

In the course of the civil rights movement's relative success in the legal and political sphere, followed by its relative disappointment in the economic and social one, a number of derivative issues emerged that became integral to the black population's struggles for a fundamental change in status. These issues include the legacy of slavery, IQ-ism, the juxtapositioning of a growing black middle class and the rise of a black underclass, black male-female relations and family patterns; they became a subtext in a broad debate about relationships of race and class in American society. This chapter establishes the changing context in which these issues emerged.

The interpretive emphasis is focused through the stereoscopic lenses of race and class. Rather than accepting one or the other, or reducing one into the other, I argue that black-white conflict can best be understood by the specific interplay between race and class as they unfold in history, are constructed in theory, and, not least, are employed to make meaning out of everyday experiences. This requires looking simultaneously at race differences between populations and class divisions within the separate racial communities. Because of the failure of scholars, politicians, activists, and ordinary citizens to understand the complex pattern and structure in which race and class interact between and within communities, the oscillating shadows that both cast are not understood and identified.

America's New International Role

When World War II ended, the leaders of our political institutions inherited a cluster of embarrassments. We fought and won a war against fascism, in opposition to the idea of a master race and notions of racial superiority. We inherited the role of international police and leaders of the Western world against a backdrop of rising Third World nationalism, especially on the continent of Africa. We soon became engaged in a cold war with the Soviet Union and consequently found ourselves competing for the allegiances of these newly formed nations. Both liberal anticommunists and conservatives agreed that racial segregation and overt discrimination had to end, if for no other reason than the fact that such practices interfered with our struggle against international communism. Walter Reuther, addressing the fiftieth anniversary meeting of the NAACP, warned that segregation "can be American democracy's Achilles heel in Asia and Africa where the great millions of the human family live."[2] Acting secretary of state Dean Acheson wrote:

> The existence of discrimination against minority groups in the
> United States is a handicap in our relations with other
> countries. The Department of State . . . has good reason to
> hope for a continued effectiveness of public and private efforts
> to do away with these discriminations.[3]

Similar utterances were made by prominent black leaders up to and beyond the 1954 *Brown* v. *Board of Education of Topeka* decision.[4] U.S. officialdom was ready, even if the American people were not, for legal changes, if properly pressured.

As the patriotic outpouring of "brotherly" love among all races, creeds, and colors dwindled soon after World War II, the postwar "normalcy" patterns established themselves. American people immersed themselves in their work, getting ahead, accumulating consumer goods, and enlarging their families. On a few major university campuses, a minority of radical and liberal students struggled against the quota system in professional schools that required photographs and other such information that would clearly identify one's religion, ethnicity, or race. And while the NAACP was working arduously and continuously at undermining the legal foundations of segregation,[5] it was still possible up to the early 1950s to find nationally used high school and college textbooks writing mythological histories about happy slaves, the implications of which were extended to embrace the willingness of contemporary blacks to accommodate to their subordinate position.[6]

Stereotypical history and its depictions are always difficult to destroy, especially if the subordinate group has pariah status. Nevertheless, the landmark Supreme Court decision in May 1954, *Brown* v. *Board of Education*, triggered a chain of actions and reactions that permanently shifted black-white relations and uprooted typical images established in white minds since the earliest days of our history. The unanimous declaration, overturning *Plessy* v. *Ferguson* (1896), that segregation was inherently unequal and damaging moved key aspects of the struggle from the de jure to the de facto level.

The Civil Rights Struggle

The most significant single event to follow the *Brown* v. *Board of Education* decision was the Montgomery bus boycott, which began in 1955 when Mrs. Rosa Parks refused to surrender her bus seat to a white man upon command by the bus driver. The boycott, which lasted one year, injected a new sense of collective power and pride into the black community and brought moral and financial support from northern middle-class whites and union leaders;[7] it also represented a new combination of class forces and conflict in the southern context. Many older black middle-class leaders, whose strategies for change mainly involved appeals to and deals with members of the "responsible" white elite, linked themselves to a new stratum of young clergy who were educated and had matured in the post-World War II period.[8] These younger religious leaders had assimilated more fully the spirited struggles for nationhood by Third World nations.[9] To this must be added the new black urban working class that also emerged from World War II.[10] Last, the rise of a sizable southern business class should not go unnoticed. Unlike the rural white planters whose manifest racism could ignore the mood of the rest of the country when they intimidated isolated black farmers, the urban businessmen, with regional and national competitors, worried daily about downtown sales affected by the boycott.[11]

The Montgomery experience had a ripple effect and led to desegregation struggles in a number of southern cities.[12] Perhaps of greater importance, the boycott validated the mandate for demonstrations to integrate not only buses, but lunch counters, restaurants, libraries, churches, theaters, amusement parks, beaches, and, more generally, "any public business licensed by the state."[13] While these varied tactics were for the most part aimed at breaking down the walls of de facto segregation, which now was officially illegal, their use required considerable courage and involved a radical departure from the slower legal testing procedures and standard pressure group politics. The tactics were seen as a threat to the social order. They were perceived by many whites as a "territorial" invasion that violated the property owner's sense of prerogatives and freedom to choose, which to blacks meant white freedom to exclude. Insofar as the state has an obligation to maintain order and protect private property, the demonstrators, as a sign of their own commitment, were ready to accept violence against themselves in order to raise the moral conscience of the nation. The white majority at this time, it should be recalled, had little immediate sympathy with black causes and social journeys. But insofar as the national government had an obligation to enforce the law of the land, which included, of course, the Supreme Court decision, black struggles were legitimate. Thus, the march of events from 1954 to the march on Washington in 1963 put the national government in an ambiguous position. With TV cameras reporting violence against blacks around the world on the one hand, and the legal legitimacy of black goals on the other, federal troops reluctantly and hesitatingly were used to protect black protesters. In the course of these events, local white southern extremists (White Citizens Councils) grew in alarming strength, driving white urban moderates into a state of limbo. A race war was in the making. Polarization within the southern white community was matched by the emergence of the Student Nonviolent Coordinating Committee (SNCC) in mid-1960, a group soon perceived as a more militant alternative to Martin Luther King, Jr.'s Southern Christian Leadership Conference. Civil rights concerns previously viewed as leading edge demands of the black middle class gradually turned into social justice and black power demands under the youthful SNCC leadership. The struggle to desegregate Birmingham in the spring of 1963, followed by the march on Washington in August of the same year, marked a turning point.

The Birmingham battle called into operation every segment of the black population, including the working class, the lower class, and young children.[14] Demonstrators filled the jails; downtown business came to a standstill; Sheriff Eugene ("Bull") Connor, a symbol of southern racism, responded with "dogs, firehoses, and clubs" to some SNCC stone throwers. He also turned the hoses and dogs on perfectly peaceful demonstrators. The events of Birmingham "caused a national revulsion," leading to the capitulation of Birmingham's business community.[15] Following the march on Washington that drew two hundred thousand persons from all parts of the country—black and white, young and old, rich and poor, union and nonunion—John F. Kennedy's proposed civil rights bill was approved by Congress.[16]

The summer of 1964 marked the Mississippi Summer Project. Large numbers of northern white college students, fired up with a sense of idealism, descended on Mississippi in a voter registration drive. Whites learned personally about rednecks and life-threatening terror just by exercising what was viewed as a normal right "back home." A significant number of blacks experienced a sense that whites were taking over. It was said of whites that they were "running offices, freedom schools, and campaigns by virtue of their superior education and the sole fact of their being white, and that they thereby prevented blacks from controlling their own movement."[17] Compounding this loaded situation, some white women "became sexually involved with black men," an issue that had explosive political and racial dimensions in Mississippi.[18] In the course of the personal becoming political, a black feminist affirmation emerged—an issue to which we shall return at a later juncture.[19]

Between 1963 and 1966, the crescendo of demands for civil and voting rights rose to unprecedented levels and spilled over into western and northern urban centers. These non-southern voices were less focused on civil and voting rights and more on jobs, urban renewal, welfare, schooling, health care, job training, slum conditions, and, not least, desegregation in housing. The outcome was not only the passing of the Civil Rights Act (1964) and Voting Rights Act (1965), but also President Lyndon Baines Johnson's announcement of his War on Poverty. Some of these programs focused on race-specific problems and issues and became a source of white backlash in subsequent years.[20] These included Johnson's executive order on affirmative action, preferential treatment intent, federal funding of local control and participation to fight city hall, and compensatory education.

Simultaneous with the War on Poverty there emerged, beginning in 1966, the black power movement. The minority voice of Malcolm X, which had persisted unflinchingly alongside King's broader-based civil rights movement between 1954 and 1963, now received national attention. De facto desegregation proved more difficult to eliminate than de jure. In some situations, class differences between black and white school districts frequently appeared too substantial, given the pace of events, to sustain integration goals and interracial alliances. But in many other communities, rhetorical euphemisms developed to obstruct integration. Whites used class—even in the absence of serious class differences—when they meant race. And when class differences were clearly absent, "cultural differences" often became the excuse to prevent integration. Finally, even when desegregation occurred—with or without class differences between the races—it often led to resegregation within schools. Thus, alleged class and cultural differences between the races prevented the momentum of the civil rights movement from achieving genuine integration of the established black middle and working classes with their white counterparts.

In any event, the frustrations and expectations of the black middle class were an important factor in the emergence of the black power ideology among SNCC organizers. Distinguished by their youth and nonministerial origins, SNCC leaders such as Stokely Carmichael and John Lewis represented a new breed of southern-based, college-educated blacks.[21] They constituted yet another wave of leadership as SNCC began to compete with the Southern Christian Leadership Conference.[22]

Black Power: 1966–72

Under the general rubric of black power, four themes developed between 1966 and 1972. Although some of these themes are not novel, they were articulated with new energy and defined by the history-making civil rights movement that preceded it. Black community development, black capitalism, cultural nationalism, and revolutionary nationalism all embraced a common ideology: the need for black identity based on some combination of race and culture, the need for black self-determination, and the need to overcome white economic and cultural domination.[23] Whatever the emphasis, black power advocates always opted for independent forms of action. In the economic sphere, independent action meant controlling resources to develop some fraction of a racially based economy. Politically, race advocates argued for their own ideology and legislative agenda. For the cultural domain, they focused on the "positives" of black history and experience, returning, if necessary, to the glories of the black population's preslave roots. In principle, although not always in fact, black power advocates eschewed alliances with whites and glossed over status and interest differences within the black community.

A brief comment about each specific theme will serve to illuminate the differences among them. Black community development was discussed in terms of community control. The main innovative dimension revolved around the creation of ghetto-based resource and financial planning agencies in the form of community development corporations. The goals of these corporations were, first, to implement the creation of ghetto-based enterprises to absorb some portion of unemployed and underemployed blacks; second, to improve the competitive performance and quality of existing ghetto enterprises owned by black capitalists; and third, to acquire sufficient political power and autonomy to affect the flow of resources out of the ghetto, as well as to extract resource transfers from "foreign" exploiters.

These activities were racially unifying to the extent that they relate to the unemployed black masses, to some black businesspersons, to black professionals and technicians who sought to employ their human capital know-how in service to the black community, and to the black politicians and ideologues who saw the need to develop effective electoral constituencies and the perpetuation of black power ideas in general.[24]

Black capitalism, our second black power theme, had a more limited vision, although it was often advertised as more realistic since it had the endorsement of the white establishment.[25] Black capitalism as an instrument of black salvation has a long history of failure in a variety of guises. These range from grand visions of black retail chain stores, manufacturing plants, development banks and enterprise zones to the modest policies of the Small Business Administration for what are essentially family entrepreneurial undertakings in and on the margins of ghettos. Black capitalism is consistent with conservative self-help schemes and the urging of black workers to internalize self-discipline and the work ethic.[26]

Cultural nationalism, the third black power theme, involved a number of general scenarios: nativism, a focus on the portion of the black experience derived from Africa; a liberation struggle from the bonds of white supremacy and from the internalized self-denigration associated with enslavement;[27] and, not least, overcoming the black "identity crisis" associated with the destruction of the black cultural and historical heritage by emphasizing, publicizing, and developing black contributions to civilization and American society. An inspired cultural nationalism requires the development of a black intelligentsia on a scale much larger than that envisioned years earlier by W. E. B. Du Bois.[28]

Revolutionary nationalism, the last of the black power themes, is distinguished by its utopian economic program and its focus on direct action tactics and supermilitant rhetoric. Whereas cultural nationalists tended to say little that was specific in the area of altering the economy, the revolutionary nationalists, in the spirit of Marxism-Leninism, projected the need for black ownership of "banks and industries and stores"; control of "local, state and national governments, courts and police forces"; [and] a consequential role in the administration of "schools, and universities, churches, public places, foundations, etc."[29] Since revolutionary nationalists aimed at altering the class structure, their implicit logic required class alliances with white workers; their actual organizing style emphasized race.

The Backlash

The density of the supermilitant spirit—which was part real and part a media creation—had to have a short life.[30] It burned too fast to evolve and endure. It provoked a profound backlash among all strata of white American society, and provoked a limited backlash among some segments of the black community as well. The story of this backlash constitutes the next phase of the black struggles for full and equal status. This phase began "officially" in 1972 with Daniel Patrick Moynihan's "benign neglect" statement:

> The time may have come when the issue of race could benefit from a period of benign neglect. The subject has been too much talked about. The forum has been too much taken over by hysterics, paranoids, and boodlers. . . . We may need a period [in which] extremists are [denied] opportunities for martyrdom, heroics, histrionics or whatever.[31]

Burned and hurt by the liberal and black community's rejection of his black family plan in l968 with its reference to the pathological status of the black family whose initial dependent and matrifocal characteristics were allegedly determined by enslavement, Moynihan had drifted into the Nixon administrative fold. Under the banner of "law and order," conservatives aimed their political guns at putting down white university student disruptions and black street protests. Even before Moynihan's call for "benign neglect," the white backlash was under way in a variety of forms.

In reaction to the perceived failure of the War on Poverty, Arthur Jensen, education professor at the University of California, kicked up a storm in his 1969 article on differences in IQ between blacks and whites.[32] After "proving" through a vast array of statistics that roughly 80 percent of an individual's intelligence is inherited, Jensen concluded that compensatory education for blacks had failed because of their inferior biological endowment. Blacks are not educable in the same way as whites, and, therefore, investment in their intellectual development is a waste of resources.

As university-based black power advocates pushed for the creation of black studies departments and curriculum changes to reflect the history and nature of the black experience, white ethnic students quickly responded with "me too." If a black studies program is to be created, why not an Irish or Italian or a Greek or a Jewish studies program? Do not we white ethnics likewise have legacies and problems that need appreciation and understanding? This issue became most acute as black and Jewish interests acted out their respective scenarios.[33] Because black power rhetoric was identified with Third World peoples, it often became anti-Israel and anti-Semitic. As a result, the traditional black-Jewish alliance on campuses to end discrimination and bigotry dissolved. Thus, what started as a black academic demand to create a curriculum that would compensate for the cultural genocide experienced by blacks fed into a white backlash. Ethnic demands produced instead interethnic rivalry and balkanization on many large university campuses.

Gradually, the culturally diverse ethnic programs, often underfinanced, became a form of cultural window-dressing within the larger and typical liberal arts curriculum. Traditional departments began introducing a range of ethnic courses that further reduced the need for minority students to find identity by becoming an ethnic studies major. Perhaps, as Jesse M. Vazquez suggests, "outside forces will revitalize the reasons that gave birth to black studies programs."[34] I am more doubtful about such possibilities.

Probably the most critical backlash was stimulated by school busing of blacks into white neighborhoods to achieve the mandatory goals of integration. Busing was viewed as an invasion by blacks into white turf, which included not only "their" schools, but also "their" communities, "their" parks, and "their" shopping areas. "Their" constituted an invisible territorial sovereignty assumed in each white neighborhood when blacks moved into it. The whites most affected by these alleged black invasions were the more affluent blue-collar workers and lower-middle-class white-collar ones. It was the stratum immediately above the black community, not the upper-middle-class professionals residing in the much richer suburbs, that felt most threatened by busing orders from the courts.[35]

As the struggle for integration spread, the currents of the blacklash reduced themselves to a more general rejection of the twelve or so major central cities throughout the nation in which poor blacks had become concentrated. This was noted by the liberal urban sociologist Herbert Gans:

> Most voters—and the politicians that represent them—are not inclined to give the cities the funds and powers to deal with poverty, or segregation. This disinclination is by no means as arbitrary as it may seem, for the plight of the urban poor, the anger of the rebellious, and the bankruptcy of the municipal treasury have not yet hurt or even seriously inconvenienced the vast majority of Americans. . . . Many Americans . . . are opposed to significant governmental activity on behalf of the poor and black. . . . Not only do they consider taxes an imposition on their ability to spend their earnings, but they view governmental expenditures as economic waste. . . . In effect, then, the cities and the poor and the blacks are politically outnumbered. This state of affairs suggests the . . . most important reasons for the national failure to act: the structure of American democracy and majority rule.[36]

Between 1972 and the election of Ronald Reagan in 1980, civil rights groups activated their concern for affirmative action.[37] A new stratum of black college students had risen who were seeking entry into professional schools and middle positions in the bureaucracies that ran public and private enterprises. This effort emerged in a larger economic context marked by "stagflation"—slow growth, creeping unemployment, and inflation. Real income in this period for large numbers of blue- and white-collar workers had become stagnant and even declined. Maintaining family living standards often took two full-time income earners. The acuteness of this new condition of stagflation was accompanied, moreover, by a diminishing faith in the federal government to correct the situation with policies that would increase output and employment and stabilize prices. In fact, the government was increasingly perceived as part of the problem rather than as part of the solution.

In this context, neoconservative scholars and pundits consolidated their attack on the welfare society and reaffirmed the virtues of the self-propelled market system. Welfare policies, once celebrated for their success, increasingly became viewed as the black nemesis that maintained black dependency on state subsidies.[38] As real income declined for the lower middle classes, the tax burden could readily be blamed on the cost of the welfare system that sustained blacks who were unwilling to work.[39]

As more middle-class blacks in the seventies found jobs and acquired middle-income status, especially among two-income families,
they moved to the periphery of the central city or into marginally integrated suburbs; paradoxically, some returned to settle in the South
they have traditionally fled.[40] In any event, they abandoned, like many
whites before them, the older urban neighborhoods and, in doing so,
they contributed to the increased concentration and isolation of the
black poor and underclass that continued to reside in the inner cities
throughout the nation.

These various currents of change in the seventies proved conceptually unsettling for black intellectuals and leaders. The demise of the
black power and separatist upsurge precipitated a confusing debate
about whether race or class now composed the foundation of racism
and the black malaise. The submerged civil rights leaders, having succeeded in the sixties in changing the legal structure, reemerged with a
focus on affirmative action. Both the former black power advocates
and civil rights leaders moved in the direction of integrationist goals.
Both groups tended to avoid entering into a public debate about the
continued destruction of the black family and the growing black
underclass, a matter that was finally corrected with a vengeance in the
mid-eighties by William Julius Wilson's book *The Truly Disadvantaged.*[41]

Imamu Amiri Baraka's disillusionment with Kenneth Gibson's mayor-
alty in Newark led to the most celebrated black separatist conversion
of the mid-seventies, and it illustrates well the pervasive intellectual
confusion of that time. Baraka, formerly LeRoi Jones—established play-
wright, poet, publicist, and political strategist—announced in 1974 his
conversion to Marxism-Leninism and advocated that all workers, black
and white, join hands to struggle against capitalism.[42]

In the same year, a number of black intellectuals, many of whom
were strong nationalists, were driven to debate the relationship between race and class at the Sixth Pan-African Congress in Tanzania. The
African-based socialists, to the dismay of many American blacks,
equated the degradation of their position to class rather than race.
Race advocates, on the other hand, were "suspicious, even disdainful,
of alliances with whites."[43] The class analysis was seen as "a way out, a
way to take off their African clothes, change back to their names, refry
their hair, pick up white friends again."[44] Less disdainful arguments returned to a position articulated by Malcolm X years earlier: blacks must
organize separately and then integrate from a position of strength.[45]
One participant shunned all ideologically motivated positions and insisted that pragmatism should determine the extent of black-white col-

laboration.[46] Finally, it was pointed out that black unity was an illusion because of class differences within the black community: "Regardless of chit'lins, fried chicken and soul, dancing-doin-it and rhythm, there are basic conflictual differences among blacks and those are class differences."[47] This last observation received increasingly more attention as the decade of the seventies came to a close.

With more individual blacks acquiring the benefits of college education—one of the major fruits of the whole black upsurge from 1954 to 1970—it was natural for civil rights leaders to reflect the interests of this group and shift their attention to affirmative action. While the evidence suggests, contrary to some neoconservative claims, that affirmative action efforts to recruit and upgrade blacks to middle-level jobs were successful,[48] the affirmative action ideology was not without its contradictions. First, it was increasingly viewed as reverse discrimination. A few highly publicized cases proved to middle-class whites that affirmative action was unfair; it violated rules of merit by putting less qualified blacks into positions that otherwise would have gone to whites.[49] When seniority and some promotional rules in white-dominated unions were challenged by black affirmative action advocates, fears of affirmative action acquired a wider base;[50] they entered the spontaneous rhetoric of the white middle-class backlash. Second, affirmative action that was initially race specific became generalized. When women, Hispanics, and Asian-Americans became defined as minorities and eligible for affirmative action regardless of their respective income and status differences, the concept of a minority representing more than 50 percent of the population lost some of its logical meaning. Third, the singular focus of affirmative action, an interest namely of middle-class blacks, ignored the truly disadvantaged blacks who possessed neither education nor skills to compete effectively.[51] Finally, it has almost become fashionable among some contemporary black conservative scholars to argue that affirmative action is demoralizing to blacks themselves. It accents black inferiority on the assumption that promotion or entrance into a good college would not have occurred in the absence of preferential treatment. It lowers self-esteem and induces the acceptance of lower standards. It indirectly "encourages blacks to exploit their own victimization. Like inferiority, victimization is what justifies preference, so that to receive the benefits of preferential treatment one must . . . become invested in the view of one's self as a victim."[52] And not least, it creates an illusion among blacks that "they [whites] owe us this" and that living blacks should be paid "for the historic suffering of the race."[53]

The first book to give serious theoretical and empirical attention to the rise of the black middle class in the post-civil rights period was William J. Wilson's *Declining Significance of Race*, published in 1978.[54] Although vituperatively received by many black intellectuals, it stimulated a vigorous debate about class and race and the growing integration of the black middle class in the work sphere of American society.[55]

Wilson argues that the rise in demand for white-collar workers in the private and public sectors, combined with the success of the civil rights movement in removing the barriers for black entry into white-collar jobs, spawned a new, black middle class. The top third of the black population has now achieved integration in the economic sphere. Blacks, especially young college-educated ones, have acquired equal chances in the labor market to exchange their skills, goods, or services on the same basis as whites. Race has ceased to function as an important screening mechanism in the allocation of educated blacks. Income differences, therefore, between whites and blacks in the middle white-collar areas of employment have almost disappeared. Thus, it is class, not race, that increasingly determines the economic fate of blacks. By implication, the race category per se loses its theoretical relevance.

The situation that defines the bottom third of the black population is somewhat different. While historic racism may account for the lack of skills and education of poor blacks, their concentration in our central cities and their current isolation and impoverishment are due to the impersonal forces of technological change, capital flight, and demographic movement out of the inner cities on the part of both whites and better-off blacks. Insofar as these poor blacks are at a disadvantage, they compare to poor whites who likewise have been bypassed by technology and job upgrading in the postindustrial era. More neutral class policies, rather than race-specific ones, are the order of the day.[56]

Unjustifiably in my judgment, many of Wilson's black critics viewed his interpretation as completely dissolving race considerations in his explanation of the current nature of black subordination. In contrast to black reactions, white liberals and conservatives saw virtue in the direction of Wilson's analysis. It legitimized the liberal and conservative political inclinations to yield further to their working- and middle-class white constituencies who were "tired" of hearing about the special needs of black people. Allegedly color-blind policies enabled white politicians to avoid allusion to race-specific programs; perhaps it even enabled them to justify avoiding policies for the poor in toto.[57]

By the time the 1980s rolled around, the incremental retreats from the early civil rights days to the election of Ronald Reagan had accumulated into a well-formulated backlash, a revision, if you will, of the

meaning and impact of the black struggles in the post-World War II period. The individual who most clearly summarized the delegitimization
of the whole black struggle was Thomas Sowell, a prominent black
conservative economist and intellectual. Writing thirty years after the
historic *Brown* v. *Board of Education of Topeka* decision in 1954 and
twenty years after the Civil Rights Act of 1964, Sowell's book *Civil
Rights: Rhetoric or Reality?* raised the following questions:

> How much of the promise has [the] judicial and legislative
> events [brought into being by the civil rights movement] been
> fulfilled? How much has it been perverted? How well has the
> social vision behind the civil rights movement been
> understood—or even questioned?[58]

Sowell's answers to these and related questions have become the litany of America's neoconservative doctrine and, perhaps, the inner
speech of many liberals silently drifting to the right.

The civil rights movement in Sowell's eyes ultimately failed. What
began as a movement specific to blacks soon became a universal vision
that failed to serve black interests. Contrary to his intention, Thomas
Sowell proves the extent to which America is a racist society—the extent to which white America is capable of putting the lid on the black
American quest for social justice.

Sowell's arguments and "observations" delegitimize the process by
which the civil rights movement specific to blacks was transformed
into a civil rights vision allegedly applicable to all oppressed people. In
the absence of any knowledge of Sowell's race, background, and intentions, readers of his *Civil Rights: Rhetoric or Reality?* often assume
that he is a white scholar venting his disgust with blacks.[59] While bla-
tantly untrue, Sowell's arguments can be interpreted to feed such a
view. From his perspective, the civil rights movement has spawned a
race relations industry with leaders who do more harm than good,
whose interests are to perpetuate themselves, and who use and are
used by the mass media to sensationalize issues that have a dubious
reality and may even do damage to black causes.

The civil rights vision has linked black economic success to black
politics. This is unfortunate, since little evidence exists to show that
political activity and economic success are related. "It would perhaps
be easier to find an inverse correlation," writes Sowell, "between political activity and economic success than a direct correlation. Groups
that have the skills for other things seldom concentrate in politics."[60]
Sowell repeatedly cites the economic success of Asian-Americans who

allegedly "made it" like many immigrant groups of the past, that is, through hard work and no politics.

Sowell charges the civil rights vision with being simpleminded. It reduces the explanation of black-white statistical differences to only two alternatives: (a) innate inferiority, which, of course, the civil rights vision rejects, or (b) discriminatory practices by our social institutions, which it accepts.[61] In putting all its emphasis on the latter assumption, the civil rights vision becomes simplistic and unable to stand up to scientific scrutiny, especially when one seeks to explain the relative progress of other ethnic groups. By "scientific scrutiny," Sowell means comparing income and occupational differences among groups after consideration of other "causal" factors such as age, region, time of entry into the United States, migration patterns, cultural habits, and wasted energies devoted to pursuits other than hard work. His conclusion is always in the direction of reducing racist and discriminatory factors in accounting for black failure to "make it" relative to other "equally" discriminated against racial and ethnic minorities who have "made it."

Perhaps Sowell wails most strongly against affirmative action. He argues that once the civil rights movement was transformed to defend the aged, the disabled, women, Native Americans, Hispanics, and so on, 70 percent of the population became minority groups, an absurdity that makes affirmative action useless.[62] Instead of viewing the broadening base of affirmative action as the leading edge in an effort to change our national priorities about which, where, and how people work—as an effort, even if momentarily not successful, to establish deep changes in the ground rules guiding our goals to achieve social justice—Sowell sees it as solely inducing a white backlash, as discouraging employers from hiring blacks or other minority groups, and, finally, as nurturing black inferiority because affirmative action suggests that blacks are unable to make it by the merit standards that judge the majority. He makes a similar interpretation about busing: busing for school integration is an axiomatic disaster, since it not only leads to a white backlash but also speaks to the idea that it is impossible for all black schools to be of a high quality.[63]

In sum, by pushing confrontation with the white power structure too far, by making overt efforts to acquire economic progress through affirmative action that benefits middle- but not lower-class blacks, by seeking to use the government to correct today's statistical discrepancies that are a result of past wrongs and not of present institutional practices, blacks could lose everything. The black civil rights vision in action is pushing the majority of white society into a corner from which it may lash out with an antiblack reaction that could bring down the promise of freedom for all.[64]

What should blacks do? Blacks should, according to Sowell, accept the system as it stands and do what all other past and present immigrant groups have done. This general prescription involves the following specific recommendations: (a) Let businesspeople apply their own criteria for organizing the efficient use of workers within their enterprises; too much interference with their prerogatives will increase their hiring and promotion costs and lead to a decrease in demand for black employees. (b) Blacks should throw themselves into the competitive jungle like everyone else, even if it means accepting menial, low-paid work; by learning work discipline and being forced to shape up in a real world, blacks will do better in the long run than by accepting government handouts. And finally, (c) instead of black power and civil rights ideologies, blacks should adopt the work ethic, become work addicts, and seek self-sufficiency through establishing small businesses. Besides, suggests Sowell, these propositions are more consonant with the real basis upon which black progress has always rested: hard work in the context of rapid economic growth. Black opportunities are more a function of the pushes and pulls of impersonal market forces and less a result of black political and social posturing about racism. If posturing is necessary, black leaders should emphasize positive black achievements and the success of the black middle class.

Sowell's overall assessment of the evolution of the civil rights movement from the early fifties to the present is, in my view, an articulation of white America's drift to the right based on the judgment that blacks have pushed whites beyond their limits of toleration; it constitutes the rationalization of rising neoconservative forces. It is as if Sowell were hired to articulate what "responsible" white conservatives would not say for fear of being accused of overt racist sentiments. This judgment has been poignantly made by Derrick Bell, a black Harvard University legal scholar. In discussing the way white policymakers are currently seeking to abandon the enforcement of civil rights laws and the blaming of black poverty either on blacks themselves or on the social policies upon which they rely, it is always a good practice to obtain some black experts for achieving "deceptive authenticity."[65] Thomas Sowell, in the view of Derrick Bell, is one such black expert:

> [Thomas Sowell], knowingly or not, dispense[s] a product that
> fills the present national need for outrageous anti-black
> comment. Many whites welcome it. . . . Spout[ing] . . . white-

racist rhetoric . . . obtains a spurious legitimacy because it emanates from a black mouth.[66]

Whether or not Sowell has acted as mouthpiece for the racist undertones of the conservative drift over the past fifteen years or so is not relevant for the immediate purposes at hand. I personally believe that the "mouthpiece" castigation is unwarranted. He no doubt would dismiss the accusation as an ad hominem attack. Nevertheless, our racist heritage includes the way whites use color and then stand back to observe how blacks devour each other, as if whites were not a part of the fray or the problem it represents. Be that as it may, Sowell has performed a service, insofar as one might wish to view it as such, by articulating in a coherent form the way many white backlashers and conservatives view black struggles.

One last comment is required about Sowell's civil rights revisionist interpretation. Sowell's overall perspective has an unintended contradiction that undermines some of his glib comparisons between blacks and other ethnic groups. In chapter 4, "The Special Case for Blacks," Sowell argues that "blacks have a history in the United States that is quite different from that of other American ethnic groups. The massive fact of slavery looms over more than half of that history.[67]

This fact of slavery, he continues, was followed by Jim Crow laws and virulent, biologically defined racism relegating blacks to membership in an inferior subspecies of the human race. As a result, Sowell reminds us, "blacks are black for life. They do not have the option simply to change their names and life-styles and blend into the general population."[68]

An origin and history as profoundly unique as Sowell claims militates against facile comparisons between African-Americans and other ethnic groups. Not only may black history and its legacy be unique, but white racial sentiments toward blacks may be uniquely different from the white majority's chauvinistic attitude toward other ethnic minorities.[69] All chauvinism is not equal in character and intensity.

As the current wave of ethnic affirmations is paraded under the rhetorical banner of multiculturalism, the unfinished economic and social agenda stimulated by the civil rights movement is being aborted, if not completely abandoned. It is ironic that the declining economic position of at least 30 to 40 percent of the black population throughout the 1980s should coalesce alongside rising antiblack sentiments. As one supporter of the known ex-Klansman, David Duke (who received 40 percent of the vote in his campaign for the state senate in Louisiana), stated: "Blacks are just taking everything. They're taking everything from us, and the white race is going down the tubes. It's about time someone spoke up for the white people."[70] Extreme overt sentiments, of course, are not the norm, however close they may be to the private thoughts of others. They are, in my judgment, part of a white backlash continuum: witness the fact that President Bush vetoed the 1990 civil rights bill, which focused on enhancing certainty in employment for minorities. The veto, according to informed opinion, was related to the social and political climate that enabled President Bush to "alienate black leaders, but [placate] the much larger number of whites" with references to the bill's reliance on quotas.[71]

Conclusion

Assessing the critical events that marked the civil rights struggle and its metamorphosis into a civic disgrace evokes endemic issues that perennially emerge in the conflictual history and experiences of black-white relations. Black affirmations and white reactions to them reveal the changing faces of our latent and manifest racist impulses. The issues, as the struggles from the fifties to the nineties illustrate, range from the meaning of the slave experience to possibilities for a new era of black-white relations beyond the derogatory dependency status allegedly established by the welfare state.

In attempts to explain black subordination and understand black-white conflict, there is a long-standing debate between those who view the enduring black malaise as rooted and defined in terms of race from which socioeconomic status is derived, and those who see it as primarily anchored in the black population's class position from which cultural characteristics are derived. The shorthand mode in this debate is simply race versus class. How to allocate the respective roles of these two opposing organizing principles, repeatedly employed to explain racism and the relative subordination of blacks, involves looking at the vacillating shadows cast by the interaction of race and class. These interactions have changed as one explores the entrapment of the black population from its African roots to North American enslavement, from enslavement to the development of a rigid agricultural tenancy system, from rural impoverishment to ghettoization. Consequential portions of the black community have been periodically locked into social and economic enclaves that nurtured subordination and racism in a variety of vulgar and subtle forms, including self-denigration and dependency. In the course of historical shifts in circumstances, we have witnessed the use of race or class categories to explain the subordination of blacks. Whites use myopic race perceptions to produce class differences, or employ class differences to rationalize racial exclusionary practices. Blacks, for defensive and offensive reasons, vacillate between racially oriented themes that transcend class and class themes that subordinate race.

Illustrations abound. The origin of slavery is seen as an outgrowth of the class exigencies of the southern plantation owners; it is also understood as arising out of a deeply rooted racialist mind-set that constitutes a part of Western cultural tradition predating black enslavement.[72] In a parallel manner, the evolution and manifestation of black cultural habits are viewed as tied to a history that transcends the slave experience, thereby directing our focus to the black population's African roots; or they are seen as more reflective of the white domination of blacks in the American context.

Dimensions of this debate never seem to die. Moynihan raised the ghost of the slave legacy to account for the state of the black family's deterioration and dependency; black power advocates asserted that it was the racial-cultural legacy, despite enslavement, that sustained the black family's survival.[73]

Comparing black-white differences in income and occupational achievements, especially as they relate to schooling and scholastic performance, social scientists periodically turn to the notion of inherited mental capacities. Hereditary explanations have a long, checkered, and seamy history in which there is little cause for pride. Nevertheless, biologically driven arguments appear to be a cat with many lives, re-emerging with different and more subtle stripes. Why and when this approach gets injected into the social equation of black-white differences illustrates, frequently with a vengeance, how class conflicts can be transformed into racist social instruments by professional academicians and scientists to affect the allocation of resources to blacks.

In the political and civil rights struggles of the 1960s there emerged an implicit debate between Martin Luther King, Jr., and Malcolm X that centered on class versus race. King, in orienting blacks, often reminded his followers that they were mainly working people, and they therefore shared common interests with unions and all other working people. Class ought to transcend race.[74] Malcolm X, in contrast, advocated organizing around race. Whites in all classes, and especially those in the working class, despised blacks.[75] Progress in dealing with issues that confront us required that we first organize as blacks. In the tradition of black power advocates, this meant emphasizing the need for black identity based on some combination of race and culture shared by all blacks—regardless of the specific class, status, education, and income differences within the black community. It is precisely here that William J. Wilson's analysis intercedes with the argument that class has replaced race in "determining life-chances in the modern industrial period."[76] Middle-class blacks now have the same goals as middle-class whites and poor blacks now have shared interests with poor whites. Discrimination based on race, in one interpretation of Wilson's argument, ceases to become a vital determinant; race affirmations and explanations lose their appeal.[77]

Whatever doubts Wilson's well-argued thesis cast on the continuing influence of race, a virulent strain of social racism in everyday life appeared to rise and spread throughout the eighties. It was noted by the very same black middle class that Wilson identified as having acquired equal economic life chances.[78] This social racism outside the work sphere is unlikely to proceed without affecting the status of the blacks who are "making it" economically. Beyond the underclass and the style of life it conjures (a major source of social racism), there are "everyday" occurrences in black life that are transmitted through the mass media and defined in racially degrading terms. Teenage pregnancy, for example, is rarely described as simply a problem of young poor women. Black teenagers are generally identified, along with a possible motive for pregnancy, for example, the acquisition of income from the welfare system in order to avoid work.[79] Is this alleged adaptation explicable by race or class? In the popular mind there is often little doubt.

The swelling undertones of hostile racial sentiments and the need for racial pride perhaps constitute the basis of Jesse Jackson's political rise in the current period. His political mobilization of blacks sometimes involved the employment of class and race themes in a single voice. On the one hand, in his speeches made in 1984 and 1988, Jackson called for the need to "leave the racial battle ground and come to the economic common ground."[80] Class commonality is what will unite blacks and whites. On the other hand, Jackson's idiom, cadence, and incantation are that of a black preacher talking to his people. For the most part, Jackson's message is geared to the racial and cultural experiences of blacks.

Jackson's rise to the status of a power broker in the Democratic party is viewed by many white Democrats as an embarrassment; that feeling is a self-evident, if veiled, reflection of racist sentiments. The Democrats need to turn out the black vote in larger numbers and, of course, also need the more volatile white middle-class vote.[81] To the extent that the party is too race specific, it will lose the white vote. To the extent that it avoids race issues or substitutes a race orientation for a broad or vague class one, it will fail to enlarge the black vote. This dilemma is part of the unsolved race-class tension that drives black-white relations.[82]

Underlying my major themes—the economics of dominant-subordinate relations and their aggregation to produce a race-class nexus that affects many aspects of American life—is a historic foundation that necessarily requires a statement about the legacy of slavery. Since the mid-seventies, unfortunately, the discussion of the unique slave roots shaping the trajectory of black-white relations has diminished.[83] A correction of this lapse is in order.

AMERICAN SLAVERY: CONTEMPORARY MEANINGS AND USES

A lmost all discussions of black issues inevitably make reference to the legacy of slavery. In this allusion to the past, one becomes aware of the extent to which the present makes history. The past is forever being discovered and rediscovered — almost as if it were in fact changing because of present exigencies and events. "One must reflect uneasily," writes a southern historian, "that there was a connection between the long hot summers of the violent sixties, those dreadful academic quarrels, and the publication of some good and very bad books on slavery."[1] The human need to adapt to contemporary conditions, and to get moral and ethical solace as well as guidance for the future, requires justifications for and rationalizations of the past. In the course of confrontation with the here and now, we "invent" history. History is inescapably a social construction shaped by the present. No matter how fixed and deterministic the past may appear to some historians, the present engages our thinking about it and restructures history's meaning.

Reconstructions, moreover, change over time and as new events emerge to upset understandings derived from the past. Just as current circumstances periodically induce individuals to rethink the meaning of their lives — to reconstruct or create personal histories — the rush of unforeseen events or the dramatic emergence of perceived new opportunities for change might spur whole groups to seek a "new history."

As I noted earlier, aspects of the legacy of slavery have often been invoked by individuals representing a variety of viewpoints in the course of struggles to overcome barriers of race and class. The frequency and ease with which allusions to past slavery appear in contemporary discussions about blacks underscore the fact that the slave experience constitutes an omnipresent shadow that affects the perceptions whites and blacks have of each other. It is important to note that there are significant differences about how and why the legacy of slavery relates to the present status and behavior of blacks.

In this context, the challenging and currently relevant questions are: Did the slaves *accommodate* to the slave system that evolved in the United States? Were the slaves severely *damaged* by the system of servitude? Did they *resist*? If resistance occurred, was it based on class exploitation in the sphere of production? Or did resistance manifest itself in constructions based on race and culture that stemmed from preslave history or from family relations of slaves that operated outside the immediate work domain?

Another major question that has relevance for current perceptions and judgments of, and by, contemporary blacks is framed in sharp moral terms: Was the system of slavery *benign* or *evil*? However self-evident the answer to such a question might seem to ordinary citizens living in a free society, it is not so evident to many past and current scholars who reconstruct history in their endeavors to cope with present and often unanticipated events.

The terms of the slave debate are defined by such key words as *benign*, *evil*, *accommodation*, and *resistance*. These terms are more than mere classifications of the dead past: they are categories that are used to make sense of what happens in the present and to promote policies concerned, on one hand, with ameliorating the subordinate position of blacks or, on the other, with justifying it. One authority writes:

> There can be no doubt that the civil rights struggles of the 1960's exposed the racist bias of much of our most respected written history. Emancipated whites vowed to set the record straight. Blacks voiced a broader demand to recover their own history and to institute programs in African American Studies that would cut across the conventional subdivisions of Euro-centric history, literature, and social science.[2]

Given the added impetus of the civil rights movement, it appeared almost as if historians, debating the dimensions and consequences of slavery and antebellum society, kept one eye on the status of the contemporary black-white conflict while focusing the other eye on rearranging the past so that it would be consistent with, and relevant to, current events and trends. In an effort to bring a semblance of balance to the slave debate, it is suggested that

> a more complete absorption of the realities of human nature at work . . . in a slave society . . . would appear to depend to a great extent on continued progress in the social arena: on solid gains in civil rights, jobs, and educational opportunities. If these are not forthcoming, there is still cause for alarm that history may again be employed in the service of "politics and social action."[3]

It seems that a "balanced" view of past reality is no less a function of the present than a less "balanced" one. In the present context, like it or not, the disposition to use the shape of current events in reinterpreting the past stems from a pervasive presumption that the legacy of slavery continues to influence black adaptations to and struggles against current conditions.[4]

The social and political forms of the struggles under review here are guided and fueled by race and class interests. These interests themselves are in turn opposed or obstructed by different configurations of such interests; thus, it is only natural that the views and uses of slavery's legacy vary along racial and ideological axes.

The manner in which reflections on African-American history are filtered through present prisms of race and class results in different kinds of research on the slave system. The concern here, therefore, is to examine those aspects of the contemporary slave debate that relate to the issues laid bare and reinforced by recent civil rights struggles and the subsequent backlash.

Social Holocaust

The background of slavery is a palpable and distinct fact of life for most blacks in the United States. Ancestors of today's blacks were abruptly and violently abducted from their native lands; the fact that the ancestors of other citizens were not is a difference to be forever remembered and understood. When invidious questions are asked about why African-Americans have not succeeded or have not followed the route of other ethnic groups, the answer is inevitably that those other groups were not forced onto these shores as slaves.[5]

Although different arguments might be made about the nature of the U.S. slave system and its long-term consequences, no comparable debate has developed about the effects on slaves of being uprooted from their African soil. The violent separation of the "African from the social tissue that held all meaning for him" constituted a catastrophe of holocaust proportions.[6] This sudden separation of individuals from their collective network exposed blacks to a form of raw economic exploitation in the American context not comparable to that experienced by other exploited immigrant groups. While general class and economic needs motivated the dominant white rulers, they did not perceive black laboring hands as members of a single subordinate class. Neither did black slaves perceive themselves as such a class. However harsh the circumstances were that white immigrants faced, those groups viewed their ocean voyage as an "opportunity" that was "chosen," however uncertain it might be. Blacks, in contrast, necessarily saw their fate as a "journey" into an abyss they did not choose.

Slavery Defined

Before examining the more specific items and issues of the debate about slavery and its effects, it is wise to set forth a formal definition of slavery. This keeps us from making loose and faulty comparisons with other forms of exploitive class systems, thereby missing the full ramifications of what it means to be enslaved. Further, a formal definition may help to dispel a too common view that casually equates slavery with a state of poverty—with a class condition similar to that experienced by poor immigrants. If the slave system is viewed simply as "just" another port of entry characterized by poverty, one consequence is that the inability of blacks to extricate themselves from an interim class position is often linked to biological or deeply flawed cultural traits.

Orlando Patterson, social historian and sociologist, has developed a carefully articulated account of the elements that define slavery. He cites the following distinct features:

. . . powerlessness, a condition "in which the powerful is free to use naked violence";[7]

"natal alienation" that results in "social death," the loss of connection to past kin and absence of a capacity to link with future kin;[8]

. . . the absence of official honor, manhood, and free choice;[9]

. . . the support of the master's power by the nonslave community, i.e., using the authority of the state to enforce ownership of the slaves;[10]

. . . the reinforcement of the master's legal right and privileges through the manipulation of cultural and ideological symbols in order to cultivate shared values between the master class and the nonslave community.[11]

The characteristic physical features and conditions of slaves, it should be further noted, determine whether the slavery is legitimized by the masters in cultural, class, religious, national, or racial terms. The closer the enslaved outsiders are in physical features and conditions to the master and nonslave-owning constituents, the more likely will the enslaved be demeaned by class symbols rather than symbols that are based upon putative distinctions and "unique" features of the slave. Sustained degradation linked to race and culture makes it qualitatively more socially insoluble than when it is based only on cultural difference. This makes the black experience fundamentally different from that of other groups—a fact sometimes noted but then readily neglected or forgotten.

Although the above definition of slavery is formal, it is highly probable that all actual slave systems would be marked in some degree by each of the elements cited above. This discussion, therefore, provides a useful backdrop for our examination of the force and role of the slave debate in American social and intellectual history.

The Debate about Slavery

Was slavery in the United States benign or evil? When asked in this form, the question unfortunately ignores human beings. The question focuses on slavery qua system, rather than on its impact on persons. We begin this examination of the great slave debate by identifying three major views of the U.S. slave system's effects: first, that the system had benign qualities; second, that its effects were inherently evil and damaging; and third, that the resistance of slaves was more common than is usually acknowledged by many scholars.[12]

The benign view more or less dominated the perceptions of many white historians until the early 1950s. The chief authority for this position was Ulrich B. Phillips, who asserted that "on the whole the plantations were the best schools yet invented for the mass training of that sort of inert and backward people which the bulk of the American negroes represented."[13]

The efficacy of the plantation system as a training institution for African blacks rested on two diametrically opposed assumptions about their character. One assumption was that blacks were by nature sub-

missive, light-hearted, amicable, ingratiating, and imitative; and therefore, what that friendly race needed was the systematic drilling that the
institutions of the plantation provided.[14] A second, and opposite, characterological assumption was that blacks had barbarous, savagelike
qualities that similarly needed conditioning, training, and, above
all, control. And further, in this instance, slavery—like prison and
torture—could transform intractable and willful people into meek
souls.

Not so coincidentally, this historically articulated perception of the
black male, especially as "savage," has a continuing and current life as
it fits and reinforces character assumptions about today's street-wise
young black criminals.[15] This latter assumption and its accompanying
perception have perhaps received less formal academic endorsement
than their counterparts. The depiction of slaves as "happy-go-lucky,
sweet-smiling" Negroes existing on benign plantations was a standard
image up to the end of World War II.[16]

The benign assumption about slavery and the "sweet" picture of
black "folk" are most compatible with the accommodationist interpretation of the ways blacks allegedly adapted to the realities of the slave
system. Blacks, in this view, accepted the parameters of a closed system because the system itself was not all that bad and because blacks
had a "friendly" nature.

The accommodationist view is based on an ideology that was useful
to plantation owners and others who sought to legitimize the slave system. Possible (or even highly probable) alternative responses to
slavery—such as running away, revolt, sabotage, and work slow-
downs—could be dismissed as aberrations from the norm or induced
by outside agitators. It was held that such responses did not represent
the essence of the way blacks experienced the system.

In examining facets of the debate about slavery such as the characterization of the slave personality and the manner in which it was
molded, it is revealing to look at the way some social scientists reflect
and help shape popular sentiment in their responses to current issues
that relate to blacks. Notable among these overlapping problems and
concerns are black youth (schooling problems and crime), the black
underclass (dependency and crime), black families and parenting (dependency and lax work habits), and other seemingly intractable difficulties that threaten the equanimity of whites' social existence. James
Q. Wilson, for example, a leading neoconservative, writes:

> Public problems can only be understood—and perhaps
> addressed—if they are seen as arising out of a defect in

character formation. . . . The black people whose behavior we wish to change do not have right "tastes" or discount the future too heavily. To put it plainly, they lack character.[17]

Wilson's depiction, unfortunately, reflects private thoughts about blacks, both now and then, that are held by many far beyond the neo-conservative fold. A good deal of public discourse, as well as private exchanges, conveys and supports views of black character as rooted "in the blood." One important implication is that once character depictions are isolated and taken out of their social context, they are readily viewed as intractable and unamenable to change by public policies.

Evil and Damage

The view that slavery was necessarily evil and damaging to the person has a long history. Among the chief exponents of this theme, each of whom has contributed an influential variation, are historians Kenneth M. Stampp and Stanley M. Elkins, and novelist William Styron.

The long-standing argument concerning whether the slave system was benign or evil in practical as well as abstract terms was emphatically put to rest by Stampp in his pivotal book, *The Peculiar Institution* (1956).[18] This book injected the damage thesis into the debate, even though it also features resistance as a subtheme. Stampp makes the point that what the slaves lost upon emancipation was not the nurturance of a benign institution—a training ground for the "simple" and the "savage"—but their chains; and, further, that however second-class and flawed their subsequent citizenship was, it was distinctly less a burden than had been the chains of bondage.[19]

Three years after the publication of Stampp's book, Elkins extended and enlarged the damage thesis in *Slavery: A Problem in American Institutional and Intellectual Life*.[20] Elkins argued not only that slavery was physically harsh, but also that it had infantilizing effects similar to those that the closed system of the concentration camp had on Jews.[21]

Elkins's thesis of infantilization and the generation of a Sambo personality type has had important scholarly and political fallout. It has led directly, for example, to uncomfortable and sometimes bizarre dialogue between blacks and Jews concerning, among other things, questions about which group has suffered more, and whether slavery was more or less catastrophic than concentration camps;[22] to the resurrection of the detestable Sambo stereotype;[23] to providing cues and support for Daniel Patrick Moynihan's controversial depiction of the pathology of the black family;[24] and to influencing Styron in his controversial fictional depiction of Nat Turner in the prize-winning novel *The Confessions of Nat Turner* (1967).[25]

Resistance

The resistance theme came to the fore in 1968 in strong opposition to the damage view. The prominence and influence of the assertions by Elkins, Moynihan, and Styron stimulated a flood of responses. These were sharp, sometimes heated replies that, in underscoring the nature of black slave resistance, bordered on denying any significant and enduring damage.[26] Notions of black docility and accommodation, even if explained by environmental and class forces, were anathema to proponents of black power in a renewed search for historical sources of pride and community. Such judgments by writers and their followers necessarily fell under suspicion, given the strong reaffirmation of African-American cultural traditions, including religion. Participants in the civil rights movement, and notably advocates of black power, sought both to destroy the residuals of the slave mentality persisting in contemporary institutional racism and to get rid of a long-standing social etiquette.

The resistance theme received an important, albeit qualified, boost from John W. Blassingame's carefully documented book *The Slave Community* (1972).[27] In refutation of Elkins's conclusions, Blassingame shows that the slave community was complex and that it produced and reproduced a variety of responses, modes of adaptation, and personality types. In addition to the Sambo type—representing total accommodation—there were rebels, reformists, and escapists. Blassingame emphasizes the manner in which preslave black culture and religion preserved personal autonomy and prevented "total identification with planters, and internalization of unflattering stereotypes."[28]

The book that has probably done the most to develop and reinforce the resistance theme is Herbert Gutman's *The Black Family in Slavery and Freedom, 1750–1925*.[29] In direct opposition to Moynihan's thesis concerning the contributions of slavery to the pathological character of the black family, Gutman argues that the black family was the main instrument of survival and that the black family, in general, was alive and together from 1750 to 1925.[30] Gutman set forth three general conclusions: the behavior of the slave was not determined as such by the sponsorship or treatment of the master; the habits of the slave were neither imitative nor a direct internalization of the master's ideological dominance; and the culture, psyche, and social arrangements were conceived and transmitted independently of the master class.[31]

The presentation thus far has shown how the debate about the effects of slavery on blacks in the United States has been anchored simultaneously in the past and the present. The terms of the debate evolved from arguments stressing either the docility or the resistance of slaves. The assumptions and interpretations underlying this long-running debate have shifted back and forth between class and race perspectives. For some students of slavery, severe and raw economic exploitation produced permanent cultural and personality damage that has had significant effects on the adaptations of contemporary blacks; for others, adaptive responses and survival mechanisms of blacks were anchored in culture, family, and religion—all of which enabled blacks to endure and counter class exploitation. This suggests that the affirmative side of black politics is rooted outside the work domain, a fact that has implications for contemporary black struggles.

Examination of this evolving debate brings to the fore two developments. One is the emergence of research and analysis that focuses on the interaction among effects that are categorized as benign, damaging, and featuring resistance; a second is the appearance of efforts to achieve explanations that integrate race and class. In the following sections I describe and comment on these developments and their current ramifications.

Combining Themes of Adaptation to Slavery

The ideological, as well as scholarly, confusions prevalent in historical interpretations of black experience in the United States are illustrated by two books that cite a mixture of adaptive themes: *Time on the Cross* (1974) by Robert W. Fogel and Stanley Engerman, and *Roll, Jordan, Roll: The World the Slaves Made* (1976) by Eugene D. Genovese.[32]

Time on the Cross, which relies heavily on manipulations of statistical material, advances three propositions. First, the slave system was benign; white masters rarely brutalized blacks, as generally claimed by some historians. Second, to the extent that the slave system was not benign, the slaves protected themselves, perhaps even resisted oppression. Third, to the extent that there was damage, it was of the amorphous psychological variety associated with the lack of free choice.[33]

According to Fogel and Engerman, the belief that "slave-breeding, sexual exploitation, and promiscuity destroyed the black family is a myth."[34] To the contrary, the family was the basic unit of organization under slavery; moreover, it was in the interest of the slave owners to keep black families together in order to maintain them as productive units and prevent disincentives from taking place through demoralization.[35] In view of the efficiency of the plantation, the hard-working nature of the slave, and the desire on the part of slave owners to maintain their stock of human capital, the slaves had material (not psychological) conditions of life that compared favorably to those of average industrial workers of the North; in general, slaves had health care better than or at least comparable to that of their white counterparts.[36] The authors of *Time on the Cross* conclude that the legacy of slavery cannot be used to explain many aspects of the present; this position contrasts with that of white liberal scholarship. To the extent that blacks currently represent our system's failures or rejects, according to the arguments presented in *Time on the Cross*, we need look no further than the present nature of the system for an explanation. In the hands of Fogel and Engerman, the legacy of black slavery is denied its contemporary influential role: to the extent that blacks were miserable in their slave status, it was because they were denied free choice and subjected to psychocultural deprivation. This produces a crude dualism that has blacks "basking" in a materialistic near-utopia while experiencing a mental prison. It resembles in a fashion the way some social critics describe modern America: a land of material abundance and spiritual emptiness.

An unintended conclusion of the Fogel-Engerman thesis is that American slavery was more efficient and, in many respects, more humane—at least in the paternalistic sense of having a "big daddy" to look after you—than much of capitalism in the nineteenth century.[37] This is an odd interpretation, since perhaps the most important attribute of a capitalist-driven price system combined with a free labor market is its claim to efficiency; here, in Fogel and Engerman's unintended view, capitalism fails by comparison. Since Fogel and Engerman clearly do not suggest a return to or the incorporation of those superior attributes of the slave system they identify, there are no policy implications or possible normative judgments in their thesis. Their venture into theorizing has no meaning.

Aside from the fact that their statistical evidence has been proved false, their conclusions, if not their methodology, touched all the basic themes.[38] They agreed with Gutman about the importance of the African-American family, although their reasons are somewhat different. They agreed with southern paternalists, but likewise for different reasons. They concurred with Elkins's psychological personality-damage argument insofar as they stressed ego damage to the slave rather than material exploitation; and, not least, they concurred with the interpretations of many African-Americans who saw the enemy as current racism and economic exploitation. The authors of *Time on the Cross* suggest that the present plight of blacks should not be blamed on the past; the lot of the slave was not so bad by past standards. If there is a black malaise, and if blacks are objects of race degradation and class exploitation, this was true not only in the past; the present system also bears responsibility.

In *Roll, Jordan, Roll*, Eugene Genovese—unlike Fogel and Engerman who pasted together the themes of benignity, damage, and resistance as might be done in a poorly constructed paper collage—synthesizes the same themes into an organic whole. Although Genovese is a self-proclaimed Marxian historian, his Marxism differs from more orthodox interpretations. All the actors in and around the slave system (master, slaves, and the more peripheral yeoman and free laborers) were affected by a closed system in which "natural" forms of cooperation and conflict, love and hate, suspicion and trust, resistance and obedience prevailed simultaneously. Employing the notion of paternalistic hegemony inherited from vagaries of both the slave owners' alleged feudal heritage and the traditionalism of the slaves' own preindustrial past, Genovese shows how the slave and master worked out a modus vivendi in the context of a two-class system. Paternalism served as the organic, noneconomic adhesive that kept the overall system working. The factors that induced "functionaries" in the system to cooperate were not solely material incentives or coercion or common ideas or moral commitment. Slaves' obligations to work hard stemmed partly from necessity and partly from loyalty. In return for cooperation and loyalty, the slaves received not only maintenance, but rights and privileges. Undergirded by that bundle of rights and privileges, slaves found common interests among themselves that represented "freedom" of spirit, pride, and meaning as human beings in a community of people. Slave resistance was, therefore, always muted by an acceptance of the benign, genuinely caring paternalism of masters. The paternal dimensions of the system were aimed at resolving inherent tensions between masters, on the one hand, who wanted perfect control over the slaves' working time in order to enhance the plantations' surplus output for export and, on the other hand, slaves who sought more autonomy over their own working time.

The material class interests of masters and slaves were opposed. This was logical insofar as the slave's reproduction wage was independent of his work effort; leisure was a free good in the sense that its acquisition involved no loss of material well-being. In this general context, slaves internalized the master's paternalism and also sought means to protect themselves from its effects. Since the production of this paternalistic ideology is something less than an exact process and cannot be completely relied upon as a means of controlling primary producers who have contrary material interests, coercive mechanisms must be available and used in the event that hegemony turns out to be imperfect and uncertain. The exercise of the rod in the context of Genovese's version of paternalism can be and has been exaggerated.

The slave community was not homogeneous; and since there was some division of labor and status differentiation among slaves, there were forces at work, however incipient, that were used by the dominant ideologues of the system to divide and conquer and, therefore, further weaken the slaves' resistance impulses and knowledge of their general interests. House slaves, field slaves, black slave drivers, men and women differed among themselves as well as differed from the master who dominated them. Genovese infuses relational opposites and conflicts of interests into his notion of integration; these conflicts are "resolved" by ideological forces that sustain the system.

Genovese used the backdrop of the prevailing major themes (accommodation, damage, and resistance) in order to show that the system, in its paternalistic and antibourgeois aspects, had benign dimensions. Racist Southerners did not completely misunderstand slave history. In its systematic reliance on brainwashing techniques aimed at imposing subservience and in its employment of overtly violent coercion when the former failed, the system was not without physical and mental brutality. Inasmuch as slaves were locked into a system in which their immediate material interests were clearly opposed to the control and domination the master class sought, the emergence of mechanisms of protection and resistance should not be surprising.

Genovese's thesis, in essence, represents a grand and successful synthesis of that portion of the slave debate that revolves around the presence or absence of benignity, damage, and resistance. Insofar as slaves internalized the prescriptions from above, there was characterological damage; insofar as they escaped from working themselves to death—either through the "kindness" of the master's heart or the slaves' own forms of resistance—they survived in this sphere of class antagonisms; and insofar as they could affirm life's possibilities, they created their own cultural and religious forms outside the work sphere but within the boundaries of the paternalistic system.

Debate about the Debate

The great slave debate is important in its own terms; however, as I have argued, it is by no means solely about the past. The central issues and themes of that debate—benignity, damage, and resistance—are concerned with the nature and character of slaves, and with their capacity to struggle as a class within a closed system. These very same issues and themes have been brought forward in present discourses concerned with race relations and efforts to close gaps between blacks and whites.

The current relevance of old themes is illustrated in some of the ostensibly simple questions that are periodically raised about the status and behavior of blacks in today's society. For example, what kind of remedial educational efforts beyond those available to everyone should be made to help African-Americans close the various skill "deficits" or income gaps that exist? While answering this question does not require reference to the issues of the great slave debate, such references do in fact occur regularly among both black and white scholars.

If the assertion is made that the effect of slavery was all damage, it suggests not only that blacks have lost their capacity to fight as a group but also that remedial and special programs are necessary.[39] Like those who have been crippled in war, they need a protected environment because they cannot compete in normal situations. While this may justify and in fact produce more than the normal amount of remedial efforts and resources, it also justifies white liberal paternalism. Dependency states are not conducive to demands for autonomy. Moreover, some assert that it is precisely the institutionalization of dependency by the liberal welfare state that is at fault. This is a major source of criticism among conservative white and black scholars.

While the motivations of conservatives who advocate the precepts of old-fashioned puritanism or those who emphasize unique black traditions are not necessarily suspect of overt biologically determined reasoning, their criticisms are frequently racially and culturally based: the black community lacks intellectual and entrepreneurial traditions related to a "communal" past, or black children have different learning styles from those of white children.[40] These illustrations are derived from cultural habits within the family or from sources outside the work sphere. They are not class interpretations emanating from exploitive plantation relations.

It is not immediately clear why the market system would produce more damage to poor blacks than to poor whites. To the extent that blacks have not succeeded in achieving parity in the many decades following emancipation, it is then their own problem—so goes the argument; their present status is due to their inability to pull themselves up by their own bootstraps like other groups that have been impoverished and discriminated against. In this reasoning, the victims again become the source of their own victimization: blacks must be reflecting their biologically or socially inherited destinies. The biological argument becomes the source of a race-based argument; one of its guises is "scientific" IQism, as I explain in the following chapter. The emphasis on social inheritance is part of the cultural deficiency school. Overcoming this barrier leads members of this group to emphasize self-help, cultivation of a work ethic, and the need to develop small businesses, all of which are consistent with individualism and the market system.[41]

Finally, the suggestion is made that if the whole history of the black struggle has been dominated by resistance, there must not have been any serious damage. If no damage occurred, then no special parity or reparation programs are warranted; what is justifiable and should prevail is the general axiom that everyone, African-Americans included, should have the equal opportunity to become unequal. Unjust barriers need elimination, but no special treatment or consideration should be given.

If the opposite assertion is made that the dominant effects of slavery were benign, the conclusion follows then that blacks were not damaged and no remedial or special programs are justifiable. If slavery produced no damage, it is difficult to argue that its termination did. The assumption would follow that market freedom should provide opportunities for advancement. The market jungle, if sufficiently free and open, stimulates the extra effort of the downtrodden to overcome disparities. Since past immigrants allegedly needed no crutches, neither do African-Americans. The competitive market is marked by the use of color-blind cash nexus principles that reward efficiency. The operation of these, it is assumed, will eventually divide the African-American community into entrepreneurs, professionals, and workers in proportions that prevail in the dominant society. These various black strata will find corresponding common ground with their white counterparts. This logic is the basis of an implicit expectation that class similarity will eventually eliminate status differences related to race.

The examples above show how the slave debate can be, and is, used in selective ways to legitimize or delegitimize specific policies aimed at correcting black-white inequalities. The determination of the emphasis centers on whether race or class is the chosen lens for inspection and evocation of the past.

A significant facet of the debate is concerned with issues about the origins and virulency of racism in the United States compared to Latin America. Kenneth Stampp indicated some parameters of this debate:

> In the main, Maryland and Virginia masters first subjected their Negroes to the customary forms of servitude. Like white servants, some of them gained their freedom after serving a term of years, or after conversion to Christianity. . . . Moreover, the Negro and white servants of the seventeenth century seemed to be remarkably unconcerned about their visible physical differences. They toiled together in the fields, fraternized during leisure hours, and, in and out of wedlock collaborated in siring a numerous progeny. Though the first southern white settlers were familiar with rigid class lines, they were as unfamiliar with a caste system as they were with chattel slavery.[42]

In this view, class obliterated race differences both *between* the dominant and subordinate layers of society and *within* the subordinate layers. Stampp goes on to argue, however, that as the landholders acquired an appreciation of the advantages of slavery "over the older forms of servitude, [it] gave a powerful impetus to the growth of a new labor system."[43]

Eric Williams had established the direction of this position in orthodox Marxian terms with even more force some years earlier when he argued that the origin of Negro slavery, and therefore of racism, was "economic, not racial."[44] This line of reasoning suggests that prior to the perceived profitability and general advantages of a plantation system, racism as an ideology was either nonexistent or inconsequential. Class exploitation prevailed for black and white workers equally, without "coloring" intraclass distinctions. But once the economic viability of a forced labor system made itself visible, racism with all its implications began to emerge as an ideological justification of the newly established plantation elite. With the development of such a system "color had become . . . [not only] evidence of slavery but also a badge of degradation. Thus the master class, for its own purposes, wrote chattel slavery, the caste system, and color prejudice into American custom and law."[45]

The counterargument to this line of class reductionism, stated simply so as to maintain clarity, is that differences between black and white indentured servants were sharply established at the very beginning of the colonization of the North American seaboard, long before the slave system became a compelling possibility in the South. This counterargument holds that racism predated the colonization of Africa by Western Europeans.

The evidence employed to buttress this position is of two kinds. The first kind argues that the Elizabethan Englishman "had an acute sense of the hideousness of color, barbarous customs and hypersexuality of Africans. All the associations of the color black with evil and filth . . . were projected on to the Negro race."[46] The English required no agonizing reappraisal of values to legitimize slavery; they were only acting out a deeply entrenched belief system. The second type of evidence stresses the fact that white indentured servants from England were protected as English subjects through indentured contracts. Blacks, in contrast, had no governments and therefore "did not have the benefit of written indentures which . . . limited their terms of service."[47] Prejudice toward black indentured servants would have developed because of the deeply rooted English cultural mind-set, but it would not have led to the slave system. Both positions suggested that "objective" class commonalities between black and white indentured servants by themselves were not sufficiently powerful to block the black's road to enslavement.

The consensus position in this debate about which came first, the racism or the slavery, is that there was a convergence of racist predisposition with the availability of land and the need for cheap labor. Black enslavement gave a qualitative impetus to preexisting racist attitudes.

A distinction that those who argue the existence of preslavery racism fail to make in their efforts to refute the economic determinist position concerns the difference between latent and manifest hatreds and mythologies. At what point do latent fantasies and ideas of a mythological nature cause the emergence of real social practices? It is only after the fact that it is possible to say that a general constellation of ideas floating vaguely in the culture caused a particular reality to come into existence. Many latent symbolic configurations in the history of a society never materialize.

Perhaps what the advocates of preslavery racism are explaining is the intensity rather than the emergence of slavery, and in doing this, they compare the nature of English racism, for example, to that of the French or Spanish. The possibility that racist sentiments may have manifested themselves more profoundly because of preslavery, Elizabethian England's cultural backdrop leads to still another aspect of the debate within the debate, namely, perspectives on the relative virulency of racism in the United States.

An important and paradoxical note relates to the fact that slavery developed within a democratic society; thus, an extraordinary rationale was required to justify it. To declare that all people are entitled to certain inalienable rights and then deny such rights to large numbers of persons needed an ideology that debased blacks. Racism became such an ideology. Blacks were subhuman, congenitally lazy, irresponsible, and dishonest in the judgment of the Virginian plantation owner Landon Carter.[48] Personal qualities were attached to color per se. Since each slave counted for only three-fifths of a person in the words of the Constitution, the slave's lack of comparable rights did not violate the general rule. In other areas of the world where slaves, peasants, and workers were all subjugated by a repressive hereditary totalitarian political system, there was no need for a special rationale to justify slavery. The differences between slave and nonslave were less dramatic.

In this respect, free blacks, even those who were economically better off than poor whites, had less status on the basis of color. The inferior economic status of the black slave majority spilled over, cast a shadow so to speak, to affect the social and political status of those blacks who were not in bondage. This is not dissimilar, as I argue in chapters 5 and 6, to how the overcrowding of blacks in the lower class filters upward to affect the social position and economic mobility of blacks above the lowest level, and, in particular, in the middle class.

To maintain a slave system, the nonslave citizens, as we have suggested in the course of defining slavery, must support the maintenance of the system. Because slavery was a regional formation that rested on local control and lacked a national community, the plantation owners were more insecure in the United States than elsewhere. The American slavocracy had a fairly reliable regional community but an unreliable national one. The South's justification of its deviation from the national system needed not only a more debasing racist ideology, but more exacting social surveillance of the slaves relative to other areas of the world. A chronically insecure and defensive landed class, envious of the rising commercial and capitalist interests, needed to assure itself that somehow it lived a good life. Its genteel facade, built on the rock of social and physical exploitation of slave labor, increasingly depended on the vagaries of an international market.

As a result, the internal structure of the South needed stability and predictability. The system over time gradually became less violent as it became legally tighter.[49] Laws that recognized the slave's humanity proliferated, but in ways that defined slaves "as lesser humans in a dependency assumed to be perpetual. Now they were to be treated as children expected never to grow up."[50] As the American plantation system became "less harmful to the body, [it] could be more afflicting to the soul."[51] This conclusion is not dissimilar to the sentiments occasionally expressed that, in spite of material gains experienced in the recent period and the elimination of crude racial barriers and their justification, a subtle racism continues to grow unabated.

The demographic pressures studied by Carl Degler in the case of Brazil need to be considered in the United States also.[52] In contrast to the American South, manumission was easier and miscegenation was more common in Brazil. The shortage of white Brazilian women, along with their inferior status, encouraged interracial marriages and liaisons generally. Less restricted sexual relations involving both races produced more mulattoes in the population. The result was that Brazil developed a consciousness of degrees of blackness; Brazilian society failed to develop the "strict and sharp line between the races so characteristic of the United States."[53] Long before general emancipation, Brazilian mulattoes found their way into dozens of trades and crafts because there was no large white middle layer of workers to stop them. This gave more social and economic space to Brazilian nonwhites, both slaves and ex-slaves, than was the case in the United States.

Conclusions and Implications

Interpretations and assessments of the consequences of slavery in the United States range from those that stress the simpleminded and docile nature of the slaves to those that emphasize rebellion and slave resistance. They aid in understanding the legacy derived from slavery. The description of this legacy facilitates the direct analysis of issues of race and class embedded in the debate about the slave system; the analysis is developed in subsequent chapters.

In the context of our examination of the past and present significance of the slave heritage and of the continuing debate concerning slavery, we have developed a cluster of key conclusions that includes the following:

Feelings of white supremacy are an inheritance from perceptions of the U.S. system of slavery as benign.

Thus, the ideas that legitimated slavery ranged from characterizations of presumed docility of blacks through allegations of animal-like qualities to the assertion of genetic inferiority.

Complementary to the belief in white supremacy is the opposite belief in black inferiority. The latter is a likely outgrowth of profound damage suffered under slavery. It is difficult to believe that the oppression of slavery did not leave psychological scars and forms of self-denigration.

In efforts to escape from both the supremacy and inferiority legacies, blacks used a variety of means to protect themselves—culture, music, poetry, literature, folklore, and religion.

In the struggle to achieve freedom, equality, and social justice, blacks acquired pride from endeavors to make their own history; and in doing so, they also contributed in telling ways to the national debate about the contrast between the nation's professed ideals and its actual practices.

The issue of class versus race is embedded in the major themes that are used to interpret and state the meanings of the slave experience. The Marxian view is that the elimination of class exploitation at points of production will eliminate race-based conflicts in general.[54] Marxists devote insufficient attention to race and culture as an independent secular force with its own meaning and roots outside the work sphere where community and family relations are established.

A variant of the class position that emphasizes natural market forces is sometimes the focus of conservatives. The current poverty of blacks is depicted as similar to that experienced by yesterday's immigrants who moved into urban areas. Race is less important than the "timing" of black migration to urban centers and the "temporary" deficiency of skills and diligent work habits.[55] In this view, blacks over time will acculturate and succeed; race-specific programs are not needed. What *is* necessary are general opportunities afforded by economic growth. Insofar as blacks do not succeed, genetic factors or deeply rooted cultural habits are often suggested.[56]

In contrast, those who stress the dominant part played by race argue that "economistic" approaches chronically underestimate the ways in which culturally rooted experiences that are related specifically to race perpetuate themselves; they operate somewhat independently of "objective" material interests.[57]

This line of reasoning is stretched backward by those who argue that racism predates slavery. It is carried forward into the slave debate by those who argue that one major support for the survival of African-American humanity under the brutal conditions of slavery derives from black religion, black communal traditions, and black social inventions developed in the community and family spheres. This focus is projected into the present by those who are advocates of black power and non-Eurocentric culturalism.

There is irony in the fact that the race and culture emphasis often appears more relevant to successful blacks in the middle class and intelligentsia. Can it be that the meanings of racism outside of the work sphere—for such persons who have acquired all the economic class credentials—become more acutely experienced, understood, and resented?

Probably the most sinister and obdurate race-related legacy of the U.S. slave experience is the use of biology to explain alleged intelligence differences between blacks and whites. Especially noteworthy in this regard are the interpretations and uses of differential performances on a battery of standardized tests. The profound popular and scholarly confusion that prevails in the sphere of intelligence testing warrants special consideration.

SCIENTIFIC RACISM AND SOCIAL CLASS

Majority opinion would declare, I believe, that "intelligence" is inherited in the same axiomatic way that majority opinion once believed the world was flat and the planet Earth was located at the center of the universe. Parents believe that they often see "inherent" differences among their children whom they erroneously think are raised in identical environments. Not uncommonly it is said that "Mary Ann has the brains of her grandmother." Folk wisdom abounds with examples of family members and friends who suffered equally from poverty but, like cream, only some rose to the top. It cannot be all environment. While tribute is often paid to hard work, it takes only a small amount of provocation to induce individuals to view some groups as born smart and others as born even stupid. Intelligence is widely spoken about as a trait, not unlike eye and skin color. The idea that intellect is inherited has a large popular market. It should not be surprising, therefore, that a biological interpretation of black intelligence, under the guise of science, is periodically used against the black population. One example appeared in a shareholder proposal of the 1988 annual meeting of the American Telephone and Telegraph Company. A proposal was introduced asking the board of directors to discontinue its affirmative action program because it was lowering the quality of the personnel. Citing a recent psychological study, the rationale for the proposal was stated in the following terms:

With the importance of intelligence in a career at AT&T, an I.Q. of 114 or above would seem to be a desirable characteristic in most job applicants. Yet, we must objectively consider Dr. Gottfredson's estimate that only 1.1% of the Black population, compared to 23% of the White population, has an I.Q. in this range. We believe that to ignore data such as this in employment practices, sacrifices the essential long-term benefits of personnel quality, for the short-term approval of pressure groups.[1]

A more blatant statement about black intelligence was recently made by a professor of philosophy at City College of the City University of New York:

It has been amply confirmed over the last several decades that on average blacks are significantly less intelligent than whites. [Moreover] black representation in a field can be expected, absent any discrimination, to decrease as the intellectual demands of the fields increase.[2]

I suggest that scientific IQ research is related less to the quest for truth and more to the marketability of biologically determinist ideas. Well-documented racist motivations aside, black-white social and class conflict periodically induces members of the scholarly community to undertake research aimed at justifying the social system's need to protect itself against this perceived inferior and disruptive black threat in our midst.[3] Intentions to the contrary, the biological hereditarians—in their endeavor to isolate the biological factor from social relations—illustrate the power of class and stratification in their explanations of black-white differences.

By illustrating how scientific racism was employed in the 1830s, 1850s, and 1890s to justify a white supremacist social order, by showing how good minds were influenced by other good minds to articulate racist theories in the name of science for reasons that had little relation to scientific "truth" seeking, I hope to diminish the most recent vogue of racial geneticism. The replay of history may help those who are unfamiliar with it see themselves in a different light.

Historical Backdrop

Until approximately the 1830s, an environmental school of thought ascribing black-white differences in "mental, moral, and psychological characteristics" to "climate, state of society, and manner of living" had some respectability in scientific circles.[4] At this juncture in American history the older political elites, those whose lineage was traceable to our founding fathers, were losing power to the lower-level "upstarts." This changing of the guard, so to speak, is one feature that characterizes it as the Jacksonian era. It was an era, among other things, that represented a "peoples' movement" in the sense that it extended liberal democratic rights to a poorer class of the white population. Related to this process was "anti-Negro sentiment . . . violence against free blacks and the elimination of Negro suffrage in some Northern states."[5] Jackson's emphasis on "*laissez faire*, decentralized democracy, states' rights," and, not least, on "egalitarian and competitive individualism" functioned against the abolitionist impulses and invigorated a racist social climate associated with "status anxieties among whites."[6] The overarching mood of this era stimulated the attack against environmental scientism and the rise of its biological counterpart.

The new doctrine of polygenesis, in which species were assumed to be derived from more than one ancestor, was first articulated in 1837 and became more acceptable in the decades that followed. It mustered new scientific data to prove that the "races of mankind had been separately created as distinct and unequal species."[7] This new scientific theory not only represented an "assault on environmentalism," but it spread "at a time . . . when it was found to have some influence on the discussion of slavery and Negro prospects."[8] Democratic egalitarian principles (as exemplified in the U.S. Constitution) needed special rationalization to justify their nonextension to blacks. Since "Negroes were creatures set apart, [they] did not have to be conceded any social status at all within an officially homogenous and egalitarian . . . community."[9] As scientific polygenesis gained influence, the advocates of scientific environmentalism accommodated to the hard "facts" by suggesting that "the races had diverged as a result of environmental factors . . . [and had] now reached the point of irreversibility; therefore Negro inferiority was [an] unchangeable fact of nature."[10] Thus, divergent scientific schools of thought, employing the best procedures and facts available, found a way of synthesizing their disparate approaches. A crude sociobiology emerged in the 1860s that suggested that social traits become embedded in specific groups to become thereafter inherited traits. If ascribed white characteristics such as "good principles and habits, intellectual culture . . . [and] industry" can eventually acquire a biological base capable of transferability from one generation to another so that they "become thoroughly inbred in the stock," so can ascribed black traits such as bad principles, laziness, and criminality become inbred in the stock.[11] Thus, various schools of scientific thought—from about 1830 up to the rise of social Darwinism—found ways to demonstrate that there were some obdurate innate biological dimensions that constituted the bases of why blacks were unworthy of the democratic promise. Race biology, even when the environmental conditions for blacks and whites admittedly differed significantly, became an invariant rock upon which to justify the social and economic subordination of the black population.

Science is not static; the theory of polygenesis and its offshoots gave way to Darwin's more modern idea that the human species evolved over a long period of time from a common ancestry. But good ideas, like good seeds, develop deformities as they mature in bad environments. This was the case with Darwinism as it was "socialized" in the American context.[12] Species survive, with variation, from parent forms through natural selection of the best adapted to triumph in the struggle for existence. The "survival of the fittest" provided rugged individualism and competition with a scientific rationalization to justify black subordination and, in fact, allayed white fears by projecting black extinction. In a competitive social and economic jungle, blacks would prove unfit and eventually fade away, the ultimate solution to the white man's burden. In contrast, whites—especially those captains of American industry who were consolidating their power—assured the American public that the law of the fittest, however "hard for the individuals, . . . is best for the 'white' race, because it assures survival . . . in every department."[13]

Even before the culmination of social Darwinism in the last quarter of the nineteenth century, Thomas Huxley, one of Britain's more prominent scientists and a disciple of Charles Darwin, addressed himself directly to Darwin's theory of evolution and its relevance to emancipation in the United States. Huxley assured his American brothers:

No rational man, cognizant of the facts, could deny that the
Negro was inherently inferior. Consequently, it is simply
incredible "to believe that" he will be able to compete
successfully with his bigger-brained and smaller-jawed rival, in
a context which is to be carried on by thoughts and not by
bites.[14]

American society, of course, did not need any prestigious imports to assure it that blacks were endowed with inferior brains and would not therefore successfully compete with the white population. Many homegrown scientists were led by their own investigations to ineluctable conclusion that the morally and intellectually weaker blacks would become victims of the stronger whites in the natural selection process. Once natural selection did its job in producing race traits, moreover, it became important to assert that innate traits such as immorality, criminal behavior, and degeneracy could not be rectified through religion, education, and philanthropy. Such compensatory use of resources was a waste "because . . . external influences did not affect basic hereditary characteristics."[15] Leading students of American demography were quick to latch on to this proposition.[16] As one can see, Arthur Jensen's "disillusionment" one hundred years later with compensatory use of resources for black development is not new; it is part of a long, if not venerable, history.[17]

Darwinism applied to race endowment not only suggested the possibility of black extinction and warned against squandering of resources when dealing with an allegedly incurable problem, but it also proved to be a viable social philosophy for "anti-Negro thinkers during . . . the [whole] post-emancipation 'competitive' state of race relations."[18] Its function was to justify a policy of repression and neglect. The white racist view of black reconstruction and its demise "served to underline the alleged futility of the kind of policies that the racists had espoused, . . . [and] even raised doubts whether blacks should receive any help at all from paternalistic white . . . reformers."[19]

For those who required hope that social intervention was of some consequence without losing the scientific "soundness" emanating from hereditarians, Lamarckian evolutionism momentarily filled the gap. It permitted "social influences to affect [the] genetic make-up of individual[s] and races."[20] Such thinking characterized a new group of scholars who argued for a notion of "plasticity," although they were quick to articulate the view that the genetic drag would never really permit blacks to acquire anything resembling the achievement of the Nordic races.[21] Thus, even a qualified environmentalist view proved to be inapplicable to blacks. Race endowment stood as an immutable factor against success. The Lamarckian view, in any event, was short-lived; it was overshadowed by attacks from "strict hereditarians who denied the plasticity of the races."[22]

Did the facts validate the numerous arguments put forth by the "scientific" racists? It cannot be denied that there was a "terrible truth in the figures demonstrating black 'degeneracy' "; [but] to the extent that they were valid they constituted a powerful indictment of white injustices. . . . Few whites read them that way."[23] More common among hereditarian scholars was the belief that their theories were being validated; the factual outcomes of white supremacy appeared to be the "inevitable unfolding of biological destiny."[24] Social and class oppression produced the data to "validate" racial theories that sustained the need to subordinate blacks.

Just as scientific theorizing is in a perpetual state of flux, so is the social climate that either nurtures new theories or revives old ones. Between 1920 and 1940 there are two interesting interludes that moved in almost opposite directions; both illustrate the importance of social forces on "scientific" truth seeking. In the 1920s, "value-free" cognitive tests aimed at measuring intelligence were used against immigrants, especially non-Nordic ones (southern Europeans, Asians, etc.). Prominent professional psychologists, Americanizing the use of the Stanford-Binet intelligence test, showed, for example, that "83% of the Jews, 80% of the Hungarians, 79% of the Italians, and 87% of the Russians were feeble-minded."[25] For a short interval, newly arrived ethnic whites were lumped with blacks who, a few years earlier, received a similar judgment as a result of their performance on the Stanford-Binet test. To the idea that criminality is innate, a notion commonly employed against blacks, was added the idea that dullness of mind is also innate. In 1916 the famous psychologist Lewis Terman wrote:

> Their dullness seems to be racial, or at least inherent in the
> family stocks from which they came. . . . The writer predicts
> that . . . there will be discovered enormously significant racial
> differences in general intelligence . . . which cannot be wiped
> out by any scheme of mental culture. Children of this group
> should be segregated in special classes . . . They cannot master
> abstractions, but they can often be made efficient workers.[26]

In the late 1930s and early 1940s, the social atmosphere, itself the product of a struggle against the racialist theories of fascism, was conducive to scientific environmentalism. Numerous studies and social experiments conducted by social psychologists and others in related disciplines showed how different environments affected the perceptions, academic achievements, and values of identical twins, blacks and whites, Southerners and Northerners, and views of young children. All roads led to external influences associated with the group mores, class, or culture. It was the heyday of humane environmentalism articulated in scientific terms. This environmentalism was buttressed by anthropological ideas that were popularized in the animated film *Brotherhood of Man*, based on Ruth Benedict's widely distributed pamphlet, *Races of Mankind*.[27]

By the latter part of the 1950s scientific racism reemerges inside the scholarly establishment as a reaction to the 1954 U.S. Supreme Court decision that led to the desegregation of southern schools.[28] The historian Idus A. Newby points out:

> Segregationists who took a second look at the Brown ruling remembered earlier charges that it rested not upon law and constitutional precedent but upon works and theories of a few social scientists. [Urged on by a group of scholars affiliated with the U.S. National Academy of the Sciences, a small group of scientists] became convinced that social science was the Achilles' heel of the Brown ruling. A challenge based on science, they decided, might succeed where those using states' rights and constitutional literalism had failed. Thus the two elements in the story of scientific racism converged. Academic scientists joined segregationists in a concerted effort to overturn the Brown decision. The shift of emphasis from legalism to science . . . was to destroy the legal basis of the civil rights movement.[29]

As in the past, contemporary strains of scientific racism begin with a reaction to socially charged civil rights struggles. It is not a new pattern. But history never quite repeats itself. The role of the scholar, the function of the academy, the relevance of public sentiments, and the class profile of contemporary American society are fundamentally different from those that prevailed in the nineteenth and early twentieth centuries. Moreover, old theories dressed up in new garb are marketed with different labels. For this reason we must explore anew the wave of scientific racism in the post-World War II period.

Two societal developments are relevant to our immediate purpose: the rise of a new middle class and the growth of the academy. Both formations led to generalizations that do injustice to particulars. Nevertheless, the drift of events in these respective spheres, however selectively portrayed, captures the critical reasons for the revival of biological determinist theories and their use against African-Americans through the issue of measured IQ differences.

Meritocracy of the New Middle Class

Between 1950 and 1970, American society experienced tremendous growth in material well-being. In the process, the composition of the output and of the labor force changed — generally from goods to services, from blue-collar workers to white-collar ones. Within white-collar occupations, work routines, so it appeared, required more mental labor involving coordination and communication skills from an array of professional, semiprofessional, and technical workers. This trend, observed by a number of writers, began to define the post-industrial society.[30] Among its essential features was the link between upward occupational mobility and the acquisition of formal knowledge. Those who had the ability or capacity to achieve more education, a sign of measured merit, would also succeed in achieving better jobs with higher monetary rewards. With the growing importance of schooling and its tradition of IQ testing, the present revitalized a past habit by attributing black-white differences in economic status to black-white inherited IQ differences. On the assumption that all the relevant discriminatory barriers were broken by the civil rights movement, and armed with new scientific and statistical ways of separating discrete environmental factors from innate hereditary ones, scientific racism was born again in the 1960s. More will be said about the implications of meritocratic logic and IQism at a later juncture. My immediate aim is to provide an interpretation of the growing status anxiety of America's broad white middle class—an anxiety that turned meritocratic posturing into a class-race issue.[31]

As the national product mix and occupational profile changed, well-being for a growing number of middle-class persons (including those in academe) increasingly became tied to the acquisition of what Fred Hirsch has called positional goods.[32] This fact has greater ramifications than the economic changes recorded by postindustrial observers. For positional goods, unlike necessities, demand increases more than proportional to increases in income. The critical quality of positional goods (used here to embrace jobs, services, and education) is that their private utility is determined by excluding others from acquiring them. A good, safe, quiet, undensely populated community is possible only on the condition that it has restrictions that screen its accessibility. Many kinds of goods and services in fact can be enjoyed only if there is restricted availability. Education begets special privileges, and therefore special kinds of job considerations, only if relatively few people are so educated. Once 40 percent of the labor force has a B.A. degree, such a credential carries increasingly less distinction and therefore warrants less special consideration for job acquisition.

In the course of rapid economic growth and increases in demand for professional and more skilled white-collar workers, colleges and universities were used by a rising middle class to achieve mobility and relative affluence. As economic growth began to taper off near the end of the twenty-year period, the egalitarian thrust that was set in motion by the 1954 Supreme Court decision became more fully apparent. The comfortable but increasingly anxiety-ridden middle class began to feel greater uncertainty about its acquired success.[33] The scale of the egal-itarian movement triggered a social defensiveness among important portions of this self-conscious middle stratum that requires elabora-tion.

The civil rights and black power egalitarians realized that genuine equal opportunity needed more than political and legal rights; it re-quired equality in outcome. While arbitrary distinctions associated with ascribed status were eliminated, those related to inherited wealth, extremely high incomes, and family environment prevailed. As Fred Hirsch noted:

Neither in the cradle nor at the school gate do different
children have an equal start in life. And then what of other
differences in inherited or environmentally influenced
characteristics which in individual cases may be of decisive
importance for economic achievement—differences in health,
in capacity for self-control and discipline . . . ? Clearly once the
concept of economic opportunity is taken seriously, it expands
without natural barrier toward equality of outcome.[34]

This is why a serious demand for equal opportunity is rightfully feared by those who have acquired a psychological status closely linked to the possession of goods and economic position. Equality in life's starting place at birth, given the freedom to achieve as much as possible in one's own life span, requires addressing a host of economic and social inequalities that are not readily eliminated by the competi-tive market and equality before the law. Such equalities in initial life chances would most likely reduce inequality in outcomes between in-come groups and thereby affect the status of the white middle classes.

Those who entered the labor force in the late fifties and early sixties with degrees in this or that—who passed their tests, displayed cogni-tive skills, and acquired positions in the middle and upper-middle lay-ers of the income-occupational structure—felt the need to preserve their newly acquired social status. This variegated white-collar middle class acquired jobs that provided comfortable material and psychic in-comes and secured important positional goods such as relatively un-crowded suburban homes or small country retreats that were pro-tected by legal covenants or high prices.

But as the possessors of good fortune became excessively visible to those not far below them, competitive emulation in a democratic soci-ety nurtured a general question: why shouldn't everyone have a sub-urban home, a country retreat, a college degree, and a satisfying job that provides both psychic and material well-being? The social question became a widespread demand and produced status anxiety among the newly formed middle and upper-middle classes. It threatened the quality and use of their positional accumulations. Opening the doors to everyone in the positional marketplace destroys the utility derived from positional advantages. The suburban gem that you so carefully protected looks increasingly like the overcrowded city from which you sought escape.[35] The development of this process produced a backlash of fear.

Privilege, whatever its nature, finds a way of defending itself, especially from the "hordes" immediately below. The very rich, of course, use the price system with a vengeance: a cliff dwelling on the ocean near a major city is simply not affordable for even the moderately wealthy. The middle classes that made it after World War II, especially as their dream of positional goods began to wane, saw the need to defend themselves more forthrightly against the pressures from below for upward mobility. Theories of excellence aside, their social point was that "not everyone" can meet the merit criteria to get into the upper middle class. "Not everyone" meant, in particular, the sons and daughters of that working- and lower-middle-class stratum whose scores on cognitive tests were lower than those of the middle class's own offspring. As social and political pressures accumulated from the bottom of the social hierarchy for more economic equality, the academy sooner or later found ways of responding with considerable high-sounding finesse. Subtleties aside, either higher degrees became necessary for elite or professional slots, or educational costs rose sufficiently to ward off lower-income applicants, or nonmarket criteria were called forth to distinguish "good" degrees from "bad" ones.[36] In plain words, the academy divided up its functions so as to ensure the interests of the middle class, although it would be a distortion to simply equate changes in middle-class moods and needs with changes in the academy. This peculiar institution is more paradoxical. It reflects the system and undermines it at the same time. My concern is with the former and not the latter.

Given the diverse, often conflicting, social moods that prevailed in the early seventies, the "fragile" administrators who worried about bureaucratic disorder and the sanctimonious professors who felt that their classroom decorum had been violated were only too eager to join the larger backlash that was in the making among the middle layers of American society.[37] Many in academe had stored up resentment because they felt they had silently yielded to the white radical transgressors of the late sixties and early seventies. Those activists, who allied themselves with the rising black "masses" and Vietnamese peasants, changed the curriculum and routines of the university system to which the professors owed their material success and enviable way of life. How else can one explain the dramatic shift to Richard M. Nixon on the part of a significant number of academics who had never before voted Republican?[38] A despised presidential candidate won their support for reasons unrelated to the Republican party; their vote was almost totally related to disruptions in the university led by militant whites and to disruptions in the larger society led first by blacks and later by an assortment of both blacks and whites. Academics, like the middle layers of American society, had a visceral need for "law and order." Within the academy, they advocated "tougher" standards and a return to required courses. The intent of such proposals was frequently aimed at rolling back changes brought about by the disorderly sixties and early seventies, not unrelated to the civil rights "revolution."

Exactly how social and political moods were translated into research agendas (private foundations and government grants aside), how egalitarian advances in one period begat their opposite in the following, how an old dogma like biological IQism acquired research respectability and managed to strike a chord for large numbers of scholarly bystanders are questions that do not lend themselves to easy answers. My own rather harsh judgment is that the academy is an institution occupied by specialists with considerable amounts of knowledge about a shrinking fraction of a growing subject. As specialists who tend to know more about less, they are prone to accept without critical judgment what experts conclude about other areas.[39] If the methodology appears rigorous, conclusions—especially if they correspond to intuitive biases and casual experience—pass unexamined.[40] More often than not, academics are followers rather than generators of new ideas. On matters of social values, they have a cast of mind similar to that of the wider public.[41] This fact is contrary to the popular perception of professional social scientists as forerunners of liberal and egalitarian thought and, perhaps, as threatening to public values and the hard-earned income of ordinary citizens. While there is some truth to this popular notion, it is exaggerated and misunderstood. Within the academy, an internecine war erupted in the seventies in which scholars representing a variety of disciplines peddled overt racist notions about the determinants of black-white differences in IQ. Their ideas tended to conform to the requisites of the social structure and paralleled the larger white backlash that developed in the social arena. A brief, admittedly selective, look at social science inside the academy will help us get to the heart of scientific racism in this period and ultimately to the related race-class debate.

The Academy

In a peculiar way, the academy is an ideal place for the rationalization of the meritocratic society in terms of scientific IQism. The academy itself has grown into a mass social hierarchical system with its multiple layers separated by tests and cognitive performances. There are elite schools where elite scholars enjoy special dispensations for research and the teaching of elite students. Their style of life is the envy of those lower in the hierarchy. There are lesser schools, state universities, state colleges, and smaller private colleges that enroll less-prepared students whose scores on cognitive tests are lower. There are converted state teachers' colleges that accept those in the next rung of the ladder. Finally, we must not neglect to mention community colleges and vocational schools where anyone who can set an alarm clock to get up in the morning can enroll. The faculties are ranked in accordance with the rank of their respective institutions.[42]

Within schools, and even within academic divisions and departments, there is further hierarchy. We all "know" that the physical and natural sciences attract the "brains." In the social sciences, economics represents the queen because of its rigorous theoretical tradition and its "natural" quantifiable units that make it akin to a natural science. Those in economics who do economic history or comparative systems, especially if they do not run numbers through a computer, are the lowest on the totem pole.[43] Sociology and history are "merely" descriptive, soft as velvet—although they too have their "number crunchers." In the humanities, people are difficult to classify; they are like artists with idiosyncratic temperaments. Close to the very bottom of the heap are the departments that educate prospective teachers. Here we find the least qualified members of the academy teaching the least qualified students. The former assimilate the cognitive IQ tests generated by the educational psychologists, teach their use to the least qualified students who become public school teachers. Those in the public school system who most detest teaching for lack of ability or interest become administrators who administer the tests that ultimately are employed to demonstrate that black-white measured intelligence differences are rooted in biology.

A caricature of the academy? Undoubtedly! Yet it is one many of those in it experience with a frequency few care to admit. Many, if not most, teachers from grade school to graduate school do not have much knowledge outside their speciality. Beyond their own area of concern, their thoughts are often as banal as the next person's. Some, of course, may have more cultivated tastes in this or that sphere. But when it comes to the frustrations derived from the teaching experience as such, especially when viewed in the average, impersonal context in which it occurs, the teacher's visceral judgment about many students who cannot learn what they as teachers have so "valiantly" sought to communicate is that this or that "kid is not up to it." Not being up to it can mean many things, the litany of which has been repeated often. But the bottom line of its meaning, especially when it is learned that such a student did not do well on one of a variety of cognitive tests taken, is reserved for black students: "The work is over their heads; they ought to be working at something simpler. . . . They don't belong here. . . . They haven't got what it takes" are some random remarks culled from my colleagues.

"Over the head" is reduced to what is "in the head," and what is in the head requires simple tasks. Some heads are limited in what they can absorb. The *limited* head and the *simpler* tasks are the experiential elements that induce members of the academy to accept as common sense the notion that measured IQ differences are on some level biologically determined, a view not too different from the prejudice of "ordinary" folks.

Worse yet, academics have acquired a faith in scientism that perhaps leads them to accept some of the basic IQ fallacies with conviction. They believe in tests; they believe in the outcome of tests; and they believe, even in the absence of direct knowledge, that when their fellow scientists in other fields report findings that are derived from adherence to the most rigorous procedures—which means controlling for as many variables as the social context will permit—truth has been established. While social scientists in the academy have not debated IQism publicly since the 1960s and 1970s, in private, according to one survey, "many of them tacitly [have ceded] the argument to those who claimed that the disparity was traceable to some deficiency, such as in genetic endowment."[44]

The process of establishing truth in the academy, or at least establishing the respectability of certain ideas about a phenomenon, is complex. There is a strong tendency among social scientists to model their research designs after the physical and natural sciences and, thereby, to elevate the status of their findings. Without any pretense at delving into the subtleties of this problem, I shall simply invoke my own sense of why this is an incorrect direction.

One of the major differences between the science of nature and a "science" of society is that "nature is not manmade, is not produced by man."[45] Intuitively, it is relatively easy to imagine a raw nature with regularities independent of man's contribution. Anthony Giddens raised the problem:

Human beings, of course, transform nature, and surely transformation is both the condition of social existence and a driving force of cultural development. But nature is not a human production; society is. While not made by any single person, society is created afresh, if not *ex nihilo*, by human beings. It is indeed only made possible because every . . . member of a society is a practical theorist.[46]

As practical theorists, everyone has value judgments about what the "real" society ought to be and how the actual society really works. This does not mean that there is a consensus among physicists and chemists about how nature functions or that what is observed is independent of theoretical constructions. Observations of the nonhuman world change as different theories with different categories change. Theories and categories are human creations, and, therefore, subjectivity is inevitably introduced in the organization of nature, however impersonal the instruments of measurement in the "hard" sciences. But, as Lester Thurow critically pointed out, no contemporary astronomer, upon discovering the regularity of some celestial body, ever commented that the body ought not behave that way.[47] Nor have zoologists, I might add, ever been forced to reconsider the phylogenetic rank of forlorn dogs because of dog protests. Only social scientists—along with religious leaders, politicians, and ordinary folks—believe that people ought to behave in accordance with this rather than that rule; or that we must reconsider our understanding of this or that human group, given the current situation or the anger in the community.

This is so because social science is fundamentally about the moral dimension of human relations. It is not above society or value free. Its language may be technical and imbue those who understand it with special status. Nevertheless, social scientists in their professional work manifest the conflicting prejudices of the larger society.[48]

Our brief excursion into the nineteenth and early twentieth centuries illustrated the ways in which scientific pretensions were little more than a camouflage to rationalize race and class prejudices in the context of social, regional, and national conflict. In retrospect scholars look back and moan about what a disservice it was to the cause of science that biological theories were used to justify "class and caste hierarchies" and to help "maintain slavery . . . and the slaughter of the American Indian."[49]

But is all this a matter of history? Are we blind to its current repetition? Are social scientists still capable of achieving a respected place in the academy with arguments that explain race and class division on the rock of biology? The answer to these questions must be, of course, yes. As long as there is class subordination intertwined with racial differentiation, there will be an audience for biological racism. And, moreover, social scientists will be available to communicate it.

The Hereditarians

There are class hereditarians and there are race hereditarians. Although there are differences between them, distinctions are lost in a society in which blacks are overrepresented in the lower class. Moreover, the way that messages are conveyed from specialists within the academy to generalists and ultimately to the public is an unrefined process. Subtleties may abound in professional journals, but as they filter into the public arena, all discussions of IQ in contemporary society end with noting black-white differences. When, moreover, it is reported that blacks do significantly worse than whites on SAT tests (whatever qualifications are made about improvements from some previous year), the innate mental deficiency of blacks is close to the surface of white minds and, perhaps, is silently shared by some blacks who have internalized white society's doubts about black intelligence. Our obsession with testing has intensified our interest in "innate" mental abilities and their relation to upward mobility.

In the postindustrial society, a meritocratic middle class and its academic spokesmen invented a way of socially legitimizing their own rise to and maintenance of status. This legitimization is in the form of a syllogism that is more widely diffused throughout the branches of the social sciences than is openly admitted. Richard Herrnstein, a Harvard University psychologist, stated the case as explicitly as possible in a 1971 *Atlantic Monthly* article; his view is at the very center of much that propels the concern with IQ, which has little to do with the pursuit of truth and the advancement of science:

If differences in mental abilities are inherited; if success requires those abilities; if earnings and prestige depend on success; then social standing (which reflects earnings and prestige) will be based to some extent on inherited differences among people.[50]

To this syllogism, Herrnstein cites a number of postindustrial corollaries: First, as the social environment becomes more uniform for all groups and individuals, intelligence—as a heritable trait—will increase; genetic differences will be more manifest. Second, as modern, technocratically oriented societies eliminate "unnatural" (economic, social, political) barriers to mobility, actual (natural) barriers will increasingly take the form of innate differences. Third, as the size of the elite necessary to manage complex, industrial societies grows, more individuals from the lower depths will be called upon to manage. Those in the lower classes who have the innate ability will rise to the top; those who do not will stay behind. The result will be an increase in the "[IQ] gap between upper and lower classes, making the social ladder even steeper for those left at the bottom."[51] And fourth, derivative of this growing gap is the fact that unemployment—and therefore its related social miseries—will no longer be a matter of "dislocation" or "retraining" if the new "jobs created are beyond the native capacity of the . . . bottom layers. . . . [Being] unemployed may run in the genes of a family as certainly as bad teeth do now."[52]

The difference between Herrnstein's logic and that of Nobel Prize-winning physicist William Shockley is that the former emphasizes class and genes and the latter race and genes.[53] Since blacks are overrepresented in precisely the class categories with which Herrnstein is dealing, there is little practical difference.

Gary S. Becker, a prominent conservative economist and human-capital theorist, reasons similarly and perhaps typifies in sharper focus what is generally believed among his lesser-known colleagues. Becker's implicit logic is as follows:

Income differences are determined by human capital differences.

Human capital differences are, among other things, closely connected to differences in the stock of knowledge individuals accumulate.

One major source of differences in the stock of knowledge among individuals and groups is formal education.

Since everyone has more or less equal access to the same system of education as a matter of political right, it follows that those who acquire less knowledge in a given period of time— before entering the job market—must be less capable, that is, endowed with an inferior capacity to acquire knowledge.

It follows that income differences that reflect productivity differences are ultimately explained by biological differences that are assumed to be inherited.

Finally, the whole process outlined above is perpetuated throughout institutional practices of marriage, or, to use Becker's phrase, the marriage market.

As Becker states it:

An important result of population genetics is that positive assortive mating of inheritable traits, like race, intelligence, or height, increases the correlation of these traits among siblings; the increase would be greater the more inheritable the trait is and the greater the degree of assortive mating. . . . The correlation by intelligence is especially interesting since, although intelligence is highly inheritable, correlation between mates is about as high as that between siblings. Apparently, the marriage market, aided by coeducational schools, admissions tests, and the like is more efficient than is commonly believed.[54]

Informed by the findings of biological determinists, human capital economists can celebrate how fortunate we are that our educational institutions through their screening and stratification mechanisms have accomplished what the 1920 eugenic movement could not—the efficient economic distribution of "innate" talent.[55] The fact that this distribution happens to correspond to the existing racial and class disparities is "fortuitous." Becker's argument has been put more succinctly in a reaction to a special report on human capital in *Business Week:*

The human capital problem . . . discussed is totally unsolvable by the techniques that the various writers suggested. Intelligence is largely hereditary. Smart people have smart kids. To expect the average kid from the ghetto to compete with the offspring of the upper middle class—you can't be serious.[56]

Biology and social institutions; nature versus nurture; race versus class; these are the main foci of the black-white difference debate. Must we accept one or the other?

Nature versus Nurture/Race versus Class

The nature-nurture argument under a variety of guises has a long history and no resolution in any abstract sense is possible. With respect to black-white differences, the argument is flavored with deeply felt value-laden presuppositions that are fed in the context of social conflict and the struggle for social justice and economic equality. Scientific findings represent a quest for legitimizing differential life chances among groups, classes, and segments of classes. The degree of equality sought or deemed desirable in a democratic society that holds out extensive promises to the mass of its citizenry is a topic fraught with anxiety. Issues of justice and equality involve profound ethical and moral choices that ought to be independent of biologically defined differences. One way to simplify the whole problem and bypass the complex democratic route is to employ the reductionist mode of reasoning characteristic of the "scientific" hereditarians.

Assertions like the above, although perhaps obvious to some, are necessary because the IQ genetic advocates deny their racist or ethical involvement; their charade is that of "value-free" scientists collecting evidence to validate a hypothesis in the most rigorous possible way. Yet, "despite their pretensions, 'they are constantly' engaged in making political and moral statements about human society."[57] As a group, they tend to devalue equality, the potential of common people, democratic participation, and positive accomplishments derived from changing the structure of society.[58] To deny, therefore, that examining black-white differences in IQ is without ethical intent is simply to camouflage sinister motives.

Scientific IQists aside, it is now time to turn to the structure of the nature-nurture debate by identifying the range of possible interpretations that are employed to analyze black-white IQ differences. In developing a more sophisticated set of possibilities, the racist significance of scientific IQism will be more intelligible.

The general consensus is that blacks and whites manifest differences. Beyond that, much of the agreement dissolves. There are five root positions, each with its implied cures and commitment to egalitarian goals (see the accompanying tabulation):[59] (I) IQ hereditarians; (II) external environmentalists; (III) developmental geneticists; (IV) internal physiological environmentalists; and (V) black autonomists. Among these, only the IQ hereditarians justify class subordination on biological grounds. The following three (external environmentalists, developmental geneticists, and internal physiological environmentalists) either avoid biologically driven explanations or embrace social and class ones. The fifth approach (black autonomists) returns to a race-based, but not an anti-egalitarian, perspective.

The heritability school (row I) has been elaborated earlier in this chapter. A brief summary for purposes of this section will suffice:[60] Differences in socioeconomic status are a result of differences in inher-

Positions	Cures	Implications
I. *IQ hereditarians:* Intelligence is inherited and relatively permanent	None; or by implication better breeding or two-track educational system	Equality impossible
II. *External environmentalists:* Human organism plastic; manipulation of external stimuli will completely condition human behavior	Control and modify environment in as many specific ways as possible	Egalitarian
III. *Developmental geneticists:* Intelligence not a trait; no meaning to mental behavior being determined by genes; holistic approach to genes, environment, and organism	Open; changing organism approached from variety of directions	Egalitarian
IV. *Internal physiological environmentalists:* Emphasis on fetal environment producing birth defects often mistakenly interpreted as inherited	Improved health care, prenatal care, and general well-being among the poorest	Egalitarian
V. *Black autonomists:* Language distinction; different value system; no deficit, just difference	Society should accommodate to ghetto children as if they spoke foreign language; end domination of imperial culture; black development	Separate and equal

ited mental abilities that are measured by IQ tests. Because about 80 percent of the variability between individuals in intelligence measured by IQ tests is genetically determined, mental ability is relatively fixed and unchangeable. It is reasoned that inherited intelligence differences *between* groups (blacks and whites) can be understood from heritability differences among individuals *within* groups.

The external environmentalist school (row II)—which may be thought about as the "complete nurture" school in opposition to the "complete nature" (hereditary) one—puts the emphasis totally on factors external to the individual organism. The individual is assumed to be virtually plastic, malleable, or like a "blank sheet." Human behavior is shaped by factors in the environment defined in terms of "sensory inputs, responses, rewards, and punishments 'administered' from birth."[61] These microstimuli can be viewed as part of a larger environment consisting of family circumstances, neighborhood, and class.

Vulgar Marxists frequently focus on the role of class in the context of the whole economic system. The class structure is employed to determine the politics and culture of the society that impinge on the individual's consciousness and behavior. In this way individuals become mirror images of the social order. External environmentalists, whether followers of Skinner or Marx, view individual behavior as the product of either a manipulated microenvironment or a structured macro one. Insofar as external environmentalists fail to explain behavior, they tend to fall back on the durability of old habits inhibiting adaptations to a new environment or, in the case of Marxists, "false consciousness."

Between IQ hereditarians and the external environmentalists are the developmental geneticists (row III). While the main thrust of their argument is against the IQ hereditarians, they are in principle against the external environmentalists. Developmental geneticists argue that the "relation between gene, environment, organism, and society is complex in a way not encompassed" by hereditarians and environmental reductionists.[62] Developmental geneticists suggest that the nature of the interaction between the genotype (gene or gene structure) and the environment is such that it makes no sense to predict the makeup or appearance or behavior properties of the organism "from a knowledge of [the] . . . genotype or environment taken separately. . . . No one has ever been able to relate any aspect of human behavior to any particular gene or set of genes, and no one has ever suggested an experimental plan for doing so."[63] The reasoning behind such assertions is illustrated by looking at the potential of two gene structures (G1, G2) on the potential growth of organism O in two different environments. Assume that the environment consists of two possible temperatures, high and low. Changing the environment simply involves changing temperatures. As the accompanying bar graph indicates, G1 produces an organism that reaches its known potential in an environment defined by its low temperature, but fails to do so in high temperatures.

The opposite case is the organism with G2; here organism O achieves its potential growth in high temperatures but not in low ones. Since G1 and G2 relate to the organism's growth in opposite directions as the environment changes, it is *impossible* to say that G1 is superior or inferior to G2. All one can say is that an organism's growth is a *simultaneous* product of a genetic structure and an environment.[64] This explanation is different from that employed by hereditarians and extreme environmentalists. There are simply "no generalizations that hold consistently about the way in which different genotypes will develop in different environments."[65]

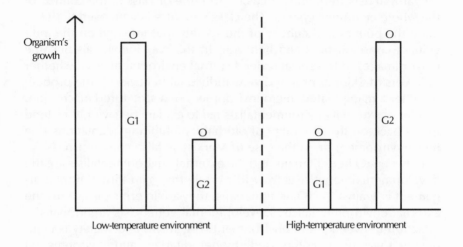

In essence, from knowledge established by developmental geneticists, the IQ hereditarians misunderstand the very genetic foundations on which their arguments depend. They fail to grasp the core process by which genotype, environment, and organism are interlocked into a whole. This process, moreover, is the technical basis that undermines the crucial assumptions of the IQ hereditarians. Once these assumptions are cast aside, the host of propositions that IQ hereditarians employ to deduce differences in inherited intelligence between blacks and whites as measured by IQ tests become untenable.

Closely allied with the developmental geneticists are medically oriented physiologists who emphasize the components of the organism's internal environment (row IV).[66] Unlike external environmentalists, they do not view the organism as passive or perfectly malleable prior to environmental impact. The internal physioenvironmentalists accept the technical foundations of the geneticists, but choose to identify environmentally induced or related disorders that are frequently mistaken for purely genetic ones. Their contribution is to enlarge the frontier of what is usually meant by environment. All kinds of minor, unobserved birth defects affecting brain development or functioning, previously interpreted as inherited (and therefore unchangeable), are now understood as caused by a defective fetal environment produced by poor diet or malnutrition, inadequate medical attention, and, not least, drug or alcohol intake during pregnancy. The argument is that some portion of black-white differences in testing may be caused not by genes but by factors in the internal physiological environment during pregnancy and/or birth.

The fifth position—identified as black autonomist (row V)—is a response to both the IQ hereditarians and to those social scientists who argue that blacks suffer from some kind of verbal or cognitive deficit associated with an inadequate environment. Adherents of the black autonomist school, it should be noted, enter the debate from a very different angle of refraction compared to the other orientations. Nevertheless, they warrant consideration because their position is germane to my general concern with how social scientists perceive the world from the perspective of race or class; or, perhaps more accurately, with how they confuse the world because of the inadequate understanding of the relationship between race and class.

The black autonomists are divided into two groups: psycholinguists and culturalists. The main proponent of the psycholinguistic argument is William Labov. The origin of the low academic and intellectual functioning of ghetto-reared children is the absence of "an appreciation of the uniqueness of the language, family style, and ways of living of inner-city children. What is lacking . . . is an accommodation by the inner-city schools to the native communication style of the inner-city child."[67] Labov, in other words, argues that inner-city African-Americans speak black English and are forced to confront a "learning" situation in a "foreign" tongue. No remediation is necessary, since blacks do not lack verbal stimulation. "In fact," writes Labov, "black children in the urban ghettos receive a great deal of verbal stimulation, hear more well-formed sentences than middle-class children, and participate in a highly verbal culture; they have the same basic vocabulary, possess the same capacity for conceptual learning, and use the same logic as anyone else who learns to speak and understand English."[68] A current variation of this school argues that black children have different learning styles that are not understood by white teachers or, perhaps, black teachers as well. If teachers adapted to black learning styles, the assumed deficit would disappear.[69] The problem is that teachers respond to black students as if they were retarded, when in fact the main problem is a language or style difference. But sooner or later, a self-fulfilling prophecy actualizes itself. Teachers who act as if they were dealing with deficient children produce inferiority feelings and a defensive stance that block the capacity of black inner-city children to develop.

The cultural wing of the autonomist school is in fact a variation of the psycholinguistic one—except that it embraces more than language and more than simply inner-city children and families. In the culturist

view, all blacks—regardless of economic circumstances—function below their potential in American society because American society is racially oppressive and offensive to black culture and values. Oppression
could lead to the accumulation of repressed anger, which would obstruct learning.[70] If blacks could rid themselves of the oppressive and
inhibiting qualities of the imperial culture, they would develop without
remediation or special aids. Blacks are not damaged and therefore
there is no skill or capacity deficit. Independence is all that is required
for black development, which may be different but not inferior to that
which characterizes white society.

The accumulation of criticisms aimed at IQ hereditarians exposes
both their vulnerability and their scientific claims. A brief discussion of
a select number is in order.

On the broad statistical front, it has been shown that education and
income levels of achievement are correlated with family socioeconomic background.[71] For white nonfarm males between the ages of
thirty-five and forty-four, studies (controlling for IQ or cognitive test
scores) indicate that success is predictable by family rank.[72] Contrary
to Herrnstein's suggestion that unemployment may be due to innate
intelligence, it is more likely related to class background. For African-
Americans, of course, class background is compounded by degradation based on race. Achievement levels are affected by both class circumstances and racial experiences. Similar class experiences may not
produce similar outcomes because of racially induced experiences in
the family, community, schools, and labor markets. Even when overall
achievement levels appear identical, conviction and confidence about
personal effectiveness may vary along racial lines.

On the more technical side, statistical measures of IQ differences
between black and white children at various ages require that the socioeconomic status of the parents be identical, that is, held constant.
While many studies claim adherence to such standardized procedures,
the socioeconomic class indices commonly employed conceal the fact
that a significant portion of blacks categorized as middle class are in
fact similar to white working-class adults. When adjustments are made
for this error, measured IQ differences between children of different
races with genuine middle-class backgrounds disappear.[73]

It is conceptually incorrect to equate the terms *genetic* and *inherited*
with *unchangeable*.[74] Many known inherited degenerative processes,
like Wilson's disease, are completely curable through the use of drugs
if the disease is diagnosed early in life.[75] Thus, even if IQ were inherited, it would not necessarily imply the kind of permanency suggested
by the hereditarians.

It is erroneous to think of genes as setting limits, as giving the organism a potential capacity beyond which it cannot develop—equating the brain to a bucket that has an upper limit to how much water it can hold. As the developmental geneticists have shown, the potentials of genotypes vary dramatically in different environments.

It is wrong to talk about intelligence as if it were a trait or "thing" like eye color. Taking a composite of unlike qualities and reducing them to a single number derived from test scores that is identified as IQ—meaning the "ability to learn" rather than what has been learned—conceals far more than it reveals.[76] In substance, the mathematics of IQism is technically miscontrued. It is akin to adding up unlike things. What do four apples plus two elephants divided by the average age of each equal? No meaningful figure.[77]

The claim that a certain percent (0 to 100) of IQ is heritable is based on a correlation of factors concerned with rank order that erroneously suggests causation or similarity, when neither may exist.[78] Suppose three boys (B1, B2, B3) were separated from their extremely poor environments at birth and raised by affluent families. Suppose the mothers (M1, M2, M3) were all very short, but M1 was marginally taller than M2 and M2 marginally taller than M3. Suppose that the boys who were raised in affluent circumstances measured six to eight inches taller sixteen years later than any of the boys in the poor families of M1, M2, and M3, but the rank order of the boys corresponds to that of the mothers (B1 > B2 > B3). The correlation would be perfect and would suggest, in accordance to the heritability statistic, the profound influence of inheritance. In contrast, the absolute average size increase that in fact occurred suggests the importance of environment.[79]

Another fatal error made by IQ hereditarians is to "suppose that the heritability of IQ within populations somehow explains the differences in test scores between [populations, for example, races and classes]."[80] Neglecting momentarily the monumental problem of what constitutes a separate group when one is dealing with the human species, geneticists inform us that the causes of differences between groups cannot be validly inferred to be the same as causes within groups.[81] The alleged genetic determinants of white middle-class scores cannot be assumed to operate for another racial group.

A related problem, as I intimated above, is the question of what is a group when one is talking about the human species? Put differently, on what basis do we categorize blacks as a group? What percent of one's ancestors must be African-rooted to qualify one as a member of the black group? Would we do better to organize people on the basis of blood type or on the basis of the existence of a certain protein X that may not be universally found in identical proportions among all individuals?[82] If all blood type A people were put together and given IQ tests, would not that be a more scientific grouping than skin color, which not only varies widely but is socially structured?

"African-American" is a social category applied to those who are raised in a particular environment and share a history of experiences. For this reason, it is necessary to differentiate between African-Americans and, for example, West Indian blacks. It is more than skin color that defines the black experience in the United States. Although West Indian blacks often are made to feel like "niggers" after living in the United States for a few years, sometimes developing a bitterness toward white society as a whole, they possess a culturally more confident posture toward their racial maltreatment than do African-Americans.

On a different level of inquiry, there are the separated identical twin and adoption studies, both of which bear on the IQ-hereditarian position. The twin studies have been used to "prove" the "fixity" of mental ability. Upon close examination it has been shown that the facts do not reveal what was originally advertised about a large proportion of these studies. The gross fraud of the infamous Cyril Burt case aside, it turns out that many of these studies involved twins who were separated but neither raised in very different environments nor separated for very long periods of time in the formative years.[83] In the few cases in which there were dramatic shifts in the environment, the results did not support the claims regarding heredity.[84]

In fact, the best adoption studies done by behavior geneticists in which careful control groups were built into the design yield strong findings against the notion that IQ is highly heritable.[85] These studies compared the parents of the biological child with those of the adopted, as well as the children from both the adopted and natural parent. The results strongly suggest that "children reared by the same mother resemble her IQ to the same degree, whether or not they share her genes."[86]

When we move on to the IQ tests themselves, we find that a battery of criticisms has accumulated. One criticism begins with the observation that "IQ scores of many children vary as much as 15 points over the course of their school years, and for one in ten children, it varies by more than 30 points."[87] Even Arthur Jensen admitted that "in some extreme cases variation is as much as 60 to 70 points."[88] The explanations of variability are in several directions.

Some studies have shown that African-Americans do much better when tests are administered by blacks or by computers, although white scores remain the same.[89] Others suggest that "IQ test scores among Blacks . . . can be raised through various devices including coaching, training . . . changing the test environment, rewording the language of the test, and most important of all, by a combination of these."[90] This kind of attack is again aimed at the alleged immutability of IQ.

Many of these criticisms raise questions about the tests themselves and precisely what is measured. Is it intelligence or acquired knowledge? Closely related to this kind of inquiry is the argument that IQ tests are culturally and class biased: there is no such "thing" as a culture-free test. Thus, if African-Americans are deeply rooted in a cultural subdivision of a society that perpetuates values and styles governed by other rules (the black English and learning arguments), changing the tests in line with the culture would improve the scores, a fact that has been demonstrated by those who pursue this line of inquiry. In this respect, we should not forget another observation already noted. The poor performance of Eastern European immigrants in the 1920s was due not only to cultural difference but also to the intimidation of the immigrants by the test conditions and the testers themselves. Why should we not assume the same for African-Americans?

My final remark in this inventory of criticisms against IQ hereditarians is philosophic. IQ biological reductionists may have a problem for reasons other than their veiled, and often explicit, racial biases. Reductionists proceed from the unwarranted ontological assumption that in the beginning there is the gene from which emerges the formed or "determined" individual from whom group and societal patterns may be discerned and explained.[91] By starting with the assumption that knowledge about the whole is derived from aggregating knowledge about individuals, and that knowledge about individuals is reducible to gene structures, reductionists lose sight of the fact that individuals and the social structures of society coexist, that is, exist simultaneously. This is not simply a matter of one modifying the role of the other, or a case of a mechanical interaction between two separately conceived elements of a system; it is rather that the very roles of differently organized parts of a system cannot be defined, cannot be conceived in a coherent and meaningful way without simultaneously understanding how they are interlocked in a conjugal arrangement. In this sense, we are back to the problem of conceiving of a gene without an environment, or an environment without an organism. Once thinking moves out from under the reductionist rug, immutability disappears; hitherto unseen possibilities open to the development of the human species.

Hereditarians and autonomists both make race the center of their focus, although the former constitutes an attack on blacks and the lat-

ter represents a defense of blacks. The two variants of environmentalism reason in a mode consistent with that of class determinists; life
chances of blacks are determined by crude and subtle environmental
influences. And finally, the developmental geneticists include both environmental and endowment factors in their analysis, but in ways that
undermine the approaches characterized by biologically oriented social scientists.

Conclusion

What I have argued in this chapter is that much of the "scientific" racism about black-white mental differences is derived from the social
structure that social scientists help create, both as citizens and as members of a professional group. They then proceed to contemplate and
measure the black-white differential consequences of an unjust social
structure and conclude that there is a significant biological factor unrelated to the social structure that determines these black-white measured differences.

   When one examines the long history of the misuse of biological
"scientism" against African-Americans, when one considers the history of scientists actually doctoring and falsifying their collected data to
prove black inferiority,[92] when one considers the gaps in knowledge
about genetics that characterize its use by social scientists, when one
includes the large variety of ways that assumed endowment observations can be misspecified because of the prevalence of numerous environmental subtleties that are omitted from consideration, one
reaches a simple conclusion: racially biased scientists are normal. Like
"ordinary" folk living in a racially charged and stratified society, they
have their racialist theories that relate to social policies and practices.
Unlike ordinary citizens who are up front about their racial sentiments,
hereditarians are sinister; they use the scientific enterprise as a screen
to conceal racial biases. Since racially biased scientists are active respondents contributing to a racially biased social and class structure,
changing the former must go hand in hand with changing the latter.

ECONOMICS OF DOMINANT-SUBORDINATE RELATIONS

S lavery not only produced a legacy that justified the use of scientific IQism against blacks; it also generated a frame of mind, however modified over time, legitimizing institutional racism—a phrase that has been overused and ill-defined.

My concern in this chapter is less with the wide range of diffuse discriminatory practices that prevail in a variety of areas, and more with the way institutional racism operates to produce or reproduce dominant-subordinate relations in specific situations. While mechanisms (e.g., conforming to the racial preferences of others), sources (e.g., employers, employees, and consumers), and manifest forms (e.g., black-white differences in career ladders) vary, they all operate to inhibit the kind of job opportunities that empower blacks over whites in ways unlike the process by which male whites acquire empowerment over other whites. This process works, moreover, behind a veil that eliminates the individual's sense of responsibility for his or her action.

In the course of making decisions, people are rarely aware of the nature of their racial biases; very few individuals wear a sign on which is written "I am a racist." Most people in contemporary American society think they, and not others, are exempt from this affliction.[1] People often express the view that they are only adapting to a larger constellation of forces that they as individuals cannot control. If so few people admit to racist attitudes, why does a belief exist that there are so many "other" people with such attitudes? The answer, I believe, is that racism is normal; it is so completely institutionalized in our routines that it escapes our conscious attention. It is built into a myriad of decisions that have degrading consequences, even when they do not reflect intentions, "inner" sentiments, or personal values. Much racism, which is part of our everyday exchanges, is not perceived as unjust. My focus is on the nature of this process.

By institutional racism, I mean that people, as individuals or in small decision-making groups, are induced to behave as if they were employing a racial criterion for reasons of self-interest or protection — even when it may be contrary to their personal preferences, values, or tastes. If such a process is to function effectively, the following implicit conditions must prevail to one degree or another. First, the dominant group in aggregate must have the means, the wherewithal, to effectuate their decisions; that is, there must be power differentials, otherwise racism reduces itself to "all talk and no action."[2] Second, in any particular social context, color must have a sufficiently pejorative connotation to enough members of the dominant group so as to be capable of overriding other considerations. Third, a double standard needs to operate in the sense that similar behavior by blacks and whites is evaluated differently. These interrelated conditions combine to produce a propensity to relegate blacks to subordinate positions vis-à-vis whites; nuances are important in this tendency.

Organizations are structured in terms of lines of authority, by degrees of equality involving personal empowerment. The structure of dominant-subordinate relations in authority arrangements are both formal and informal. My concern here is with organizational situations in which blacks appear to be integrated in the sense that they are working under the same roof as whites. I am not, in other words, concerned with upward mobility along completely or partially segregated lines, for example, black personnel managers managing black employees. The extent to which manifest racism has been made inoperative, in my view, is measured only by the degree to which blacks have equal opportunities to reverse dominant-subordinate relations, or to establish relations that are equally empowering between the races for any given general line of activity. This point has not gone unnoticed by black scholars:

Whites [do not necessarily] seek to distance themselves
physically from blacks. The assumption that they did, which
forms the basis of . . . [many models], misses the point
completely. The whites did not object at all to having blacks

around them so long as the blacks always behaved deferentially and occupied subordinate positions.[3]

The impulse on the part of whites to maintain dominant-subordinate patterns generates overcrowding of blacks in particular occupations and within general occupational categories, sectors of the economy, or residential sections of the metropolitan area. Once this occurs, the status of individual blacks whose capacities are above the group's average is affected. That is to say, in any particular situation, if a large percentage of blacks are perceived to occupy the least desired place in the hierarchy of an organization, then black individuals who are above the average in such a situation face barriers to upward mobility if such mobility requires occupying positions of authority that reverse dominant-subordinate relations. The aggregate consequences of this process in dynamic terms are analyzed in chapter 6. My concern here is primarily with the application of the dominant-subordinate rule within individual organizations.

By examining the nature of racially determined decisions inside enterprises at various levels, it is possible to observe how dominant-subordinate relations between white and black employees have become institutionalized, even when integration appears to prevail. While most of the decisions affecting the black worker's subordinate position are made by employers, they are derived not only from considerations about the productivity or qualities of black workers as such, but also from the assumed perceptions of consumer, employee, and competing employer responses to the use of black workers in positions that alter dominant-subordinate relations.

Consumer Discrimination

A white employer operates a small TV repair service in a large metropolitan area in which about 25 percent of the population is black. Most of the employer's services are supplied in the homes of white consumers as a consequence of residential segregation. The company hires nine white service workers and one black one; the black worker is employed to repair sets brought into the shop. The employer in this example is assumed to be free of racial bias. His or her employment policies are determined by customers who are assumed to have concerns about blacks entering homes in certain capacities. White consumers may have general fears that are broadly defined, or they may link the quality of the service with the appearance of the person who provides it. Technically the customer in the example purchases only the repair of the TV set. But since consumers in this market are not expert buyers, they also purchase the assumed "extrinsic" qualities of the person supplying the service, a fact that may have little relationship to the actual service being performed. It is similar to mistakenly equating the good bedside manners of surgeons with their operating abilities.

Extending this understanding that the owner of the TV repair company has about his or her customers, the owner further assumes that white customers have an aversion to blacks entering their homes, and especially an aversion to blacks supplying services that reverse the dominant-subordinate relationship whites expect when they "deal" with blacks. While whites, for example, may prefer white window-washers, at least they "deal" with black window-washers in terms that are consistent with white black-white hierarchical expectations and social practices—whites tell the black service worker what to do or how to do it. Washing windows is a service in which the consumer can pass immediate judgment about whether the job has been done appropriately. TV repair workers essentially reverse this dominant-subordinate role. They become, in relation to the consumer, technical experts whose diagnosis and decision must be trusted. White consumers are not readily induced to have a relationship with blacks in which the dominant-subordinate pattern is reversed. Because of these considerations, our white employer does not employ black TV repair workers, since to do so may lead to a decline in demand for the company's services. Even if black TV repair workers were available at lower wage rates, this fact alone might not offset the change in demand experienced by the company. As a consequence of dominant-subordinate considerations, job opportunities are not available to blacks in this kind of service industry, unless, of course, it proceeds along segregated lines; that is, blacks are relegated to the service solely of other blacks.

Lest this be considered an isolated example, it is worth noting other examples of "pure" consumer-determined discrimination that are mediated by the impersonal decisions of employers. Brokerage firms are hesitant to hire black brokers to give advice to white clients. Black lawyers, doctors, and dentists do not have white clients or patients. Black insurance salespersons sell insurance primarily in segregated markets, especially if it involves face-to-face personal consultations. In all these cases, consumption of the service is connected with personal characteristics of the suppliers of the service. In the words of one West Coast personnel officer, the problem with respect to some kinds of jobs is not that the black employee lacks skills, "but that he is aesthetically objectionable—he spoils the decor, so to speak."[4] This "spoilage" is rarely noted in situations where the black relation to whites is subordinate. In the business decision, the personal views of the employer may become irrelevant; the concern is the loss of sales by putting black workers in positions that reverse the lines of authority when dealing with consumers.

It should be noted that in many cases where black professionals supply services, an income effect is associated with the consumption sphere where there is residential and/or social segregation. Blacks will buy services from white professionals, but whites avoid or rarely have the opportunity to purchase services from black counterparts. Black professionals, operating in independent primary markets, tend to be dependent on black demand, which is limited by the generally lower income that prevails in the black community relative to the white one, and by the asymmetric nature of the demand for black professional services. In this way the income of black professionals is lessened—not necessarily by their human capital characteristics, but by the segmentation that prevails in the consumption sphere. This segmentation, in turn, can affect the long-run self-investment in professional growth on the part of blacks operating in the independent segregated markets. Eventually, therefore, black professional market capacities may be adversely affected. In this sense, the poverty of the black population casts a shadow that circumscribes the economic status of black professionals.

Another kind of consumer discrimination produces differentials in career ladders between black and white workers. This can be exemplified by a large department store that employs blacks as salespersons in proportion to their numbers in the larger metropolitan labor market. Moreover, the employment pattern is not only on an integrated basis, but it is one in which there is equal pay for equal work. No discrimination appears to operate on entry level jobs. But that is where the matter ends. Upon close inspection one finds, appearances to the contrary, that black employees are not randomly distributed among the store's occupations.

Although there are particular sales jobs that both blacks and whites perform (i.e., class integration at the lowest level), there are also sales jobs that are "reserved" solely for whites. What determines this relatively subtle job-caste arrangement is related, as with the TV repair example, to the dominant-subordinate relation that is technically defined by the nature of the commodity being sold. Blacks are most commonly found at those sales counters where the consumer requires little advice, guidance, or information from the seller. Blacks tend to sell those commodities or provide those services where they act mainly as instruments in the collection of money after the consumer has made an "autonomous" decision to buy. The salesperson simply conforms to the decision of the consumer; the dominant-subordinate relationship remains intact.

In contrast, the purchase of electric appliances or other durable goods, which need to be explained to the consumer in order to facilitate a decision to buy, requires sales personnel who can maintain a dialogue with potential purchasers and interpret their needs. In these kinds of jobs, salespersons tend to be white. Thus, the ostensibly unbiased employment practices of this department store result in racially determined placements within the store. This process operates to limit the career ladders of blacks, although entry level jobs are available on nondiscriminatory terms. As this reality becomes experientially internalized on the part of blacks, a lack of motivation to fulfill more than minimal job requirements may begin to operate. Consequently, productivity differences between black and white workers may begin to be perceived by the employer, and thereby legitimize the employer's differential career ladder policies on grounds other than the way that they might affect consumer sales. Productive effort, it should be emphasized, is elastic and—in contrast to the way most economists argue—not a bundle of fixed characteristics. Productivity is either stretched or contracted by the individual's belief in the opportunities to develop and advance that are part of the work-site environment. This includes an ambience provided not only by management but also by the quality of interaction and networking among employees themselves. If blacks are socially isolated and have minimal affective social relations, which are vital to job satisfaction, networking for improving skills and nurturing motivation will be negatively affected.

Another example of the dominant-subordinate barrier in operation was observed by Frederick Douglass in the ninteenth century when he pointed out that prejudice against blacks was far greater among mechanics than among lawyers.[5] This is illustrated by the pattern observed in an office equipment supply company. The company's hiring policy, perhaps contrary to expectations, exhibits a willingness to hire some blacks at higher technical-level jobs, while not employing blacks for the lower-level sales positions. The clue to understanding the company's unwritten policies is knowing who participates in the purchase of technical, rather than nontechnical, hardware and services. Large computer systems are bought or leased for use by technical experts. Buyers for companies that use computers spend tens of thousands of dollars on a single item or system and have experts do their buying. As an expert, the buyer is concerned only with the specifications of the product as it can be observed or explained by another technical expert.

The expert buyer, by definition, is a person who avoids confusing the commodity or service with the extrinsic characteristics of the person who is doing the selling. Therefore, given pressures, the office equipment company does not resist hiring qualified black computer experts who deal with comparable white experts. Once "expertise" is necessary in a situation, it acquires respect in the same way that the extrinsic rank of a police officer—independent of the person—acquires respect.

In the case of the company's less sophisticated products purchased by companies or small store owners, the consumer ceases to be an expert. Appearance, presence, and rapport might be considered important attributes of such salespersons as they explain the virtues of particular pieces of equipment to its actual users. Low-level buyers for companies are even known to socialize with their sellers in exchange for their patronage (not to mention the acceptance of gifts). As a black entrepeneur complained, "[My] main frustration is a lack of social connections that a white rival might enjoy."[6] In any event, the relationship behind these kinds of transactions is one in which the subordinate position of the purchaser needs consideration. While the salespersons wish to please their customers, they also are assumed to have superior technical knowledge about the commodities being sold. Buyers at this level are capable of confusing color with the products being sold, especially if white salespersons are competing with black ones. This possibility leads the equipment company managers to employ primarily whites in these lower-level but skilled positions.

An observation of a very different nature involves middle-class black consumers, as reported by white contractors who solicit jobs in a section of Queens, New York, known as St. Albans. In general, consumer discrimination, as we have indicated, is asymmetrical; white consumers avoid specific kinds of exchange relations with blacks who supply the services, but black consumers are generally willing to deal with white suppliers of services. Yet, it has been known for black consumers to turn against their own cohorts who supply services, although perhaps for reasons different from those of their white counterparts. A white contractor who does outside home repairs (siding, storm window installations, roofing) in a middle-class black community recounts the following conversation with a prospective black consumer:

CONSUMER: You do good work?
CONTRACTOR: The best.
CONSUMER: I mean you have good workers?
CONTRACTOR:: The very best with lots of experience.
CONSUMER: I mean that they don't waste time and do quality work.

CONTRACTOR: Yes sir. They are workers who have been with me for a long time. Joe McKenna and Harry Klein are two of the best workers in the business.

CONSUMER: McKenna, you say. Good to hear that. That's what I mean.[7]

When I queried whether the black consumer's concern with the quality of the workers whom the contractor employed really was a question about the race of the workers used, the contractor said: "No doubt about it; they didn't want to say it outright; that's natural; but they wanted to know whether I used black workers. Had I suggested I used them, I would have lost the deal."

One can suggest various interpretations of the way the dominant-subordinate preoccupation in a racist society affects even its victims, for example, either how blacks project onto other blacks internalized white perceptions used against blacks themselves as one possibility, or how they get some psychic satisfaction in reversing who is working for whom as another. This latter possibility was enunciated in Alice Walker's *The Color Purple*: "Do her peoples [referring to a white family] know, I ask. They know, say Sofia. They carrying on just like you know they would. Whoever hear of a white woman working for niggers, they rave."[8]

Employee Discrimination

As in the area of consumer discrimination, blacks in the production sphere are often limited in upward mobility by the "enforcement" of the dominant-subordinate rule. Within the workplace of a large firm, discrimination becomes more subtle in the absence of overt exclusion practices by a white-dominated union. A personnel manager who operates from the apex of a large, impersonal bureaucracy is probably socially neutral with respect to the color composition of his or her labor force. But there is no neutrality with respect to the collective performance of the enterprise's labor supply. Managers see their employees as a unit that must work in harmony if daily routines are to proceed smoothly. For this reason, even employers in a large, nationally established business might come to develop race rules for job allocation and promotion that are related not necessarily to their own views but to those that conform to the preferences of the employees. This is clearly seen in the case of the automobile industry, whose management, while preaching nondiscrimination, readily adjusts its policies to the local-market racial biases of its employees. Auto plants in Detroit, Baltimore, and Atlanta all have different employment policies.[9]

Enlightened employers like those who manage the automobile industry adjust to the preferences of their nonsupervisory employees in order to ensure interemployee "harmony" between the races. They do this by relegating blacks to the occupational lines that are subordinate to the occupations assigned to white workers, and by segregating the workforce between plants or within plants. In general, whatever the particular form of adjustment, the employer, reflecting the preferences of his or her employees and not wishing to disrupt the harmony of the labor force, avoids putting blacks in positions in which they supervise whites. Blacks can, of course, supervise blacks; in such cases upgrading is along segregated lines. But this promotional route does not tend to challenge the expected dominant-subordinate relations on the job. The fact that employers consider "harmony" when they have an integrated labor force leads to the exclusion of blacks from more skilled jobs, since such jobs often entail authority over others or necessitate more complete equality in work relationships. If promotion does not require authority over whites, it becomes a more likely occurrence.

Let us take an example of two industries with the same number of semiskilled positions. In the first, the semiskilled positions exist in a technical context dominated by machines involving minimal human interaction. In the second, the context is one in which cooperative human interaction is required on equal terms in the production process. The employer in the more impersonal, technically driven industry, whatever his or her personal racial attitudes may be, would not have to consider the racial biases of the machines that are operated by blacks. But this is obviously not the case for the second employer, who manages a firm that requires a great deal of cooperative human interaction. Even if the latter employer is personally more "enlightened" in matters of race than the one in charge of the mechanized industry, he or she might be induced to hire fewer blacks in occupational lines involving interemployee cooperation because costs increase if interemployee conflicts on the job interfere with production.

Another way management is induced to adjust to employee prejudice is indicated by the following event. An opening for a foreman's position in an auto plant occurred. The general manager, via the grapevine, learned about Sam Joseph, a black worker with leadership capacities. Unfortunately, the pattern of segregation in the plant greatly limited the opportunities for black foremen. When the general manager suggested to the second in command that "Sam be considered"—even though it meant that he be placed in a section that was predominantly white—the assistant manager replied, "You put a black guy in there and all hell will break out."[10] Sam was put on ice for a more "propitious" time.

The preceding illustrations, of course, do not exclude those most blatant manifestations of employee racism involving white networking and quasi nepotism among skilled workers. The well-recorded past history of such practices aside, current practices function to exclude blacks or obstruct black advancement once employed in entry level positions. Informal training on the job and the acquisition of knowledge about new openings within organizations become the protected "property" (cultural capital) of white networks.[11] There are both economic and social motives underlying white worker's interests. Controlling the supply of skilled workers enhances wage rates; preventing excessive numbers of blacks from moving from semiskilled to skilled positions is perceived as protecting the social status of the job.

Employer Discrimination

Thus far I have argued that because of their overriding concern with profits, employers act as proxies for consumers and employees. Insofar as consumers and employees are viewed as instruments or objects to be manipulated or pacified by producers with no other end in view than profit, producers have little direct interest in the development and perpetuation of racial discrimination as such. As a matter of principle, businesses see little value in making strong moral commitments to causes that adversely affect their economic interests. As individuals, their habit is to calculate possible losses or gains from this or that choice. As a matter of practice, businesspersons "adapt" to the political and social structures that shape the moral and value-laden perceptions of others. In the course of doing this, they naturally perpetuate the economic conditions deemed necessary to their survival and development. Their inclination is to avoid disturbing the flow of money to their coffers. In matters of social change, the business vision is limited. If there are small individual costs associated with changing biased racial practices and little prospect for gain, there is no motivation to inhibit long-standing practices, personal views aside. Or, to state the matter in more active terms, if making money requires racial barriers, businesspersons will create them. If making money requires conforming to the general prejudices of society, business managers will conform. If making money requires "divide and conquer" tactics, those too will be used. If fighting for racial justice to eliminate racial discrimination involves direct costs, businesspeople will be hesitant to incur them. Thus, the market logic that argues that the profit motive is color blind offers no axiomatic reason to eliminate the importance of the way business perpetuates racial discrimination.

Because employers are, above all else, cost-conscious creatures, and because most economists believe in theory that rigorous competition ought to eliminate discriminatory wage differences, the relation between competition and discrimination warrants an extended discussion.[12]

One of the first empirical studies using competitive, microeconomic theory to explain racial discrimination was done by Gary Becker, who, as I have already noted, is a leading representative of the rational individualism school. His reasoning proceeds as follows. Suppose there were two employers in a competitive industry, one of whom discriminated against blacks. If blacks could acquire employment by selling their labor below the market-determined wage, then white employers who had the least "taste for discrimination" would hire blacks, have lower costs and greater profit, and drive discriminating employers out of business. Thus, market logic would predict that blacks would be employed in competitive but not monopolistic industries, since those who managed the latter would experience no pressures to eliminate the extra costs incurred for indulging in discriminatory tastes, a kind of noneconomic "perk" that only enterprises with surplus or protected profits could afford. Not surprisingly, Becker found evidence to validate competitive logic.[13]

Michael Tanzer used Becker's data and found no evidence to validate competitive logic.[14] By disaggregating the way Becker lumped industries into one of two categories, monopolistic or competitive, Tanzer found that black males were concentrated in only a few of the twenty-nine competitive industries. When he eliminated those few, differences in the distribution of black males between the monopolistic and competitive groups disappeared. When Tanzer ranked all of the forty industries by degree of monopoly or competition, the correlation between market structure and discrimination became zero.

When Tanzer examined the distribution of black females, he found that, if he were to retain Becker's two-category system, most were employed in the monopolistic group. Since Becker never examined the employment of black females, he never had to face the paradoxical question of why white monopolists had negative tastes toward black males and positive ones toward black females. There is nothing in Becker's competitive, disutility approach that would enable him to explain this riddle. Tanzer's conclusion is that the market structure per se has little explanatory power in the determination of black-white industry employment or income differences. The explanation, to continue my argument, is along the axis of dominant-subordinate relations within enterprises and organizations.

Given that the market structures as such do not explain discrimination, and given the strong propensities of employers to "adapt" to the racial preferences of others, can more be said about the microlevel of business behavior? Is there a business interest or attitude that requires racial subordination as instrumental to the pursuit of profit? The answer, I believe, is yes, and what follows are some illustrations that parallel those identified in our discussion of consumers and employees.

Small businesses, to take one example, are aware of their cheap labor needs and therefore have been known to oppose educational and reskilling programs for marginal workers.[15] Blacks are conceived in this context as being part of a subordinate reserve labor pool that must be forced by circumstances to perform tasks that whites tend to resist. This understanding extends beyond just the needs of small marginal businesses. "Negroes do work white men won't do," says a superintendent of a Kentucky plow factory, "such as . . . heavy, hot, and dirty work; pouring crucibles; work in the grinding room; and so on. Negroes are employed because they are cheaper. . . . The Negro does a different grade of work and makes about 10 cents an hour less."[16] Or, as a northern steel foreman frankly admitted in more paternalistic terms than his southern counterpart, "Blacks are well fitted for . . . hot work, and we keep them because we appreciate this ability in them."[17] Subordinate jobs are viewed as "fitting" for subordinate workers.

Just as there are subordinate jobs within enterprises, there are subordinate firms within industries "reserved" for black and/or marginal workers. Corporate giants may subcontract some portion of their output to small firms that employ black labor. In slack seasons or downward swings in the business cycle, the subcontracted portion of the larger firm's output is discontinued. The corporations, in this relatively simple manner, avoid some of the costs related to business uncertainties. This leads to higher unemployment rates and lower annual incomes for black workers compared to those employed in larger enterprises. These decisions become possible, not because of malice toward blacks per se, but because blacks are trapped in subordinate segments of the labor market, and therefore, individual firms are free to use them as a reserve to avoid increases in their variable costs.

In addition to satellite firms dependent on subcontracting from larger enterprises, there is the more general case involving small, competitive, labor-intensive firms that employ black and white workers. Because such enterprises function with low profit margins, they are extremely sensitive to minor changes in business conditions. As a result, owners of such enterprises are induced to lay off their black workers more frequently than they are their white ones. The reason is based on the enterprise owner's experience in the labor market. Because blacks are subordinate in the order in which employment opportunities arise, it is assumed that they will be available for rehire when business picks up. In this way, no additional recruiting and training costs will be incurred. As in the case of subcontracted firms, black workers, in their instrumental role as an adjustment factor, experience higher unemployment rates and lower annual incomes compared to their white cohorts within small enterprises.

In another vein that has not been touched upon in the literature is the ongoing, widespread discrimination against black workers by plant foremen in manufacturing industries. Foremen represent management at the lowest level of the managerial hierarchy and have considerable control over intraplant occupational mobility. Foremen are often the first persons to know of a new opening and are often in charge of actually upgrading an in-plant worker. All public pronouncements about compliance with equal opportunity laws to the contrary, top managers of middle- and large-size firms do not involve themselves in the numerous decisions affecting nonsupervisory employees; rather, many labor-allocation decisions are made by foremen.

Understanding the mentality of white foremen in this regard is important. Many have sabotaged a company's commitment to enhance job and promotional opportunities for blacks already employed at low-level jobs.[18] Foremen have direct personal contact with the factory hands. As a group, they come very close to sharing all the racial prejudices of the white, lower-middle class, skilled, blue-collar workers. Like them, they tend to have contempt for the class of lesser-skilled workers below them, workers who must be regulated and continuously prodded to work if the foremen are to prove their worth. Foremen also tend to resent the upper echelons of management whose members are forever instructing them with white-paper orders on how to manage in the field. The foreman's position is ridden with tension, which is readily displaced onto blacks. Foremen have been known not only to ride "blacky's back" to the point of discouragement on the job, but to exclude blacks from consideration for promotion or acquisition of information about opportunities to improve their skills on the job. In their unofficial personnel role, foremen often practice a quasi nepotism. They recommend relatives, friends, or friends of relatives for promotion or for other kinds of advantageous job moves within the plant. Since foremen are almost always white, even where considerable numbers of blacks are employed, blacks have minimal connection to this avenue of job improvement. Even when union equity rules apply to both races, and black and white workers are simultaneously eligible for promotion or for an advantageous job change that carries more authority, many such opportunities are often made available at the foreman's discretion. Bypassing eligible white friends and acquaintances who are part of an unofficial in-plant network that operates to "get things done" would simply mean trouble for a foreman, even if he or she were not racially biased. It is much "safer" and more manageable to keep things as they are.

It is not only at the lowest level of management that blacks are bypassed. Black managers fairly high up in the corporate hierarchy also complain of being bypassed. In a study summarized in the *Wall Street Journal*, black managers are reported as being frustrated by their lack of opportunities to advance. What is of interest for my purposes are the reasons. In order to move beyond the levels of middle management, it is necessary to "network" in ways with which the "top brass" feel comfortable. We are back to our West Coast personnel officer's observations about blacks "spoiling the decor . . . not being aesthetically desirable"; or, in the vein of Alice Walker, whoever heard of white middle management working for black top brass? However, in the corporate world, the belief is that companies allow

> employees to conform to social attitudes and behavior that are negative about blacks. . . . Such attitudes [are called] "colorism," and many consultants say it means that [top] white executives still feel uncomfortable working closely with blacks. "Comfort and fit"—you hear over and over again in getting into the senior ranks.[19]

Turning to the apex of the professional academic hierarchy, the implicit reasoning employed for not seriously considering a black presidential candidate when the suggestion was made is in order. The presidential search committee on which I served automatically assumed that a black person, regardless of abilities or qualifications, could not effectively deal with all the "ya-hoos in the alumnae association." Do blacks who deal with whites from a superior position "spoil the decor" to the extent that the work cannot be done? The unbiased, pro-affirmative action, race-free faculty members of a search committee assumed that they did. Their actions, it is necessary to emphasize, were purely instrumental to the perceived needs of the college as viewed by outsiders; that is to say, individuals were induced to act in ways contrary to their values.

There are, of course, exceptions that are frequently identified, such as an organization in which a prominent black person presides over predominantly white employees. In my judgment, this "exceptionalism" proves the rule. Aside from the fact that even on slave plantations slave owners were known to have demonstrated their "benevolence" by pointing to examples of slaves who rose above the average, the need to advertise exceptions as symbols suggests that the normal routine is of a different nature.[20] And from the perspective developed here, the normal routine is one that involves sustaining dominant-subordinate patterns.

The symbolic use of exceptions is perhaps less relevant than the problems that middle-class black professionals encounter in integrated organizations. In the normal course of work, they can be made defensive, tense, and socially alienated along the axis of color. This matter is illustrated by the circumstances described by some black technicians who were brought into the middle ranges of corporate management in the late sixties:

> At first we were quite shy or hesitant to take initiatives with the firm's clients like our white co-workers who competed for attention and upmanship about their advice and recommendations. After about six months on the job, we were called before a vice-president in what constituted a job evaluation and were told, in effect, that we were too passive; we didn't have a go-getting spirit. "This is not the South, you know." Afterwards, we talked it over among ourselves and realized how we were holding back and not really articulating ourselves adequately. Slowly we did a reversal, competed more and talked more at group meetings about how to approach this problem or that client. Although top management appeared to be satisfied, our white co-workers began to talk about us as if we had become "pushy niggers." Little racial jibes and remarks began to seep into the lunch conversations, all of which were meant to be friendly in-group humor but were in fact putdowns. At least that is the way we saw it. About a year later, we all decided to quit and become part of an urban renewal operation sponsored by the federal and state government. We needed to do something more related to our social interests. The tension in the firm was too great.[21]

The full moral of this episode is perhaps ambiguous. On one level, there may have been a mild kind of social paranoia functioning among the black technicians. Continuous defensive discomfort in interpersonal relations, however moderate, can sometimes evoke neurotic responses. On another level, it reveals the extent to which a double standard functions, one of the main elements of manifest social racism. Aggressive behavior by middle-class whites is viewed as part of a positive, go-getting spirit. When blacks behave in the same way they are seen as "getting out of place" by acting "too pushy." At the same time, if blacks do *not* behave aggressively, they are perceived as passive and slow.[22] Identical class behavior among middle-level corporate staffers turns into a racial discussion in which the behavior of black middle-class technicians is explained in terms of some other, allegedly more negative, aspect of black life from which they were far removed. This relational association is imposed on them and is the flip side of those that appear to be internalized and more self-induced. Trying to be just normal professionals, rather than black professionals with concerns about role, is very difficult. The return of the above-quoted workers to a more segregated situation was both a retreat from hopes that were raised when they were first hired by the corporation, and a move to become socially useful citizens in a more comfortable, although insular, work environment.

Conclusion

What we have argued in illustrative terms can now be systematized. The microeconomics of racism is the economics of maintaining dominant-subordinate positions in a variety of situations where integrated relations prevail. Upward mobility along segregated lines, however important, is not viewed here as an index of fundamental alterations of race relations. In this sense, the relative success of many middle-class blacks is limited, in my view, to the extent that it is along segregated lines. The acquisition of a managerial position by a black college graduate in a national department store chain that caters to "minority" customers and has a consequential number of "minority" employees may have come about as a result of a change in the company's overall policies. This indicates some degree of income and occupational progress, although it does not represent a profound rupture in established patterns.

The structure of discrimination derived from our observations involves understanding the mechanisms, sources, and forms that I briefly identified earlier in this chapter. Mechanisms vary in any period as well as changing over time. The period between 1850 and 1920 was marked by a legally perpetuated caste system. With the industrialization of the South, two world wars, and the civil rights struggles in the fifties and sixties, the mechanisms inherited from the slave system and

rural tenancy died. The forces that at present impinge on individual decisions are more diffuse and less deterministic; they are more difficult
to excise from our society by broad social protests or general govern-
mental interventionist measures. This is why analysts who overempha-
size intentional racism per se are finding it difficult to muster compelling social arguments to make their case. For example, Michael Reich, a
respected academic Marxist, persuasively argues that past racism was
perpetuated by the business class to keep workers divided, but that
current racism, which continues to divide workers, is due to such vagaries as "the insecurities created by the decline of the American economy, by the decline of individual autonomy . . . , by the strains that affect family structure, and by the increase in individualism in our
culture."[23] The reasoning behind these less compelling, racially driven
arguments, as I have contended, is related to the way institutional life
has separated the racial consequences of decisions from individual intent. Individuals do not accept culpability for the racial patterns derived from decisions that often have other motives or concerns. This
may be one of the reasons that intent is becoming increasingly more
difficult to prove in our courts.[24]

From the perspective developed here, the individual is induced to
conform to aggregate social patterns even if such patterns are not believed by the individuals themselves. Offensive interpretations about
race differences—not infrequently falling under the guise of freedom
to choose or associate—are muted or obliterated. The overt racial content is hidden from the individual's self-organized intentions. Old-fashioned stereotyping now represents a price-quality confusion that leads
to a rational, calculated judgment about an individual's productivity in
terms of some assumed average characteristic of the group.[25] And, not
least, market circumstances enable business interests to impersonally
use black labor as a yo-yo because it "happens" to be trapped in the
subordinate segments of the labor market.[26]

The sources of discrimination may emanate from consumers, employees, or employers. Understanding the sources and the respective
spheres in which decisions are made is important for two reasons: it
suggests where policy actions and educational efforts need to be directed; and it suggests something about the tenacity of discriminatory
barriers insofar as there may be a convergence of interests in maintaining discriminatory practices among the three sources. In this latter process, business decisions adapt to consumer preferences, operate to
sustain harmony in the enterprise's workforce, and keep management
working in a "color-comfort" team context. The convergence produces more obdurate barriers in some spheres of employment.

Manifest forms vary widely according to circumstances. The ones most relevant to maintaining dominant-subordinate relations are differences in career ladders, even if equal opportunity prevails at various points of entry into the job market; unemployment differences due to layoff practices by employers; income differences for like jobs due to the subordinate bargaining position in which blacks find themselves; the requirement that black professionals be superior to the average or must be scrutinized for character or "attitude" in order to qualify for lines of work that break "tradition"; and differences in black opportunity to socialize or network on and off the job in order to enhance skills or acquire "strategic" information relevant to mobility.

Outlawing manifest forms helps, but it is important to note that the forms keep changing and adapting to circumstances. Grossly unequal pay for identical jobs has been on the wane and in fact has disappeared in many sectors of the economy where wage determination has become highly structured and standardized. Yet, as I have suggested, more subtle forms have emerged—especially as our society has become formally committed to enforcing equal opportunity.

One final consideration that has been implicit in a number of my illustrations is the organizational and technological context in which discrimination occurs. Large bureaucratic and capital-intensive industries often pose less of a problem than labor-intensive ones in which personal services are relevant and/or the enterprise is managed and owned by the same entrepreneur. In the bureaucratic, capital-intensive operation, to take one extreme on the spectrum, employment and promotion practices for a large range of jobs are impersonally and procedurally defined. Promotion frequently means a better location in the hierarchy or a chance to operate a slightly more sophisticated machine. Such enterprises pose fewer discriminatory barriers than do smaller ones in which the animus of ownership breathes into daily management decisions. Related to the large capital-intensive versus the smaller firm problem is the nature of the commodity produced. To take the extreme case again, consumers are not concerned with the color of the hands that make their cars, refrigerators, and air conditioners; employer practices are bureaucratically defined and impersonal; and many service jobs require little interaction with employees since they are processed through machinery. In this situation, external pressures to eliminate discriminatory practices are more likely to succeed than when the commodity is a service, consumers are not expert buyers, and the employment or promotion of blacks involves some degree of reversal in the dominant-subordinate relation in the production process.

Given the importance of the size and heterogeneous nature of the service sector in the economy, further comment is warranted. For many low-wage service jobs that cater to "harried" middle-class customers, the perceived inadequate performance of black workers is interpreted with racial overtones. The black supermarket cashier, to take one example, is frequently viewed by impatient middle-class whites as an example of why blacks do not "make it." "They drag their ass and have a bad attitude" expresses the common undertone of irate customers' perception. For whatever reasons, low-wage black cashiers are not experienced as routinely polite, anxious to please, or eager to speed up packaging. It is a rare white customer who inquires about what lies behind this hostility or work performance. But the overrepresentation of blacks in such jobs is a breeding ground for racial hostility derived from what is seen to be "personal character" related to race.

In this taxonomy, breaking down the microeconomic barriers involves overcoming the dominant-subordinate allocation rule. To the extent that employment and promotion do not run into this barrier because they proceed along quasi-segregated lines, they are of limited relevance to the measure of black progress. More important, the "need" to abide by the dominant-subordinate rule at the microeconomic level tends to limit opportunities for blacks in many situations. This not only breeds a relatively hopeless attitude toward the job, but it also discourages longer-run investment in job development. As both processes take place, blacks are continuously relegated to overcrowding in a range of lesser positions within and between each of the various occupational groups that make up the profile for the economy.

As individuals make marginal adjustments based on perceived patterns that appear beyond any single person's control, these adjustments aggregate to form conditions of black overrepresentation in the working class, the working poor class, the welfare system, and not least, the underclass. In a society overcast with racial signs, race-class lines are frequently blurred. We acquire myopic perceptions about blacks derived from the most disadvantaged portion of the black population. Whites devote an inordinate amount of time to thinking and talking about *all* blacks in ways that stem from their understanding and perceptions of the black working poor. Such blacks are frequently believed to be closely allied to a self-perpetuating black underclass.

This is not to suggest that white Middle America fails to understand that there are good, solid black citizens like themselves. But this black middle class is seen as a special case in relation to other, less viable, segments of the black population. As a result, the black working, lower, and underclasses are inevitably connected. This, of course, is not news to most blacks. Even very conservative black scholars who emphasize individualism and believe in unrestricted markets recognize how the differentiated internal class structure within the black community combines with race to perpetuate inequalities unrelated to the individual's productivity.[27]

The black underclass itself has acquired a special place in this whole discussion. Many now believe that the nature of the black underclass is not related so much to racism as it is to the impersonal operation of market forces responding to technological imperatives and international competition. Class, not race, is the issue.[28]

The Cosby Show may attract millions of white viewers who would raise no objections to living next door to a family like that depicted in the show. The problem for whites is what "kind" of blacks are likely to follow the Cosbys. In principle, of course, middle-class whites might and do suggest that the issue is not color; they would not want any "bad" types, white or black, to move next door. The reality that whites fear or imagine pertains to blacks, and in particular, poorer blacks who are associated with the black underclass. The black underclass has become a football in public discourse—tossed about for reasons that are more clouded than those provided by scholars whose analysis has moved away from race and toward class. Whatever the reality about the black underclass, its use by whites for reasons unrelated to changing the conditions that breed it is also a reality. To this issue I now turn.

WHITE USES OF THE BLACK UNDERCLASS

D iscussion of the black underclass brings out the worst in all of us. In the course of everyday life, white and black leaders, white and black scholars, and, not least, white and black "plain folk" hear references to a black underclass, a term that suggests the existence of an evil, threatening cancerous growth in our midst.[1] Perceptions and images are often conjured up to serve a larger agenda that is frequently far removed from the particular conditions that produce a black underclass. The most blatant case in point is the use of Willie Horton, a black convict, in the 1988 presidential campaign. Horton, who raped a woman on a weekend furlough from a Massachusetts state prison, was intentionally used to attack the alleged permissiveness of the whole welfare state, to suggest that liberal Democrats were "soft" on blacks, and, finally, to impugn the personal judgment of Governor Dukakis, as if he were responsible for individuals who are furloughed in accordance with a law that was in fact developed during the previous Republican administration.

It is not my intention to suggest that the underclass in American society is exclusively black. Latinos, poor whites, and representatives of other ethnic groups certainly can be identified in various regions of the country as fulfilling the requirements for classification in this degrading category. But this chapter is about blacks, and the black underclass sends messages that reverberate far beyond its own boundaries to affect the status of the whole African-American population in ways that do not apply to other ethnic or racial groups.

Almost all discussions by professionals and popular pundits who employ the term *underclass* commence with an apology. As if they were in another world, readers are assured either that the term underclass is not pejorative or that the term is misleading because it embraces a large variety of individuals who fall into "bad" ways or hardship for a number of reasons. Generalizations are difficult.[2] Yet, it is said, some term must be used to designate a thematic focus and the term underclass is as good as any.

I make no apology for the term underclass or for why I choose to "look" specifically at the black underclass. The reality with which I am concerned does not reflect the debates about the underclass's actual size,[3] composition,[4] origin,[5] behavior,[6] causes,[7] or location in our inner cities.[8] As important as these debates are for social scientists who write for each other and sometimes use their findings to suggest new policy directions, the reality on which I focus is filtered through the myopic perceptions white minds derive from direct "experience," the mass media, and demagogic rhetoric that plays into legitimate and illegitimate fears. Such perceptions may not be accurate by "scientific" standards, but they are very real in their distortions and consequences. The white lens that is focused on the black underclass sees general images that not only embrace the underclass but link it to the working poor who live in black ghettos, to the middle-income members of the larger black community—indeed, to the whole black population. The underclass is the first step in a process by which whites derive an "understanding" about all black people.

If the "poverty experts" who Ken Auletta consulted for his highly praised study "generalize about people they barely know," then imagine how large numbers of whites who are miscreant voyeurs of the overexposed and often misrepresented black underclass scene must generalize.[9] Such generalizations constitute racism: they feed into the economic reproduction of the black underclass and promote racial stereotypes and exclusion practices toward blacks who are far removed from the behavior and statistics that actually define the poorest and most alienated portion of the African-American population. Thus the black underclass stands at the center of the contemporary race-class confusion I have sought to clarify in previous chapters. The present entrapment of the black underclass in our major central cities casts shadows that affect the racial judgments of the whole society. But these oversized, racially constructed shadows that are visible to white minds come from sources other than the actual statistical size of the black underclass. If one accepts Christopher Jencks's provocative suggestion that the concept underclass is "an antonym to the terms [white] middle class and working class," then the black underclass must be understood in terms of the economic, moral, and educational categories employed to describe the white middle and working classes.[10] Thus, Jencks seeks to determine the growth or decline of the economic underclass (people without jobs), the moral underclass (people without middle-class values), and the educational underclass (people with little education). Jencks demonstrates that since the mid-fifties, only the economic underclass grew—both black and white. The size of the moral and educational underclass declined.[11]

If one accepts the more traditional, although severely criticized, measure of the underclass in terms of the number of people living in census tract areas characterized by "high rates of school dropouts, male nonemployment, welfare recipients, and female headed households, [there was an increase by] more than three-fold between 1970 and 1980."[12] What needs emphasis, for my purposes, is that the underclass, however defined, is a relatively small part of the nation's population; it constitutes 1 percent of the population and is mainly concentrated in our ten major central cities.[13] If one further examines what proportion is black, then we are discussing a fraction of 1 percent.

To this statistically lessened problem, we must add the fact that race as a cause of membership in the underclass "club" is not overemphasized among social scientists.[14] While it is observed that minorities — often a euphemism for blacks—suffer most from the interrelated issues of crime, welfare dependency, family dissolution, and the breakdown of binding moral values, liberal social scientists tend to attribute such conditions to impersonal forces. Thus, from a purely statistical and analytical viewpoint, the race-underclass association seems to be much ado about very little. Yet, the black underclass looms larger than life among the white majority, even in areas and parts of the country where few blacks reside. It is for this reason that the white uses of images of the black underclass warrant special consideration, independent of whether such perceptions are "really" true.

Emerging Middle-Class Perception

As early as the late sixties, following the passing of the major pieces of civil rights legislation, a white backlash was in motion. Middle- and lower-middle-class concerns were about neighborhoods, schools, parks, and streets. When you let a few "good" kinds of blacks into your territory, they will be followed by a horde of "bad" kinds. In conjunction with, but not caused by, this white preoccupation with blacks entering "their" social spaces was a status anxiety propelled by the slowing down of economic growth and rising prices.[15] Increasingly it took two incomes to remain in the same place.[16] Projections about the future did not automatically assume that the offspring of America's white middle layers would achieve more than their parents did. And the rising tax burden appeared to produce declining benefits, except for the tax revenues that were going to a large, undeserving portion of the black population.[17]

Although welfare liberals and black leaders repressed a serious discussion of a growing black underclass in the seventies, the issue grew beneath the social surface. "After a long eclipse," write two current leading scholars on the black poor, "the ghetto has made a stunning comeback into the collective consciousness of America. Not since the riots of the hot summers of 1966–68 have the black poor received so much attention in academic, activist, and policy making quarters."[18] The reasons for this comeback are complex. It is related, in my judgment, to a sharpening division between the rich and poor,[19] a growing restlessness among white middle- and working-class voters, and a more general rejection of the welfare system, which is viewed as a pillar of support to large portions of the black poor. Central to the concern with the black underclass are the interests and perceptions of the broad white middle class.

By 1970, the white middle class had exhausted its empathy with black causes and the social malaise of our central cities. This became especially true in cities that had a large number of older, less mobile, "God-fearing," affluent, working-class whites who were losing their younger members to the less ethnic suburbs. While the more affluent suburbs sought to protect the value of their homes and the character of their neighborhoods through restrictive covenants such as land-lot size requirements, "preemptive purchase, various petty harassments, implicit or explicit collusion by realtors, banks, mortgage lenders and other lending agencies," lower-middle-class, central-city whites facing a larger black population had fewer options.[20]

Impressions gathered by a reporter in the early seventies returning to his native Slovak community in Cleveland are worth quoting at some length; they illustrate the reactions of a relatively moderate white ethnic group to African-American efforts to find adequate residential space. These observations also illustrate how the Slovaks perceived more militant white ethnic reactions to the black "threat." Beginning first with an aging priest, Father Michael Jasko:

We had 2,000 families and 8,000 souls [some years ago]. . . .
Now it's 1,000 families and 3,000 souls, and most of them are
pensioners. We stopped the Canteen [a weekly dance for
teenagers] 10 years ago and hoped to reopen it, but never did.
We made $45,000 in a big year at the bazaar; last year we got
$24,000. Novenas and other night-time services have been
stopped. The old ladies of the church were getting beaten and
robbed on their way to early mass, so we stopped those. Now
the first mass is at 7 o'clock, except in the summer when we
have the 5:30.[21]

The widow of a neighborhood gas station manager who was killed in
a robbery lamented:

To many people around here, Joe was a fixture, the honest
business man who made it by hard work. We all knew that the
neighborhood was changing, but then this . . . I think of
leaving the neighborhood now, but where would I go?
Everything I know is here. I just want those killers found and I
want them to get their due.[22]

The editor of the Slovak neighborhood newspaper, a self-described
"superhawk and ultra-conservative," concluded after a long conversation:

In everything I've told you, I've not once mentioned race. It
isn't race; it's law and order. . . . There was never trouble just
because blacks moved in. In Murray Hill, the Italians told the
blacks they would kill any who dared to move in. In Sowinski
Park, the Polish pointed shotguns at them. This is not our way
of life but look at what we are reaping now.[23]

From Bill Blassman, bachelor and owner of a corner grocery:

Things were bad before Mayor Stokes, a black, was elected,
but since his election, the situation in the neighborhood has
quickly become untenable. Stokes is responsible for
encouraging blacks to come up from the South and get on
Cleveland's welfare and crime roles. Stokes has allowed a new
permissiveness. The blacks are cocky because one of their own
is downtown. . . . In Cleveland, in the old neighborhood, it is
largely Stokes' fault.[24]

Finally, a neighborhood ethnic militia has arisen in the name of the
Buckeye Neighborhood Nationalities Civic Association. One of the organization's founders reported on the planned operations of the
group:

This is our battle plan. We want to have each house with a
code number so that our police can get to any house in
minutes. The city police won't cover us, so we are willing to
give ourselves. . . . I know people are calling us vigilantes. . . .
Anything blacks say about us is out of ignorance. This
neighborhood should be preserved as a national historical
monument to mark the contributions of the nationalities.
Monuments are WASP or black, nothing for us. . . . And we
don't want blacks in our group; we are for the preservation of
the national way of life.[25]

What is most relevant about the impressions of this one ethnic
group is the range of expressed vindictive feelings and perceptions. In
their belief that they were caught between an "uppity" WASP stratum
and a pariah black one, this hardworking community of Slovaks, consisting of pensioners, older blue-collar workers, and small business
owners, lashes out in all directions. From events directly observed or
experienced at the neighborhood level, they seek concrete revenge or
justice for particular black violations. With the election of Carl Stokes
(a black mayor), they are able to justify the indictment of a large range
of black Cleveland residents who have no connection to neighborhood specifics. With considerable ease they interpret the national
economy and concoct reasons for the influx of blacks to Cleveland—
not in terms of internal immigrants looking for the jobs, higher living
standards, and better way of life that once motivated themselves to
come to the United States—but in terms of southern migrants intentionally coming to "their" Cleveland to live on welfare and engage in
crime. In a moment of self-pity, they reflect on their "softness" and express envy of the Italians and Polish who "know how" to take care of
their "niggers" through the barrel of a gun. And not least, they move
toward a paramilitary solution by organizing armed defense commit-
tees and calling for some superchauvinist rituals that would put white
ethnics on the social map. Not all reasoning by whites, of course, extends itself to a paramilitary formulation. More commonly, whites wish
that blacks had never come to these shores or that the black "problem" would just disappear.

Insofar as blacks worry about violence in their communities, it is less
due to paramilitary actions by ethnic whites (who have made their
statement with their feet by departing from the central city) and more
due to the condition facing black men. In an article, "Black Male Genocide: A Final Solution to the Race Problem in America," the concern is
expressed in statistical terms; it is worth reproducing them:

While black men account for only six percent of the population of the United States, they make up half of its male prisoners in local, state, and federal jails.

The majority of the 20,000 Americans killed in crime-related incidents each year are black.

Over thirty-five percent of all black men in American cities are drug and alcohol abusers.

Eighteen percent of black males drop out of high school.

Twenty-five percent of the victims of AIDS are black men.

Over fifty percent of black men under the age of twenty-one are unemployed.

Forty-six percent of black men between the ages of sixteen and sixty-two are not in the labor force.

About thirty-two percent of black men have incomes below the officially defined poverty level.[26]

While the combination of historic racism and current conditions accounts for the large numbers of black youth at risk, "black parents [naturally] worry that law-abiding young men—their own sons and nephews—will be rounded up with the rest."[27] The evident meaning here is that white police officers do not easily discriminate between "good" ghetto blacks and "bad" ones. It also suggests that most black parents are forever coping with the risks inherent in everyday ghetto life; their offspring need continuous protection against the "bad" black element in their midst.[28] Young black males are destroying themselves, writes Jewelle T. Gibbs, through "their own actions and activities. . . . [T]hey are continuing to kill, maim, or narcotize themselves faster than they could be annihilated through wars or natural diseases. They not only destroy themselves, but also jeopardize . . . family formation for young black woman, . . . the stability of the black community, and endanger the entire society."[29] Or, as Cornel West suggested in more interpretive terms, protection against a

> vast and growing black underclass, an underclass that embodies a kind of *walking nihilism* of pervasive drug addiction, pervasive alcoholism, pervasive homicide, and an exponential rise in suicide. Now, because of the deindustrialization, we also have a devastated black industrial working class. We are talking here about tremendous hopelessness.[30]

Complementing the quantitative and qualitative portrait of black males is the repeated characterization of black women: unwed teenage mothers, welfare recipients, women who head families because of divorce or because they have never been married. The feminization of poverty, often a euphemism applied to the condition of black women, is a commonly employed category that embraces the general condition.

Drugs, crime, street gangs, muggings, random shootouts, unwed teenagers, welfare dependency, AIDS—these are the code words that enabled a slumlord to defend his actions with a vengeance after being accused of exploiting blacks:

> Who else but me would take care of the whores, pimps, winos, addicts, hoodlums, queers—the dregs of humanity that nobody wants. It's a lousy zoo and I take care of some of the animals— but that's more than the federal government.[31]

In suggesting that he is a benign man caring for animals, Mr. Slumlord falls into a pattern that has a long history. While the dominant white majority has intermittently employed nasty epithets to describe the "lower classes" in its midst, categories of "subhumans" have been most often reserved for blacks. As Winthrop D. Jordan noted in his historical explorations of the origin of racism in the United States, "Ever since the days of confrontation in Africa the sexual connection between Negro and ape has served to express the deep-seated feeling that the Negro was more animal—and accordingly more sexual—than the white man."[32]

It was in the latter part of the nineteenth century, to continue in the historical vein, when Jim Crow laws throughout the South were instituted, that the imagery of the "Negro as beast" perhaps reached its zenith.[33] In the context of a growing agricultural crisis and the white belief that black sexuality and criminality were on the rise, numerous southern writers lamented the passing of the slave system, in which the "good darkies" knew their place, and focused on the savagery and animality that supposedly characterized the free Negro who had been let out of the cage.[34] Lynchings increased rapidly in this period, and it became less than rare to find vile racist statements about the "Negro as a brute and a savage" or "a fiend, a wild beast, seeking whom he may devour."[35] Lest this image of the "Negro as beast" be thought of as buried in our past, it is worth noting a more current remark by a New York reporter who refused, in a fit of cynical anger, an uptown assignment on the basis that he did not wish to "interview those monkeys."[36]

These crude public animal references, although relatively scarce by past standards, are not without subtle consequences. African-Americans are sensitive in unanticipated ways to vulgar, racist rhetoric. This is illustrated by the following classroom experience in the spring of 1980. I was teaching an adult education class that consisted mainly of U.S.-born black women, although there were some who had Caribbean origins. A student brought into class a current newspaper clipping about the creationist perspective on evolution and the Moral Majority's attack on the teaching of scientific evolutionism. The student queried whether I believed in evolution of the Darwinian variety. Suspecting immediately that I was about to clash directly with the class member's religious sentiment, I turned the question around and sought her opinion. The judgment was instantaneous: "It is not possible to think that we are related to monkeys."

The discussion had proceeded aimlessly for about fifteen minutes when another woman cynically commented: "It won't be long before they begin looking for our tail again." Interestingly, the few West Indian blacks refrained from either supporting or rejecting Darwinian evolutionary theory; one merely said that she "lacked sufficient knowledge to make a judgment."[37]

So here we are with the following irony: black working-class women—active unionists in a union-sponsored college program, liberally oriented on social issues—automatically side with southern white supremacist religious fundamentalists, despite the fact that the fundamentalists are bringing up the ghost of the Scopes trial and investigating high school textbooks for political reasons that can only foster a social atmosphere detrimental to the interests of blacks. The African-American reaction to the evolution issue is not simply a matter of mechanically asserting Sunday-school lessons, as may be the case for grass-roots white religious fundamentalists. Blotting out an inquiry into the validity of scientific evolution was a race-specific reaction particular to the history of U.S. blacks. It reflects the ever-present sense of subordination that produces a defensive posture and prevents a genuine opportunity to understand an important area of science.

As the 1980s unfolded, with their attendant change in political climate, the portrait of poor blacks increasingly degenerated to a depiction of the underclass in inner city neighborhoods. The debate among social scientists about causation aside, the collective portrait that is packaged in one form or another is often beyond vilification.[38] It comes across as a specter haunting us, one that cannot be grasped by normal human feelings or understood by standard cognitive efforts. It puts some portion of the black community outside the human race; this is extended by degrees to measure all blacks, a practice, to repeat, that is common in our racist history. It feeds a deep-seated racialist mind-set, even when it is offset with bracketed explanations that are nonracial or class-based in nature. Moreover, degrading images of the downtrodden black underclass used by whites are often provided by blacks themselves. The selective white use of black statements allows whites to appear less culpable for flaunting stereotypical symbols and expressing racial fears. Mass media reporting is generally not aimed at arousing passion or empathy or at deepening our understanding. Thus, we have testimonies, pictures, movies, and twenty-second TV "interviews" that frequently attribute a willful nature of those who allegedly manifest underclass behavior traits. In the current period, the prevalence of the black underclass is explained by the policies of the welfare state, and therefore is used by conservatives against liberals to account for crime, broken homes, the absence of the work ethic, and a host of other phenomena that are assumed to be completely absent from most white families.

Imaging the Black Underclass

A composite profile of the black underclass can begin either at the neighborhood level or through depictions of individuals. Be it one or the other, the details are easy to come by and are often fused into a single image in the white mind from which moral judgments are derived and racially hostile sentiments justified. From the South Bronx to the southside of Chicago to Watts in Los Angeles, neighborhoods are seen as consisting of

> currency exchanges, bars and liquor stores . . . stores [that] are boarded up and abandoned. A few buildings have bars across the front and are closed to the public, but they are not empty. They are used, not so secretly, by people involved in illegal activities. Other stretches of the street are simply barren.[39]

Moving from Chicago to Detroit, one writer reports:

> It would be hard to exaggerate the devastation that begins beyond "The Line." It's a scene of weed-choking lots and gutted wooden houses landscaped with shards of glass where teenagers gather aimlessly and children scavenge . . . from the debris. From their porches, the remaining home owners, mostly black . . . can point out a half dozen crack houses. In this neighborhood, it is easy to obliterate the present, but hard to think about the future.[40]

A *Time* magazine cover story put it in more graphic terms: "The universe of [the black] underclass is often a junk heap of rotting housing, broken furniture, crummy food, alcohol and drugs."[41] Add graffiti and dimly lit streets littered with garbage and beer cans, and the image whites have in their minds about black underclass neighborhoods (and, to one degree or another, perhaps all black neighborhoods) is completed.

Black leaders and writers, motivated to bring self-consciousness and self-help schemes into the black community, frequently feed white images, their own intentions, of course, to the contrary. "Among [black] male peers," writes the black sociologist Robert Staples, "demonstrating . . . masculine prowess in terms of sexual conquests . . . or fighting is all that is rewarded."[42] Or take some statements made by Rev. Jesse Jackson over the past decade. In a fund appeal for PUSH in 1980 he is quoted as painfully saying: "The door of opportunity is open for our people, but they are too drunk, too unconscious to walk through the door."[43] In a spirit of exhortation for self-development, Jackson continued along the same lines during one of his 1984 primary campaign addresses to ghetto high school graduates and their parents: "Don't pickle your brain in liquor—don't you put dope in your veins. . . . We must assume responsibility for our children. . . . Assure them they are somebody."[44] And finally, in his 1986 commencement address to the graduating class of Medgar Evers College in Brooklyn, Jackson dramatically called attention to additional black "sins" that have currently received much public attention. In reference to crime, he stated that "more blacks lost their lives from black-on-black murder in 1981 than black men killed in 12 years of war in Vietnam." Turning to the issue of black male-female relations, he chided both: "Brothers, you're not a man because you can make a baby," and, "Sisters, young men do not make babies by themselves."[45] Thus, his scenario ends on the sorry state of the poor black family—the unwed mother, the pregnant teenager, the irresponsible black male. Whether preaching from the public pulpit in a postindustrial "here and now" consumption-addicted society can affect the habits of ghetto-dwelling "sinners" is uncertain; no doubt the self-help motives behind the exhortations of some current black leaders are part of a venerable tradition that was crystallized perhaps most clearly by Booker T. Washington. But when issues like these, discussed by Jackson and other leaders with one set of intentions, are picked up by the same mass media for a sixty-second "show and tell," they are not always understood as intended. When a black woman interviewed on the six o'clock CBS news says, "I hate to admit this, but for a lot of young women, the only way they can get more money is to have another baby," whites come away with the confirmation that blacks do not want to work.[46] "True confessions" about the realities found in many black communities, and self-declarations about what is to be done, too often feed white stereotypes.

Such images in white minds, whatever the source, have a context. And in our present social climate, the medium of the message and the context in which it is often received provide reasons why whites respond with a resounding nay when the threat of integration knocks on their doors. A citizen of one threatened neighborhood states: "[We have paid in] blood, sweat and tears to keep our neighborhood green; to see low income [euphemism for blacks] high risers is absolutely a nightmare." Another states, "When we would see the projects go up from our kitchen window, . . . I remember my mother saying, that's the end of the neighborhood." Finally, still another concluded, "They call it scattered-site housing. . . . We call it scattered-site cancer."[47]

Cancer, of course, is an uncontrollable human disease; its use as a metaphor applies to more than just the landscape and architecture of a neighborhood. It quickly expands to include the images of black underclass persons and behaviors that range from welfare mothers and swindlers to "murderers, muggers, stick up men, chain snatchers, pimps, burglars, heroin addicts, drug pushers, and alcoholics."[48] Beyond such criminal categories spotlighting the lazy and degenerate, there are other, more "scientific" ones like "disorganized," "present-time oriented," and "rarely married." Thus, when whites fight integration, they also need to downgrade African-Americans qua persons in one form or another: "All of us have worked for our homes. Our houses are our major investment. . . . Show me some black guys who are working, and I'll go out and get people to sell them houses." "It was no longer working poor, it was welfare poor. . . . It was the way they acted." "You know how I got this house?" Mr. McLaughlin demanded. "We didn't eat out for two years. I hustled at Yankee Stadium. I was a helper on a truck. I was a bartender, a stagehand. I worked my butt off." This attitude of why can't "they" be like "us" culminated in a more general statement by the head of the civic association: "It is not a question of race but of shared values."[49] All these statements tend to be rhetorical, since few whites believed that there were in existence very many hardworking blacks capable of financing entrance into "their" white neighborhoods.

Black Families and Black Criminals

Ultimately, when popular wisdom becomes analytical, the focus turns to the black family. The family is the extent of the environment that most people intuitively grasp in search of explanations. The African-American family has been the focus of debate and contention among both blacks and whites for a long time. What was stated by E. Franklin Frazier in 1940 still appears relevant:

Black disorganized families have failed to provide for their emotional needs and have not provided the discipline and habits which are necessary for personality development. Because the disorganized family has failed in its function as a socializing agency, it handicapped the children in their relations to the institutions in the community. Moreover, family disorganization has been partially responsible for a large amount of juvenile delinquency and adult crime among Negroes.[50]

From family breakdowns arise brazen, fearless, unimaginable young toughs. Herb Denton, writing for the *Washington Post*, reports a street conversation with some young black teenagers:

They are small boys, eleven, twelve, and thirteen years old, still blushing, when asked about their girlfriends. . . . But when guns and homemade bombs explode on the street, they stand on the sidewalks with the older boys, hurling rocks and bottles at every passing white motorist. They cheer when they hit a windshield and glass shatters. . . . Alex Moore, 13, . . . talks about being on the streets, . . . about throwing rocks at whites . . . as they drove by.
"I hit a cracker cab, then a cracker came down in a van. I hit him, too."
"Why?" He smiles, sighs, gives the visitor a look of mock exasperation. Was he afraid out there with the fires and the police and the older boys exchanging volleys and gunfire? His smooth brown face hardens.
"When they shoot me," he says, "they better had kill me."[51]

Small delinquent boys grow up to be big tough youths, and big tough youths grow up to be the men who constitute the core of the underclass. Black underclass men are pictured in two ways: as unreformable criminals or irresponsible fathers. "Members" of the black underclass, from brassy teenagers to hardened criminals, terrorize the white imagination that is fed by the mass media, hearsay, or concrete incidents. Judgments are quick to come: "Some of these kids are just . . . mean human beings," writes former Urban League president Vernon Jordon.[52] Or compare the relatively benign judgment of a police officer: "I don't blame the kids. I blame the parents. If my kid came home with a watch or a bicycle that I didn't buy him, I'd want to know where he got it. But those parents are delighted. I'd lock up the parents."[53]

Whether young black delinquents are seen as simply mean or as lacking proper adult supervision, they sooner or later get classified as monstrous, as being less than human: "They'll kill you for nothing. They'll stare through you. They're cold and callous. They have no remorse."[54] The "less-than-human" category is confirmed by such boastful confessions as "I earned $1,500 to $3,000 a day as a stickup man and I wrote 'sorry notes' to the loved ones of those [I] shot."[55] Pearl Dawson, herself a black ex-convict, reflects: "One thing about Black people, when it comes to crime they don't think. A lot of crime is done without thinking."[56]

Thoughtless, sadistic, and callous are the words used to describe the black criminal. It follows that violent black crimes are often viewed as random, especially in urban communities, and the "randomness" is often seen as emerging from poor, broken families unable to supply direction to young lives. "As a result, many [big city] residents feel under a state of siege; they alter their living habits, change their locks, bolt their doors, and nervously glance over their shoulder."[57] Thus, the black-white racial discord between communities becomes a class discord within the African-American community, between decent blacks and black criminals, between the black working poor and the nonworking poor. As one old black resident of Tyler House in Washington, D.C., sadly reflected:

> I would like to say I'm black and I'm proud, but I can't say that so easily because I'm not proud of what black people are doing to each other in this building. I'm like most of the other elderly people here. I'm afraid of my own people—not only in Tyler House, but everywhere I go. The men will come up to you and say, "How you doing, sister?" Then they'll snatch your pocketbook.[58]

Downgrading the Black Male

There is one sign of "relief" among whites in this general fear of the black underclass, itself revealing of white racist attitudes. Crime statistics tell us that "95 percent of all victims of crime perpetuated by blacks are blacks. In 1980, more than 2,000 black teenagers were homicide victims, almost all at the hands of other black teenagers."[59] Are whites acting as if they were watching some "weirdo" animals in a zoo, fighting it out in a cage and thereby deriving a sense of racial superiority from the belief that they are not like "them"? It is this white posture that induced Christopher Muldor to title his *Wall Street Journal* "op ed" piece with the question, "Do Black Crime Victims Matter?" As he reported, the criminal justice system is much more lenient toward blacks who kill other blacks than toward blacks who kill whites.[60] Are not black victims people who should have their victimizers removed from society? Should we not be concerned with all victims of crime equally? The answer in a racist society is no, since black victims are not viewed as completely human or worthy of the same empathy as whites. As one cop commented, "[Blacks] are not ready for society. . . . Civil rights came too fast, too soon." Analyzing why blacks are not ready for society, and therefore do not warrant the same civil considerations as whites, the cop continues: "There's no father image. . . . There's no father who runs the family. . . . So you don't have discipline."[61] Thus, in returning to the state of the black family with its disorganization and weakness as a socializer, we blame the black male. He becomes America's number one internal enemy. He becomes not only the culprit of black crime, family chaos, juvenile delinquency, and a host of other difficulties within the black community, but also the enemy of black women. In the world of one black underclass male, his marriage "did not fail because he failed as a breadwinner and head of a family but because his wife refused to put up with his manly appetite for whiskey and other women"—appetites that rank high in the scale of shadow values on the street corner.[62]

In the words of a black male who was induced to write as if he were making observations characteristic of the whole black professional middle class:

> The truth be known, my friend was a bum whose life was an insult to black people. His death brought to public view some of the dozen or so children he'd fathered by numerous women. Always he'd dillydallied without marriage and without commitment. And once a child was conceived he was off to new conquests. Worse, he managed to glamorize his philandering so that many young blacks envied it.
>
> We [black men] are, after all, part of the problem. . . . We've indulged our sons so much that they too believe sexual irresponsibility is a rite of manhood. All the while, we have given neither our sons nor our daughters the love, trust and confidence that would make them realize how truly special they are.
>
> As a boy I remember seeing black physicians meeting teenaged girls for tawdry assignations. When the babies came,

those doctors adorned their Cadillacs with new girls and never committed even a pittance to the support of the children they fathered.

While the junior-high principal wasn't as sought after as the physicians, he also had a following. He'd leave pregnant teenagers in the lurch—too poorly educated to support themselves and with no hope of getting help from him. . . . By their actions, these men taught us that it was acceptable to use women like whores.[63]

The media technique of inducing black men to testify against themselves, regardless of the testimony's accuracy or merit, enables the white world to observe the black condition in a state of dumb disbelief and scorn. Black men are seen as the cause of the condition in which black women find themselves, and, therefore, are blamed for the fact that 56 percent of black births are out of wedlock compared to 9.4 percent for whites, a difference that identifies the black rate as "pathological."[64] This kind of statistic not infrequently turns the focus to black women and their image in white minds. While some black females, in the name of feminism and the defense of gender, may vent against black males, black women do not escape the victimization process.

Unweds, Babies, and Welfare Dependency

The media over the decade have saturated the public with stories and pictures of "black teenager birth rates, black illegitimate birth rates, and black female AIDS rates."[65] Why this state of affairs? The answer conveyed by the media, especially with regard to the unmarried teenager, is glib. It rarely seeks to offer serious insights about what it means to grow up in a socially negating society that projects a dismal future, not only for you specifically but for every acquaintance in the universe of your neighborhood. Frequently the partial explanation that is teased out of the mouth of the black teenager herself has stereotypical dimensions:

Their friends were all having babies. Their boyfriends had pressured them into it, because being a father—the fact of it, not the responsibility—is a status symbol for a boy in the ghetto. Welfare does provide an economic underpinning for out-of-wedlock childrearing.[66]

Lots of girls feel that if they get to be eighteen and they don't have a baby, they're not a woman.[67]

To white ears, the statement by a black teenager that having a child was a means of getting on welfare drowns out almost all else one might say. Thus, the more black teenagers talk about having babies, or not knowing who the father was, or why they were shipped off to a foster home, the greater is the white belief that black sexual behavior is completely indiscriminate and promiscuous. It is behavior that is inexplicable and outside the normal range of white middle-class moral deliberations. It becomes behavior specifically associated with race, with African-Americans, and is assumed to be deeply embedded in black culture in ways that transcend environmental and class considerations. This latter point is often proved by pointing to the fact that less developed countries have poor masses that manage to keep their families intact and are not sexually permissive.[68]

Out-of-wedlock births are critical to the assumed reasons why so many blacks need welfare assistance. Welfare dependency has become the public policy symbol that both reflects and causes much that ails the black community. It brings together the racist judgments whites stereotypically employ to describe the black population: ungrateful welfare cheats, laziness, absence of pride, "them" versus "us" whites who would rather starve than accept welfare. There is no end to the opprobrious phrases cast at the African-American population (and frequently accepted as partially true by blacks themselves) that are derived from the underclass-welfare linkage.

The most decisive way to chastise the character of the black welfare population is to use, as I have repeatedly emphasized, black words against blacks as if whites were unrelated to the conditions in which blacks find themselves. The welfare system has become the primary wastepaper basket to collect much of the contempt whites have for blacks. Whites are profoundly agitated by the belief that their hard-earned taxed incomes go to support black welfare recipients who "stay on the dole most of their lives," believe that there is no point to working "when you can get something for nothing," and have a "baby every year to stay on welfare."[69] The most repeated point is that welfare induces the breakup of the black family, since it "encourages husbands to leave home, knowing that public stipends will provide for their wives."[70] This, moreover, allows black males to live off their wives without working; after all, "there is no law against a lady givin' you all their money."[71] In sum and substance, the welfare system undermines the work ethic and induces the black working poor to ask:

Why work? . . . For all practical purposes, the relief check becomes a surrogate for the male breadwinner. The resulting family breakdown and loss of control over the young is usually signified by a spread of forms of disorder—for example, school failure, crime and addiction.[72]

The welfare system is indicted beyond its deleterious effects on black women, men, children, work, and learning habits. Blacks are seen as ungrateful cheats who do not care about anything:

> I remember one time my girlfriend and I got drunk and went out and bought drugs. . . . The next day, we were sick. She said: "Don't worry." She went down to the welfare center, with rags and barged in there yelling. God damn it; look at what my baby has to play in! I didn't get my check. . . . Half an hour later we were sitting at home shooting up with money from the extra check.[73]

Not only, therefore, are children had without thought, but the money acquired from the welfare system is not really used to care properly for them. Thus, the popular mind sees the welfare system as a dumping ground for those blacks who do not wish to work, for having babies in order to stay on the dole, and, not least, for institutionalizing cheating.[74]

In a country in which individuals are judged by their job, by a willingness to work even if the work pays poorly and there is little pride in the job or product itself, the overrepresentation of blacks in the welfare sector induces a profound stigma. It has become a reason that justifies why white blue-collar workers have left the Democratic party and have rejected the welfare state itself.[75] To such white workers, a "welfare recipient" is synonymous with "black." This welfare-black link, unfortunately, does not end with white misperception. Even black unionized workers, while unlikely to sever their allegiance to the Democratic party, responded enthusiastically to a white conservative speaker who had little rapport with the liberal, unionized audience until the speaker began to attack the welfare system. Thus, regularly employed black workers themselves appear to share views with their white cohorts that many welfare recipients are lazy and irresponsible.[76] In more macrological terms, the welfare system has even been indicted on the wacky belief (assumed to be well known) that it "drains most of the five-hundred-billion-dollar federal budget."[77]

The moral here is complex, although, from my angle of reflection, quite comprehensible. White workers see "race" when they think "welfare"; the link between the two is strong. Employed black workers see a "class" of people with whom they are identified and from whom they wish to be dissociated when they hear the term welfare being tossed about in the public arena. Few black employed workers, unlike their white counterparts, are unfamiliar with individual welfare recipients who might fit the publicly held stereotype.

While white workers may acquire a misplaced pride in telling themselves that starvation is preferable to accepting dole from the state, black employed workers experience something different when welfare recipients and the devalued system are publicly exposed. The overrepresentation of unemployed blacks among those who receive welfare checks calls into question the immediate social status of large numbers of working poor blacks whose income is at or marginally above the threshold of poverty. While middle-class blacks with two incomes also suffer in status from this peculiar "guilt by association," they are not as residentially integrated with high concentrations of welfare recipients and marginally employed blacks. While white workers residing in relatively homogeneous communities view the welfare sector in race terms, black workers residing in black communities necessarily view it in class terms. But this class cleavage within the black community is exacerbated by the stigmatizing white image of black welfare recipients. The black overrepresentation in the welfare sector dramatically impinges on the status of the black stratum immediately above it. In this sense, class tensions within the black population are related to the race-class differences between the populations.

Statistical Myopia

White myopic perceptions are not only confined to popular prejudices, misinformation, and manipulated media images that are devoid of endeavors to deepen the public's understanding and eliminate contemptuous voyeurism. There is also a statistical myopia disguised as value-free research or as the honest effort to find the quantitative magnitudes that underlie popular impressions. An example of this brand of representation appeared in a review of six books by Andrew Hacker in 1988 titled "Black Crime, White Racism."[78] Aside from the fact that three of the six books reviewed had little to do with crime as such, discussion of crime dominated. Without doing full justice to Hacker's quiet and buried one-line critical qualifications, what stands out larger than life is the reproduction of five tables. They constitute a story in themselves and feed the validation of popular impressions, from which academics are not excluded, that are often unsupported by numbers (see Tables 1–5).

Table 1 informs us that blacks are disproportionately arrested, a fact most whites acquire through the habit of watching TV, looking at

Table 1. Racial arrest rates

	Black share of arrests (%)	Disproportion of black arrests in population
Robbery	62.0	5.3
Gambling	49.7	4.2
Murder and manslaughter	48.0	4.1
Rape	46.6	3.9
Gambling	46.1	3.9
Prostitution	43.0	3.7
Aggravated assault	39.8	3.4
Receiving stolen property	37.4	3.2
Motor vehicle theft	34.7	2.9
Weapons offenses	34.4	2.9
Forgery and counterfeiting	32.6	2.8
Domestic violence	32.3	2.7
Drug violations	31.8	2.7
Disorderly conduct	30.7	2.6
Burglary	29.5	2.5
Vagrancy	29.4	2.5
Embezzlement	28.8	2.4
Curfew and loitering	21.9	1.9
Vandalism	19.9	1.7
Driving while intoxicated	9.7	0.8

Note: Ratios of disproportion are based on blacks' being 12 percent of the population.
Source: Federal Bureau of Investigation (1986).

Table 2. Assailants and victims (in %)

Assailant-Victim	11,099 murders
White-white	46.0
Black-black	46.0
Black-white	5.6
White-black	2.4
	100.0
	108,826 rapes
White-white	62.1
Black-black	26.9
Black-white	8.8
White-black	2.2
	100.0
	823,340 robberies
White-white	36.6
Black-black	25.8
Black-white	37.0
White-black	0.6
	100.0

Note: Victims of assailants of other races have been omitted, as have offenses where the assailant's race was not known or recorded.
Sources: Federal Bureau of Investigation and Bureau of Justice Statistics (1985-86).

Table 3. Prison populations

	Prisoner per 18-39 age group		Ratio of blacks to whites	Racial income ratio ($)	Violent crime rate
	White	Black			
Nebraska	38	584	15.4	662	26.3
Pennsylvania	32	429	13.4	625	35.9
Michigan	41	391	9.5	725	80.4
Maryland	61	528	8.7	704	83.3
Delaware	101	770	7.6	571	42.7
Oklahoma	104	569	5.5	641	43.6
North Carolina	82	366	4.5	633	47.6
Mississippi	59	292	4.9	495	27.4

Note: Rates for black and white inmates are per 10,000 men of each race in the 18-39 age group in each state. Income ratios express black earnings for each $1,000 made by whites. State rates for violent crimes include reported rapes, robberies, murders, and aggravated assaults per 10,000 population.
Sources: Bureau of Justice Statistics, Bureau of the Census, and Federal Bureau of Investigation.

Table 4. Average SAT scores for students
from families with incomes in the $30,000-$40,000 range

Asians	947
Whites	928
Puerto Ricans	844
Mexican-Americans	833
Blacks	742

Sources: The College Board (1986).

Table 5. Fourteen ethnic groups

	Family income (in 1987 dollars)	Foreign born (in %)
Japanese	43,493	28.4
Asian Indian	39,739	70.4
Filipino	37,662	64.6
Chinese	35,869	63.3
White	33,412	3.9
Korean	32,530	81.9
Hawaiian	30,522	1.6
Cuban	29,010	77.9
Mexican	23,476	26.0
Eskimo	21,988	1.5
American Indian	21,748	2.5
Vietnamese	20,415	90.5
Black	20,077	2.8
Puerto Rican	17,067	3.0

Source: Bureau of the Census (1980 census).

pictures of the ten most wanted criminals pinned on post office walls, and reading about arrests in daily tabloids. Table 2 identifies three criminal behavior patterns, of which whites must worry about only one. We see that blacks primarily murder and rape other blacks; these two categories of facts do not warrant white concern, since white empathy for black victims is minimal. But the third category of criminal information included in Table 2 does produce a white concern: the rate of black robberies of whites is higher than black robberies of blacks (37 percent versus 25.8 percent).

Moving to Table 3, we learn that blacks are incarcerated at a much higher rate than whites, with some variation in rates between states. Newsreels of prison riots keep us up-to-date on this kind of demographic data.

Table 4 is a non sequitur and represents a profound racist injection, intentions to the contrary. Blacks do worse on tests, when income is held constant. Since no evidence about black criminality is provided for those whose income range is between thirty and forty thousand dollars, what constitutes the relationship between test scores, crime, and middle-income blacks? None is suggested. If we found lower test scores among higher-income blacks compared to whites and, at the same time, found lower crime rates among higher-income blacks relative to whites, what would such a finding mean about inquiries focused on crime? Questions of this nature are not raised. Hacker quotes Arthur Jensen and Thomas Jefferson on their shared belief that African-Americans are intellectually inferior and makes reference to the complexity of the issues, but this is inadequate. Given the history of scientific IQism and its misuses, Table 4 is simply incomplete information that enables whites to confirm what is assumed to be known as hard fact.

Finally, Table 5 reproduces a standard array of numbers that feed the racist mind-set. It is a common strategy: Other nonwhite or ethnic groups "make it"; why not blacks? Why are blacks still so close to the bottom of the income heap? This table asks the same question as the offspring of white working-class ethnics: If my parents or grandparents made it in the old-fashioned way, although poor and discriminated against, why can't blacks make it without special compensation? Is there not something deeply wrong with blacks? In a postindustrial society in which people are assumed to rise as a result of merit, test scores are used to explain why blacks achieve less upward mobility. Since the poor intellectual performance of blacks has long been associated with endowment—with biology or unremitting cultural habits—race preempts class in the final analysis of why blacks are overrepresented in the criminal class. "Hard" data suggest that the "facts" of crime must be caused by the absence of "mental" traits or enduring intergenerational "cultural" transmissions; this, moreover, cannot be changed, even under favorable environmental conditions.

My point is that these are old beliefs dressed in new garb. There are other ways of presenting crime data that enhance our perspectives rather than feed our preexisting racial inclinations.[79]

Getting Tough

The avalanche of concern about black criminality and related issues naturally leads to the question of what must be done. One answer that is emerging from the white backlash perspective is the need to force blacks to "show their mettle" by withdrawing the whole support system that has been constructed over the decades; the imperative now is to come down with severe punishment to straighten out "would-be criminals."[80]

Having tried "everything" and failed, there is the turn to reliance on force. Only a few are willing to make explicit what many more secretly fantasize and wish. We need to undertake the wholesale removal of a large stratum of our black youth from the streets in our major cities. We need to lock them up for a long time, since we are dealing with "black terrorists," and they can only be dealt with in terms they understand.[81] This urge not only lurks in the minds of whites who now believe or imagine their whole way of life is threatened; it is also held by some elite black intellectuals. Harry Edwards, former member of the Black Panther party and now professor of sociology at the University of California and a national sports consultant, gave an account of his views on how to handle young drug peddlers to a San Francisco magazine. His advice, of course, need not apply solely to black youth, as any "imaginative" white might discern. It could easily spill over to include marginal blacks, homeless blacks, and all blacks who look like they might spoil the aesthetic quality of white communities. When asked how to "turn around a 13-year-old [black] kid selling crack in the street," Edwards replied:

> The reality is, you can't. You gotta realize that they're not gonna make it. The cities, the culture and Black people in particular have to begin to move to get that garbage off the street. . . . We have to take a very hard line against them, if we're to preserve our next generation and future generations. Even if they are our children, [we have got to] turn him in, lock him up. Get rid of him. Lock him up for a long time. As long as

the law will allow and try to make it as long as possible. I'm for lock 'em up, gettin' em off the street, put 'em all behind bars.[82]

The reasons that induce a prestigious black professional to spout off as if he were a redneck Southerner with a long tradition of looking at blacks as animals are different from the fears that drive well-intentioned whites, when threatened by integration, to say, "I think people in my community are not concerned about it from a racial point of view, but from an economic one."[83] The difference lies in the way the race-class nexus impinges on individual perceptions. Professor Glenn C. Loury, a conservative black scholar at Harvard University, expressed his concern about the behavior patterns of the black underclass in the following way:

> The criminal behavior of a relatively small number of . . . black men in big central cities is . . . a critical factor undermining the quality of life of [all blacks] living in those cities, and also a contributing factor to race relations.[84]

Brent Staples, a black *New York Times* reporter, put the race-class entanglement more incisively:

> As a softy who is scarcely able to take a knife to a raw chicken—let alone hold one to a person's throat—I was surprised, embarrassed, and dismayed all at once. Her flight [reference is to a white woman] made me feel like an accomplice in tyranny. It also made it clear that I was indistinguishable from the muggers who occasionally seeped into the area from the surrounding ghetto.[85]

For the white middle class, writes a sensitive suburban resident,

> to accept blacks into their ranks, they must be safe from street crime. Otherwise the middle class will continue to identify all blacks with criminal behavior. This is not a just situation. This is not a fair situation; it may be morally despicable, but that is the way it is.[86]

Middle-class blacks suffer from lower-class black life and circumstances. They suffer because whites find it unreasonable in a quasi-segregated society, where resources and social amenities are distributed unequally, to make distinctions along class lines when it applies to African-Americans. Thus, even sensitive white members of the middle class are induced to behave along racially guided lines by moving to the suburbs. In the course of this flight, they reflect on the moral injustice of treating middle-class blacks in terms of some kind of mistaken identity, a spillover, so to speak, from the overrepresentation of blacks in the lower class. Finally, our white suburbanite is resigned to the "morally despicable" reality because "that is the way it is."

This white voice represents a profound sensitivity and is genuinely troubled. The action of such suburbanites is intended to protect their personal well-being; yet the same such voices often become advocates of higher taxes and more state expenditures to help blacks, poor and middle class alike. One's personal, moral, and political interests are not necessarily congruent. There are paradoxical tensions here that need exploration, a task I undertake in the final chapter. My main point at present is simply to emphasize that even white racial egalitarians are induced to behave contrary to their convictions. That is, as we have argued, the essence of institutional racism. Most whites, in my judgment, are less morally troubled. While they believe in fairness, they may in fact be morally self-righteous about the present state of the black underclass. They may even believe that the welfare system has been too benign toward the black poor who are not viewed as deserving.[87] For this reason, among others, they are questioning the welfare state itself.

Indicting the Welfare Society

To a growing number of white minds, as well as to some conservative black scholars, the black underclass represents, as I indicated, a communicable disease that needs to be extirpated, even if it means violence and bypassing the law. Related to this urge to stamp out this disease in our midst is the disillusionment with liberal policies that are currently seen as part of the problem. The evolution of this policy-focused reasoning is described in the following directions:

> [Despite] 20 years of civil rights gain and 13 years of anti-
> poverty programs [involving] tens of billions of dollars . . .
> spent every year by the Federal Government, states and cities;
> [despite] special hiring drives, private job-training programs,
> university and affirmative-action programs . . . aimed at aiding
> [and motivating the black poor], the underclass is still with us
> and the black poor are hardly better off, and in some cases
> [are] worse off, than before the War on Poverty.[88]

Thus, so goes the reasoning, liberal policies have not only failed at considerable cost to the taxpayer, but they have abetted the growth of the underclass. Conservatives argue that changes in the "criminal justice system have decreased the sanctions against aberrant behavior and thereby contributed to the rise of serious inner-city crime since 1965."[89] Conservatives point to soft-headed welfare liberal leaders who have added to the incorrigible behavior of the black underclass by pressuring the public to maintain assistance rather than making blacks look for work. Even affirmative action efforts are held responsible for the continued growth of the black underclass since such efforts allegedly increase the demand for talented blacks and decrease it for less qualified ones.[90]

These critiques converge on the welfare system itself. The claim, initially, was that particular welfare policies undermine self-reliance, promote joblessness, and encourage out-of-wedlock births and female-headed families.[91] Ultimately, however, the whole welfare society falls under suspicion. It leads to "organized altruism" that permits "the State to supplant the family, inadvertently making parents believe they were not responsible—perhaps incapable—of caring for their progress."[92] Thus, in the revisionist history of welfare liberalism, it was the excessive "goodness" of the welfare state that created a growing, unmanageable black underclass. With a very small step, revisionist history can comfortably use images of the black underclass to delegitimize a system that had its origins in another era and currently has relevance far beyond the particulars of the black images being manipulated to challenge it.

Conclusion

I have shown in this chapter how images of the black underclass, representing less than 1 percent of the population and residing primarily in our major central cities, have been magnified to affect not only the status of middle- and working-class blacks but the legitimacy of the liberal welfare society itself. It is unreasonable to expect professional middle-class blacks, as well as working-class families, to accept with equanimity their "inclusion" in the spillover from the core of black underclass neighborhoods. It is this spillover, as well as the underclass itself, that needs understanding.

African-American reactions to the shadows cast by the underclass core are varied: self-denigrating public confessions, programs to fight racism and poverty in poor black neighborhoods, endeavors to establish more social justice for all minorities, and the advocacy of force to eliminate the "disease" in our central cities. While I have suggested that the black underclass problem is an exaggerated social construction that is manipulated for purposes unrelated to eliminating the conditions causing the black underclass malaise, I would not wish to suggest that our inner cities do not face difficulties that relate to the existence of an underclass. As Herbert Gans has rightly noted,

> An America with a [black] jobless caste would be socially dangerous, for crime addiction, mental illness, as well as various forms of covert and overt protest, some of it violent, would be sure to increase sharply. In the long run, . . . solution[s] would also be politically dangerous, because . . . people assigned to an underclass would remain an integral part of the larger society.[93]

Thus, description of any major central city generates a self-evident danger. Take one, for example, where there is

> 25 percent unemployment. One-third of the residents have moved out. There are many young men [and women] with no jobs collecting welfare checks and on the streets or playing [around] with friends most of the day. There are many young women watching television all day. There are numerous unemployed adult children living with an unemployed parent. Many of these city residents have a problem with alcohol and drugs. Older men who once did heavy labor have been laid off; most have been out of work for years. Many young unmarried women, especially teenagers, in the public housing complexes are pregnant or have already had illegitimate children. Most of the young do not expect to work in the future. They seem resigned, angry, or fatalistic about their lives. They feel no one . . . cares about them.[94]

Are these problems related to race? I believe that most U.S. whites and blacks would answer yes—even if qualifications about external circumstances like international competition, changes in technology, the occupational mix, the arrival of new immigrants, and other such factors were added to the analysis. But the problems presented in the above inner-city description are those of Liverpool, England. The people are white workers and their families.

If this can happen to white workers whose injuries, limited preparedness, and expectations are class determined, why must so much attention be devoted to the behavior of black ghetto dwellers, to their alleged character traits, to their lack of "intelligence," to their drug and crime-ridden patterns as if such qualities were in the blood or bones of the person or group? If the white skilled workers of Liverpool and their families can be reduced to behavior not unlike that of blacks trapped in American cities in a period of a decade or so, why do we need racially focused descriptions and testimonies? The answer, in my judgment, is that every society needs some categories to shield itself from its deepest shortcomings; it perhaps avoids addressing some intractable contradictions within the society. We employ the racial lens, unique to our history, to explain the special case, to explain why the equality of opportunities (embracing equality in environmental circumstances) available to blacks in principle are not so in fact. We do not escape from racial categories even when they are unnecessary in our analysis. We deny class, because we proudly believe that our history demonstrates fluidity in this sphere. Therefore, we do not wish to claim that a large group in our society suffers from grossly unequal class or environmental barriers. Thus both white and black Americans, each for different reasons, use race when they could well use class. We have done this for so long that race has become reified and intermingled with class in a complex but nevertheless coherent way.

The white uses of the black underclass are only part of the problem in which race and class interact. The race-class connection broadens to embrace the aggregate economic and social status of middle-class blacks in more general ways. I shall now examine this process.

RACE-CLASS CONNECTIONS

have argued that the civic disgrace that followed the civil rights
movement demanded a perspective that focused on race-class relational subtleties. Existing perspectives (rational individualism, class
determinism, and non-Eurocentric culturalism) were inadequate to
the task of integrating analysis, strategies, and public policies. I have
indicated in what sense the legacy of slavery still affects white views of
black mental capacities. I have shown how the economics of dominant-subordinate relations overcrowd blacks into the lower portions of
each occupational group (e.g., professional and kindred workers) and
in the lower-ranked groups (e.g., service and semiskilled operative
workers) more generally. I have also shown how the black underclass is
used in ways that affect the range of economic opportunities and quality of social life among all strata of the black population. The consequences of these processes have implications for the race-class debate, a debate that has a long history, as I have emphasized, among
black and white political activists, publicists, and scholars. But, in my
judgment, this debate has been relatively sterile; it has been devoid of
context and the experiential dimension of race-class relations. As a result, the debate has not evolved to deepen our understanding.

The present state of the race-class debate remains confused or mis-
interpreted because it fails to embrace the interplay between black
overcrowding in the lower class where race and class are sometimes
fused, and "pure" racial discrimination in the middle and upper ranges

of the economic hierarchy where class differences defined in terms of income, occupation, and education may be absent.[1] This, of course, does not imply the absence of racial criteria in the determination of the status of the black poor. To understand the importance of race relative to the absence of economic capacities among all poor, black and white, one needs to inquire whether poor blacks have fewer opportunities (life chances) to escape from comparable circumstances compared to poor whites. There is little evidence to suggest that life chances are equal. The evidence that does exist suggests that poor blacks suffer from the burdens of race and class simultaneously, while poor whites suffer from that of class.[2]

In this chapter, I demonstrate how the overrepresentation of blacks in the lower class casts shadows that stigmatize working- and middle-class blacks for reasons of race alone. This process is not, however, static; it rebounds, like feedback, to influence black economic responses in both the work and nonwork spheres and thereby affects black economic capacities as producers and consumers. The possession of middle-class educational credentials and the prevalence of racial discrimination against blacks with such credentials have ramifications not considered by those who argue for the primacy of either a race or class analysis. The reasoning developed here emphasizes the distribution of specific kinds of racial exclusion and discriminatory practices experienced by a black population that is becoming occupationally and educationally more diverse. This phenomenon, in my view, has greater relevance than overall arguments about trends in either class achievements (upward mobility) or race attitudes.

Race or Class

The race-class difference in emphasis among political leaders, scholars, professional publicists, and people more generally does not necessarily divide along the lines of race. Differences, for example, can be seen in the implicit clash between Martin Luther King, Jr., and Malcolm X in the 1960s. King, in one of his appeals, reminded his followers that the majority of blacks are working people, and as such "there is a basic community of interests that transcends many of the ugly divisive elements of traditional prejudice. . . . Negroes . . . cannot be casual toward the union movement."[3] Class is more important than race. Malcolm X, in contrast, insisted that the "history of America is that working class whites have been just as much against not only working class Negroes, but all Negroes. . . . There can be no working class solidarity until there's first black solidarity."[4] Race is more important than class.

In academic circles the debate is couched in different terms because the intentions are allegedly more analytic than overtly political. Even so, academic formulations are not without their programmatic and policy implications. Reacting to the tumultuous black protests in the late sixties, Edward C. Banfield, a conservative political scientist, suggested that turning blacks into whites overnight would change little:

> New Whites would continue working at the same jobs, living in the same neighborhoods, and sending their children to the same schools. . . . Today the Negro's main disadvantage is . . . that he is the most recent unskilled, and hence relatively low-income immigrant to reach the city from a rural backward area . . . and that the causes of the Negro's problems [are almost all economic].[5]

Clearly Banfield's message is that class overrides race.

The black liberal sociologist, William Julius Wilson, argued in 1978 that the key problem for today's blacks is the deficiency of skills and education. There is still, in Wilson's view, the residue of historical racism; but for young educated blacks living in the post-civil rights era, the acquisition of equal life chances has been achieved. In this view, class characteristics, not race, are the obstacles in the way of black progress.[6]

When Marxists attempt either to reduce racist sentiments and policies to the economic interests of the capitalist class or to prove statistically that "class structure mediates the effects of race on the income determination process," they are making racism dependent on, and secondary to, the workplace position of blacks.[7] Class is primary in the understanding of manifest racism.

In contrast to the variety of class arguments, Kenneth B. Clark, the well-known liberal black psychologist, has forcefully argued that racism in American society is still a vital negative force that determines the fate of African-Americans in all stations of life.[8] In spite of the progress made as a result of the civil rights movement, whites willfully use racial considerations to keep blacks poor, to prevent them from acquiring training, education, decent homes, and secure jobs. The existence of a black underclass is not simply a residue of the past or a current product of neutral circumstances involving capital flight from our central cities. While overt racial epithets justifying racial oppression may have disappeared, new code words are operating to justify racist actions, such as "busing," "quotas," "reverse discrimination," "meritocracy," "maintaining standards." In Clark's view, these are "shorthand terms implying that remedies for racial injustice will weaken the fiber of the society as a whole" and therefore are part of a "new racism."[9] Clark points out that even when blacks "make it" in the corporate world, "these new black managers and executives are assigned to such race-related areas as 'community affairs' and 'special markets.' "[10] The race emphasis in more general terms was articulated by various officers of the National Urban League's 1983 conference. While significant differences among blacks in income, occupation, education, and family structure were acknowledged, the consensus was that

> blacks are much more homogeneous in their attitudes and much more cohesive as a group than economic data would indicate. There is substantial agreement across all income levels as to the major problems blacks face and the reasons for those problems—racial discrimination.[11]

Race and class received a divided emphasis at a workshop (held at Sarah Lawrence College in 1979) that was part of a larger conference concerned more generally with the family in a changing world. Middle-class blacks are frequently embittered by the fact that discussions about *the* black family inevitably focus on poor blacks, welfare cases, fatherless families, and foster homes. The following is a comment by a black woman who attended a workshop led by a well-known white social scientist:

> What distresses me over and over again is that the term *the* black family presented at a symposium such as this and the diversity of the black community is never discussed. I think that much of what is said about the black family applies to any family that falls within a certain socioeconomic group.

Class, not race, determines the characteristics of the black family. But contrast the opinion of another black woman at the same workshop:

> The black family is not the issue—lower class or middle class. The black experience in this country is such that no matter what kind of black status you have, you are going to be seen as a nigger sooner or later, in one way or another. You can buy into the system only so far and not farther. That is the bottom line.[12]

The message is clear; race takes precedence over class.

Moving to the level of rhetoric in the contemporary political arena, race and class themes are sometimes employed in a single voice. Jesse Jackson's style is that of a black preacher; nevertheless, his speeches often cross the race chasm, as exemplified in his 1988 Wisconsin campaigning. There he urged blacks *and* whites to stand up against the corporate elites that rule America.[13] Class counts. Yet, viewed by the chieftans of the Democratic party with an eye on Middle America, Jackson was an embarrassment; the fear was that the black population would be seen as acquiring too much leverage in the party. Rallies aimed at enlisting the black vote were perceived as possibly inducing a further loss of white working-class support. Some even argued that Dukakis's defeat was related to racial fears among white workers. Derivative of this fact is the suggestion that the Democratic party could well split along racial lines.[14] Despite Jackson's class-directed rhetoric, he symbolized race to most whites. And in spite of Jackson's own desire to become a national leader transcending race, his idiom, cadence, and incantation are those seen as coming from a black preacher talking to *his* people; they are connected to the racial and cultural experience of blacks and not strictly to their class location.

Advocates of either class or race interpretations sometimes contribute insights, but their interpretations obfuscate the race-class interactions that are, in the view developed here, fundamental to understanding black-white conflict. Class reductionists cannot provide compelling explanations of the durability of black-white hostilities within class boundaries. Race reductionists cannot generate a viable movement and public policies that meet the economic (class) needs of large portions of the black population. Thus, my task is to develop an alternative to the limitations that characterize both the class and race determinists.

Race-Class Interactionism

My argument is that "unjust" treatment of black middle-class individuals is determined by "just" white reactions to lower-class blacks. These "just" and "unjust" valuations are entangled in the confused nature of the race-class debate. "Unjust" is used to suggest that a racial criterion is operating; "just" means real economic and social characteristics are allegedly the concern. In the jargon of economics, discrimination based on productivity differences is just; that based on race is not.[15] Putting aside the problem of how productivity is determined, and a host of other problems related to its measurement and subjective dimensions, economists generally fail to analyze how different spheres in the social system are linked to affect an individual's productive performance in the workplace alone.[16] More will be said about this linkage at a later juncture. For the present I wish to state, without cumbersome qualifications, the proposition that guides my theme. The greater the "objective" socioeconomic class differences between blacks and whites at the lower ranges of the economic ladder, the greater will be the status differences between blacks and whites in the middle and upper ranges of the economic hierarchy. Such differences among the middle classes, moreover, will stem from racial practices rather than objective characteristics such as differences in the level of skills and educational achievement. My concern here, in other words, is to explain the nature of pure racism where class characteristics cannot be employed to justify decisions. The focus is on how perceptions and actions against one segment of the black population spill over to affect another segment. The shadow that is cast and generalized from the economically subordinate portion of the black population determines the attitudes and behavior of all whites toward all blacks, and, specifically, toward the more affluent and educated members of the black population who have class characteristics comparable to their white cohorts.

Race-class interaction figures significantly, if not always explicitly, in a number of major factors that constitute the core of the conflicted dialogue between the racial populations and within them separately. It is consonant with the way whites often think about blacks, that is, in the form of stereotypes that manifest themselves either by putting too many blacks into one category or by viewing those who don't fit specific categories as surprising exceptions to the rule—"You are not like the rest of . . . I know," or, "She is really an unusual black person; you know what I mean?" These are the words of well-intentioned individuals and not blatant racists who employ overt rhetoric.

It is consistent with the way portions of the black population are induced to think about their own status. Poor blacks may chronically underestimate their own potential and therefore expend less effort trying to cultivate it. In a survey about the possession of skills, many low-income and unemployed black males, for example, initially indicated that they had none. Yet, upon further probing, it was learned that a consequential number had abilities in plumbing, carpentry, and auto-mechanics. They meant by their reply that they did not know how to galvanize their skills into steady paying jobs.[17]

It may explain why some middle-class blacks seek to distance themselves from lower-class blacks or appear preoccupied with the nature of the black image. While public statements by middle-class blacks disassociating themselves from lower-class blacks have virtually disappeared, the underlying sentiments exist in various forms—witness the cynical comment made by a black female scholar after being insincerely congratulated by a colleague upon receiving tenure at a prestigious eastern university: "I bet they thought I was not like the rest of them."

More directly relevant is the conversation I had with my black neighbor; our acquaintance is limited to nods on the street as we pass each other with our dogs. While waiting for our automobiles, which were in a parking garage that we both used, we were casually glancing at a young black youth who was hanging out, making a moderate nuisance of himself. My neighbor gratuitously commented in a strong, disapproving tone that impressed me as being overdetermined: "Why can't the bum work; there are all kinds of jobs. I'll take him to McDonald's right now and get him a full-time job. It's disgusting." He then made reference to a black woman in the neighborhood who panhandles with a child at her side and said: "That woman should be shot."

This evident need on the part of my black middle-class neighbor to dissociate himself from the "bad black element" we mutually observed reflects the assumed belief that whites judge him in relation to "them." He wanted me to know that we shared contempt for that "kind."

This kind of dissociationism, of course, is not unfamiliar to other oppressed groups, but the extent and quality of it among the black middle class are probably more common and acute than that manifested among other ethnic groups. One writer, for example, suggests that there is a tendency among blacks "to define [their] overall status . . . not by [the] average black individual or family, but by the very worst off. So even though the majority of blacks have made considerable progress in the 1980s, most blacks are focused on the fortunes of the black poor."[18]

The race-class interaction is compatible with a thread of black historiography known as "contributionism," that is, interpreting black history by underscoring positive accomplishments of blacks in American society and, more generally, in civilization.[19] Contributionism could be interpreted as a way of avoiding or glossing over the failure of the black masses to pull themselves up by their own bootstraps. Interestingly, a comparable underlying dynamic appears to operate when some whites feel compelled to identify "their" chosen blacks as race examples for emulation.[20]

In the preceding discussion, I have emphasized the way the black population is viewed through a bifurcated lens. The signs of class success in some portions of the black population are not sufficient to empower the individual in normal situations and relations. Color for such individuals is linked to the lower-class status of blacks whose signs of success are unmistakably lacking. The dynamics of this double imaging often twist the role of the race-class nexus, inducing blacks with middle-class credentials to focus on race oppression. To understand the generalization of this process, I shall explore more systematically how the class distinctions within the black population are transformed into racial practices to determine black-white differences in wealth, income, family, and street-life experience.

Residential Segregation and Wealth Accumulation

Our observation begins with observable wealth differences between black and white families whose income levels are identical. The differences measured in the 1960s were about one to five; that is, black families tended to accumulate one-fifth of the wealth that white families accumulated when holding income, family size, and other variables constant.[21] More recent studies indicate the gap has widened.[22]

The central explanation of these differences grows out of black-white differences in access to the housing market that derive from residential segregation. Excluding the very rich and the very poor, for most families a home is the single most important purchase ever made and the single most important source of wealth accumulation. Denial of access to the housing market on equal terms has meant that blacks are constrained in the type of housing they can obtain, and therefore, the homes they do obtain tend to appreciate at a significantly lower rate than those purchased by whites.[23]

Residential segregation along racial lines is a deeply rooted urban configuration and reflects a confluence of forces. Whites are willing to pay premium prices for homes in order to live in all-white neighborhoods, and surveys by the National Committee Against Discrimination in Housing have repeatedly "uncovered widespread discriminatory practices by landlords . . . [who] may not rent to blacks because [they are] afraid of losing white tenants. . . . Brokers also play an important role in the discriminatory process in the owner-occupied market."[24]

To these two sources we can add banks, insurance companies, and other financial institutions whose concern with risk factors induces impersonal decisions that reinforce segregated patterns.[25] One outcome in this confluence of institutional forces producing residential segregation is that "middle and upper-income blacks live in lower quality housing relative to their white counterparts because of the shortage of better housing in black neighborhoods."[26]

Even though there has been some exodus of middle-class blacks from central cities, the alleged flight to the suburbs has been exaggerated. For blacks who have moved to suburbanlike communities, it has not meant integration but a resegregation on the periphery of the central city or in suburbs that are in close proximity to central cities with large black populations.[27]

The dynamics that explain why middle- and upper-income black families end up owning inferior homes are well known, if often forgotten. Better-off black families frequently seek to move into white neighborhoods adjacent to their present communities in search of not only higher quality homes but better schools, cleaner and safer streets, and more extensive shopping facilities. Moreover, they can afford to do so: their occupation and education make such moves possible. Black interests in purchasing homes in better neighborhoods initially bid up prices. While the specific pattern varies within and between cities, its general contours are fairly clear. As an extensive study sponsored by the Federal Reserve System of Boston explained:

> White households will begin to move out and those
> neighborhoods will tend to undergo complete racial transition
> or to "tip." Typically, when the percentage black in a
> neighborhood increases to a relatively small amount, 10 to 20
> percent, white demand for housing in the neighborhood will
> fall off and the neighborhood will tip toward full segregation.[28]

As this occurs, middle-class blacks acquire homes that do not appreciate as rapidly in value over time as homes owned by whites. The entry of middle-class black families into white neighborhoods induces a white exodus and the eventual influx of poor blacks.

This process involves both class and race considerations, and it can be explored through the actual voices and reactions of individuals. Information is leaked that a few black families have bought homes in "our" neighborhood. Sometimes vigilantes go into action. On a less violent note, homeowners organize into an association to prevent the purchases or block entry of the black families. Intervening white families active in homeowners' associations frequently produce the following kind of contradictory sentiments:

> We are not racists. We could not care less about the color of
> the people who move on this block, be they black, yellow,
> white or what, as long as they are like us; as long as they are
> clean, quiet, and law abiding. That is why we don't want black
> families in this neighborhood. That is why we must stop these
> families from buying homes here. Because as soon as you let in
> a few black families, no matter how decent, a lot more of the
> other kind will follow. Whites will move out. They will not be
> able to sell their homes to anyone other than blacks. Some
> landlords will divide up their apartments and overcrowd them

with blacks. The city will build a low-income housing project nearby. Pretty soon housing values will fall. That is why we can't allow these black families to move into our neighborhood.[29]

A more codified version of the above statement is illustrated by a real estate broker who claimed that his area was being "sold down the river . . . to protect . . . [another] predominantly Italian, low-middle-income area from public housing. . . . Development would bring a host of social problems, crime, deterioration in schools and a population shift."[30] It should be noted that the word *black* was never used, only euphemisms such as "crime" and "population shift." Or consider the words of a lower-middle-class Irish worker who reflectively responded to an inquiry about blacks coming into his neighborhood:

Economics, I think, is the biggest strain because, in this area, a man's whole idea of an investment in the economy of the United States is the house he owns. He invests $9,000; [years later] it's worth $21,000. . . . He's really knocking them dead in the economy, right? . . . But when he feels threatened, this money, this investment that he's made, he's desperate. He says what the hell are they doing to me? This is where I put my money. I didn't put it in General Motors. I didn't . . . you know . . . A man realizes this. . . . They say—you know—they're going to devaluate on him. I don't say that it's got any validity, this feeling. What I'm saying is this is the way they feel. This is where their money went, and this is what they're trying to protect.[31]

In sum, because there is a white fear of being inundated with lower-class black "hordes" who lack market capacities, it becomes necessary to prevent the entry of middle-class black families who have market capacities. In this way, middle-class blacks are discriminated against for purely racial reasons. While white intentions may be defensive and related to protecting economic interests, white *behavior* toward middle-class blacks manifests itself as if it were racially motivated. Given the "uncertainty inherent in racial integration and racial transition," white families—unwilling to risk falling property values—leave the area.[32] This, of course, leads to falling prices, enabling poorer blacks to enter the neighborhood "until segregation becomes complete."[33]

From the perspective of white families, the actions taken to allay their fears become justified. From the perspective of the black middle class, the process looks very different. As one black manager objected:

Here I am. I've been told if I get my act together, get
credentials through a college education, get a good job, I will
be able to experience the American dream; walk through open
doors; buy a home where I want, one with a backyard, clean
streets and good schools. So I do all that and what happens? I
get turned down.[34]

The moral by this time should be unmistakable. What takes place in
the production and labor market spheres for one set of reasons may
not be similiar to what takes place in the consumption or social sphere.
This constitutes a major weakness in William Julius Wilson's otherwise
insightful book *The Declining Significance of Race*. In his argument
that young, post-civil rights blacks have now acquired equal life
chances, he makes his case primarily for the labor market. However,
the acquisition of equal incomes for identical jobs does not necessarily
produce equal wealth accumulations because individual members of
the black middle class do not have equal access to the housing market.
The overcrowding of blacks in the lower rungs of the economic ladder
induces middle-class whites to resist entry of middle-class blacks into
"their" communities, "their" schools, and "their" local parks. The
Great White Fear is that the middle-class blacks who are "good" types
will be followed by lower-class blacks who are "bad" types. As a result,
the black middle class, for reasons that cannot but appear racial, are
excluded.

Income Status of the Black Middle Class

Our next illustration shows how the relative subordination of blacks in
the lower class affects the income status of blacks in the middle class.
There are two aspects to this process: the segregation and discrimination effects. Our main concern is with the latter.

The segregation effect has already been discussed briefly in an earlier chapter. Independent black professionals — lacking access to white
markets — may be forced to sell their services or goods in segregated
markets where demand is lower and perhaps more elastic. Partially
segregated work situations or markets dampen the income potential or
limit job and/or promotional opportunities of the black middle class.

The discrimination effect is concerned with the way overrepresentation of blacks in the lower class produces racially oriented judgments
that affect the income status of middle-class blacks working in nonsegregated sectors of the economy. That is to say, the "objective" class
position and condition of blacks in the lower ranks induce a more gen-

eralized market evaluation of all blacks, including blacks whose rank is significantly above those located in the lower echelons of the system.

This idea may be set forth in a more formal mode. Assume three hypothetical urban areas—U1, U2, U3—in which blacks represent 15 percent of the metropolitan labor force. In U1, blacks are overrepresented in the lower class (measured by industry and occupation employment ranked by national income) by a factor of 6:1; in U2, the factor is 4:1; and finally in U3, it is 2:1. These interurban differentials in overcrowding will affect middle-class interurban income status differences between the races that are not explained by occupation and education dissimilarities. Overcrowding in the lower rungs of the economic ladder will generate income differences between blacks and whites where objective class credential differences are absent. As in the case of the housing market, these differences are identified here as exemplifying pure racism. Black middle-class professionals, managers, and technicians will experience less income or fewer promotional opportunities relative to their identical cohorts in U1 compared to U3.[35]

This orientation is in sharp contrast to an argument developed by Gary S. Becker, who suggested that variation in racism or discrimination between areas was caused by variation in black-white population ratios.[36] Higher ratios stimulated a greater "taste for discrimination." The speculative rationale for selecting the population ratio was due to the greater possible threat that larger black populations posed to white dominance; this greater threat could only be contained through increased racial hostility in the form of more discriminatory practices.

My critical point here is not to suggest that the relative number of blacks in an area is without consequences. It may well affect, as some studies suggest, the way whites vote.[37] But population size per se is less statistically powerful and, in my view, a less theoretically informing variable than the occupational-industry distributive differences between the populations in the lower rungs of the economic hierarchy.[38] The usefulness of these latter differences is what critically affects the race-class nexus between and within the racial populations.

Status of Black Women

The status of black women is determined by the combination of race and gender on the one hand, and by the class position of black men on the other. These dimensions of their subordinate position are interrelated, but their connections are often misunderstood or obfuscated because the mechanisms that operate in various spheres are not carefully delineated. An added complexity in depicting the position of black women stems from the fact that in the current period middle-class black women have done well relative to their white counterparts; in fact, they have not only achieved parity in many specific occupational lines, but they have done relatively better than black middle-class males when they are compared to their white cohorts.

Blacks tend to be relegated to subordinate jobs. Such conditions affect the way family, neighborhood, and life circumstances reproduce themselves. Within black social and community life, the overcrowding of black males in the lower class generates an orientation and set of expectations for black women in all strata. A configuration of forces exists that produces black male roles that serve to shape the economic, social, and psychological outlook of black women. These general male roles, influenced by the overcrowding of black males in the lower class, have led to chronic black family difficulties that have produced an overrepresentation of black women who head households. Many such women with young children face circumstances that make their lives miserable and desperate. The general characterization of the men who are linked to the difficulties experienced by poor black women is reported in Elliot Liebow's book *Tally's Corner*.[39] The individual histories of the men who make up *Tally's Corner* indicate that the men have generated a thin and tentative commitment toward their children, their wives, their women and male friends, and their jobs. This tentativeness is based on psychological assumptions rooted in experience that, in the long run, little will work out. Fear, low self-esteem, and defeat—interpersonal and other kinds—lead to decisions about marriage, personal male-female relationships, and work that reproduce failure. Whatever the humanity that characterized *Tally's* people, and there is much of it, there is also intense interpersonal exploitation, indifference, callousness, and manipulativeness, which are all related to the exigencies of surviving. Given few satisfactions and little vision of possibilities from longer-run designs in life, pleasure from personal upmanship is rampant.

One black feminist reaction to Tally and his associates is articulated in the play *For Colored Girls Who Have Considered Suicide When the Rainbow Is Enuf* by Ntozake Shange.[40] From the perspective of my argument, this play illustrates, among other things, the subculture of the black female and her suspicion of white society; the black woman's hostility toward the street machismo of the black male who can't earn a living; the black woman's suspicion of all men; her sense of determination to somehow survive alone; and finally, the black woman's sense of desperation that induces her to turn toward religion or otherworldliness.[41]

The poetry of the play, of course, obscured the stratification issues that determine black male-female relations. The limited status that defines black male workers—from union members in the more stable portions of the working class to their less certain status as full-time members of the working poor to, finally, their marginal and transient status—is such that black women are experientially socialized to believe that marriage is not an economic solution to the fate likely to await them; in fact, marriage may even be viewed as a detriment to the black female's economic success.

In substance, the subordinate class position of the African-American male has determined the differences between black and white women at all levels.[42] Black middle-class women have acquired more parity compared to black men relative to their white cohorts. One reason for this comparative success is related to the social fact that black men are not viewed as good economic bets. This knowledge is imparted intergenerationally and reinforced by experiences derived from actual circumstances. In one form or another, the black female, whatever her original class status, is told that she had better be prepared to take care of herself, support herself, survive on her own terms. As one authority observes, black parents not only avoid pushing marriage but marriage itself

> has limited importance to the black women at all educational
> levels. At low-class levels it is clear that the rejection of
> marriage comes because it is perceived as unreliable, and at
> the upper-class levels because of the small pool of eligible men
> and the competition for husbands.[43]

The historic legacy of black women—one that is still alive as a result of the condition that faces large numbers of black men—has meant that black women's income is less likely to be viewed as only supplemental to their husbands' income. The pressures on them, in fact, are in the opposite direction. As a result, black women are persons of greater consequence and power in the household compared to their white counterparts. This is not intended to be a matrifocal argument, although it has often been articulated as such by both black male leaders and white social scientists. In the late sixties and early seventies, black nationalists, in their effort to correct a perception concerning the social castration of the African-American male, often attacked aggressive black female leaders for their alleged role in undercutting the leadership positions of black men.[44] In 1974, William A. Blakey, a black director of the Congressional Liaison for the U.S. Commission on Civil Rights, noted the common "observation" that the attitude of black

men toward black women is one of disrespect and a desire to domi-
nate. Black men feel, according to Blakey, that they must persecute
black women in order to repudiate the myth of the "castrating" black
matriarch.[45] This view has been replayed, albeit in a muted tone, by the
well-known sociologist Robert Staples.[46] Some of these issues have
been dealt with most harshly by Michele Wallace in her first, well-ad-
vertised, but critically reviewed, book, *Black Macho and the Myth of
the Black Superwoman*.[47] In her effort to articulate a black feminist position that catches the dual problem of being both black and female,
Wallace exposes the black male machismo and the black superwoman
myth. While her argument lacks an adequate analytical framework and
has a number of factual errors, she nevertheless touches upon an
emerging spirit developing among middle-class black women who are
relating to the women's movement on their own terms.

This spirit, finally, is revealed in the debate surrounding Alice Walker's acclaimed book *The Color Purple*. Black men have protested and
black women justified the way Walker portrays the violent character of
black men and shows that black women need to take charge of their
own lives.[48]

The convergence of black men's subordinate position with the survival exigencies facing black women has affected the social statistics of
the black female relative to her white cohorts. Black women, for example, are:

More often single.

More often at work and employed full-time, especially between
the ages of twenty-five and forty-four, the prime working age in
the life cycle.

More often poor and the head of a household.

More likely to be divorced or separated; and if divorced, more
likely to avoid remarrying.

More likely to marry, especially for middle-class black
professional women, men with less socioeconomic status.

More likely to earn an income that is essential rather than
supplementary to the core of the family's standard of living.[49]

An inspection of these social characteristics reveals, among other
things, a highly differentiated status structure within the population of
black women. At one end of the spectrum, there is the poorest of the
poor, the black woman as head of a household with children and without employment; at the other end, there is a growing number of professional, college-educated black women, independent and competi-

tive with the best of their cohorts. The story of black women who fail has been told many times. They wade in the currents of the welfare and casual-labor market systems, along with a large number of poor black men, unable to cope with the forces affecting the context in which they raise families. For many black working-class women with steady but moderate incomes, the idea of having a husband to provide support is not a tenable expectation. This is illustrated by a sample of never-married working-class women in their late twenties and early thirties whom I interviewed as part of a union-sponsored labor education project. Most of the women agreed with the contradictory sentiments expressed by one female worker:

> I've been working at this shit job since the age of 17. I've climbed up a few notches, got some seniority, and kept myself alive. But I'm damn tired. I'd like to have a family and find someone to care for me, but I'm not going to give up what I've accomplished for any man who comes along."[50]

For educated black women, the economic story, of course, is different, but the social one is similar. Their relative success may be due to the necessity, learned early in life through one channel or another, of surviving as a single person; or, if marrying, of recognizing the need to stay in the labor force permanently if the household's standard of living is to be comparable to that of the white middle class.

Interestingly, in all the cases noted, the status of successful and unsuccessful black women is shaped by the overcrowding of black men in the lower class. A problem, often not fully appreciated, for the successful black woman is illustrated in her quest for an appropriate marital relationship. This is indicated by the situation reported to exist in Washington, D.C. It revolves around man-sharing, stemming from the fact that "both working class and professional [black women] are going after the same men and there aren't that many of them. They all want the same thing—financial security."[51]

The lack of black men who are good economic bets was discussed more systematically by William Julius Wilson in The Truly Disadvantaged; it centers on the very low marriageable-male pool index for black women. The hard fact is that there are too few employed black men per hundred black women compared to white employed men per hundred white women.[52] If class were the only barrier to the inability of black women to find suitable mates, the marriage problem (especially for professional black females) would dissolve through interracial marriages. But since this is not likely for African-American women compared, for example, to middle-class Chinese-American women, who experience more interracial marriages, black women of all classes have different life chances and opportunities of achieving congenial marital unions. While the life stories among black women vary considerably, the burdens of race prevent interpersonal integration with white male cohorts; thus, the racial burdens of middle-class black women are linked to the overrepresentation of black men in subordinate economic positions.

It is not my intention here to deny the importance of how black women suffer qua women from general black male-female inequities in the division of labor within the household. In this domain, black women share the plight of white women. My emphasis in this chapter is on the specific plight of middle-class black women whose life circumstances are shaped by the overcrowding of black men in the lower class. The black woman's class credential is an insufficient ticket to the acquisition of social equality in other realms of life.

Street Life: An Anecdote

A black working woman—standing with an overload of packages in front of a seated middle-aged white man and a younger black one— was given a bus seat by the white man. The woman thanked the man graciously and sat down. She then turned to a black woman who happened to be sitting next to her and muttered in a voice louder than she intended: "No nigger would do that." Quick glances and counterglances occurred in a moment of high tension. When I looked at the faces around me and listened to the muffled voices among those who observed the "incident," I came to the conclusion that I had witnessed an "event" that told a story far beyond its brief duration. The black woman's statement represented a self-effacing racist generalization in the form of a slur against her own people. My own immediate account of the young black male's behavior was in terms of the brashness of youth. A black middle-class woman across the aisle stared straight ahead, stoically appearing to ignore the whole scene as if she had no interest in it, as if she were ashamed of her association with black men or disgusted by the "vulgarity" of her people. A well-dressed white woman nearby whispered to her companion: "What do you expect from *them*"—not certain whether "them" was a class or "them" was a race of not-so-human people.

When I got off the uptown, Madison Avenue bus at Ninety-sixth Street, it began to rain. A white man hailed a cab going across town about twenty yards behind a well-dressed black man who had been at the corner first and was also seeking a cab. As the cab pulled away, leaving behind the man who had the right to the cab, I reflected on how I had witnessed in two simple events the articulation of the twisted interplay between race and class in everyday life. It is an interplay that constitutes blacks' internal views of themselves, black-white interactions, and white views of blacks. I have sought to link the "purely" racial dimensions of black-white relations to the oversubordination of black males in the lower class.

Conclusion

The discussion has focused on the interaction between race and class and how they affect wealth accumulations through the housing market, income status of the black middle class, the position of black women, and a race-class aspect of everyday street life. I have attempted to show how the characteristics and conditions of the black lower class, and especially, but not exclusively, black men, are translated into racial terms and thereby affect the status and participation of blacks whose credentials are above the group's average. Eliminating racial regress after spurts of progress in American society requires as a necessary condition the elimination of black overcrowding in the lower classes. Unfortunately, the black lower class does not bring forth much social empathy from the larger American public. It even breeds disdain, although for different reasons, from members of the black middle class itself. As a result, class and racial factors are closely intertwined, if not totally combined, with respect to the behavior and conditions that reproduce black lower class overcrowding.

For this reason, it is an error to view the plight of the black lower class primarily in terms of a mismatch between upgraded job requirements and urban lower-class education or skills,[53] or between where lower-class blacks reside in our inner cities and expanding employment opportunities in our suburban areas.[54] Significant portions of the black poor do in fact lack sufficient skills and education to compete effectively, but they also face race-related barriers, a condition that contrasts with that of comparable members of the white lower classes. These barriers are operative in the present context because of the dynamic interplay between class and race that I have examined throughout this chapter.

Whites employ myopic race perceptions to produce or justify racist sentiments and exclusion practices. Both perceptions and justifications acquire an "independent" legitimacy that frequently obliterates the mechanisms that generate the race-class nexus. Exclusionary practices on the basis of race act to reinforce class stratification in the black community. Because substantial portions of the black lower class are economically dislodged from the private sector, they naturally seek government-sponsored solutions to their malaise. Because the socially induced racial status of the black middle class cannot be severed from the economic conditions of the black lower class, the middle class also must view its salvation—albeit in different ways—in terms of an array of government-structured policies. Once black economic and social survival or betterment becomes linked to government actions, it is necessarily linked to politics and visions of change necessary to eliminate the breeding conditions of racist values and behavior. This constitutes the focus of the final chapter.

CITY AS PROMISE?
SHADES AND POLITICS OF
RACE, CLASS, AND GENDER

Concluding chapters frequently suggest beginnings to other books. The choice here is either to summarize my arguments in the previous chapters or try to introduce some new considerations. Although I have chosen the latter course, I shall nevertheless attempt to relate concerns about the decade ahead to what I have argued so far.

The civil rights movement, followed by the War on Poverty, was linked to the Democratic party and the extension of the liberal welfare state, which had its origins in the New Deal programs of the 1930s. In the course of the white backlash to the social justice demands by African-Americans, other factors simultaneously worked to affect the relationship between the Democratic party and its black constituency: the Republicanization of the South, the disaffection of large numbers of blue- and white-collar workers from the Democratic party, a decline of the unionized portion of the labor force from its peak of 36 percent to a current low below 15 percent, and the suburbanization of American society. As a result, the Democratic party appears to be at bay and possibly in a state of decomposition.[1] It is unable to mobilize a national community or project a coherent national agenda.

One crucial reason for this state of affairs centers on conflicts along race and class lines within the party's constituencies. Thus, assessing the role of black politics in the context of a divided Democratic party transcends election commercials that feed on white fears about blacks

taking white jobs through affirmative action or invading white neighborhoods.[2]

With the emergence of global competition in the context of unprecedented techological changes and market shifts, with the middle
classes being squeezed and with new classes and ethnic groups asserting themselves, with rising levels of unemployment associated with
sluggish growth, the federal government "for the first time in memory
. . . has no fiscal policy to deal with economic hard times."[3] The American society appears to be approaching the crossroads of a fundamental change without knowing which way it wishes to turn. This uncertainty puts the political allegiance of the black population in a pivotal
position. It makes the race and class issues that influence the shifting
involvements of black community leaders profoundly important. The
latent and manifest racism of the American people and black responses
to it will affect the nature of the new arrangements the near future will
bring. Understanding the road ahead is not only facilitated by knowing
the road we have traveled but also by a careful analysis of the evolving
conditions that are shaping the relations between the races.

In the movement from plantation slavery to rural tenancy to urban
ghettoization, significant portions of the black population have been
"locked" into social and economic positions in ways that inevitably affect the life chances and status of the whole black population differently from those of whites. While the nature of the stratification between the races changed over time, racial injustices remained in both
vulgar and subtle forms, resulting in self-denigration and dependency.
Although some racist practices have withered or fallen into disuse, others have been retained or have been transmogrified to fit new circumstances.

In the language of our theme: as the mode of production changed,
affecting our political institutions and the role of government, and
as the work force changed from producing goods to producing services and became increasingly dependent on the state in urban areas,
the black population's view of its own status in terms of race or class,
and sometimes the amalgamation of both, became highly politicized.
As a result, large numbers of white workers have acquired political and
institutional interests that make them "hostile" to black demands for
civil and civic rights, for redistributive policies that are beneficial to the
black poor, and for affirmative action that affects the mobility of the
black working and middle class. For blacks, this politicization of their
demands from the welfare state has been channeled through the Democratic party. The relative political success of black struggles through
this channel, however, has not been without a social and political

price; it has led to white workers' disillusionment with many aspects of the welfare state and their disengagement from the Democratic party.[4]

While public opinion polls indicate a commitment to particular goals of the welfare state, the system as a whole appears to be drifting without a confident rationale. Welfare liberalism as an ideology has lost its élan. There has been a decline of faith in the capacity of the state to simultaneously sustain an efficient and free market system, achieve economic security, and establish social justice. Since left-liberal alternatives appear to be less attractive and are currently without public presence, conservative rhetoric and argument have acquired public respect on a scale unexperienced in recent history. There is now a well-financed core of conservative intellectuals aggressively enlarging the vision of world society dominated primarily by markets and private corporations. Whether the upbeat quality of this conservative advance can retain its momentum in the decade ahead remains to be seen. If so, it will have a dire effect on the circumstances confronting the black population and its pattern of struggle.

Those who assume that class commonalities will eventually override race differences fail to understand how the welfare state has divided the interests of large segments of the working population. The struggles forged were often along vertical lines that separate groups pursuing divergent goals within the working class in order to acquire from the state various kinds of protection, privileges, and subsidized material benefits. The base from which these goals were projected varied; some came from work-site interests and others from residential and community needs. Since the ways by which the state responded to these working-class segments involved primarily redistributions within the working class itself, the welfare state policies often accentuated differences and furthered divisions.[5] The goals of black workers' struggle for employment rights, for the needy, and for income entitlements through the welfare system were different from those that semi-skilled and more affluent white workers sought and achieved. For these latter workers, acquiring protection around the job (contracts involving escalator clauses, pensions, and seniority rules), or the acquisition of tax-deductible government-insured loans to buy homes out of the central city (thereby increasing residential segregation within the metropolitan area), differed from the family, community, and educational interests and needs of large portions of the black population. Thus, struggles of blacks to escape from the shadows of race and class subordination through political action often set off defensive responses from the more articulate and affluent white blue-collar workers and many members of the white middle class. These latter constituencies are not ones that the promulgators and architects of the welfare state can ignore in a period when the economic resources claimed by political empowerment appear scarce.

I note these social facts and tendencies because they lead to my main scenario that underscores the structural context in which blacks are seeking to make their own political history. This context features realities not chosen by blacks themselves. Social action based on a failure to consider them will have unintended consequences as grave as those that are a result of not possessing past knowledge relevant to making one's own history. There are six such realities that need consideration if blacks are to succeed in their long-standing battle for social justice and equal living arrangements.[6] These realities concern the race-class nexus, the nature of the black ghetto, the relative size of the black population, the changing nature of the inner city, the moral conflict between white freedom to choose and black demand for social justice, and the increasingly limited ability of the welfare state to effectively correct market failures.

Race and Class

The overrepresentation of black males in the lower classes, a condition that reproduces itself in a variety of institutionally determined ways, is intimately associated with race, affecting the status of blacks other than those in the lower class (middle-income blacks specifically and black women more generally). In this way, race-class connections determine not only the myopic perceptions of the white community vis-à-vis the black community but also divisions and attitudes within the black community itself.

The black population is defined by its residential segregation in the metropolitan area, by its social segregation in other spheres of life, and by its overcrowding in low-income and relatively unskilled positions. In the minds of Middle America, race and class become juxtaposed. In everyday social exchanges, the middle layers of white America cannot readily dissociate these two phenomena, be they actual or imagined; whites, therefore, resist entry of middle- and/or working-class blacks into "their" space (communities, schools, parks, and places of work) or feel demeaned by working under black supervision or alongside blacks on equally and personally empowered terms. The possibility of middle- or stable working-class blacks integrating on genuine terms with whites of comparable class positions easily degenerates into race exclusion and put-downs, even in the absence of class differences. It is often middle-class black families fleeing from black neighborhoods who encounter pure racial barriers established by middle- and affluent working-class whites. The Great White Fear is that the marginal entry of middle-class blacks like themselves will be followed by lower-class black "hordes" unlike themselves. Thus, income, status, and upward mobility of educated blacks are detrimentally affected because of over-crowding of blacks in the lowest occupational positions in the system. Race, therefore, becomes an independently experienced force deter-mining the status of some portion of the black population who have the class credentials to integrate. But the race factor, its operative vital-ity, is not unrelated to class. Much of the discussion of whether it is race or class that determines the overall black status omits specifying the ways the two (race and class) are linked and rebound off each other; one inevitably casts shadows affecting the valuation of the other.

A similar, albeit more complex, process works to affect the status of black women. Their position is determined by a combination of race and gender factors on the one hand, and the class position of black men on the other. The degradation of the black male population affects the way family, neighborhood, and life circumstances reproduce them-selves. More specifically, it generates an orientation and set of expec-tations for all black women: lower class, working class, and middle class. Because of the black male's overrepresentation in the lowest echelons of the economic hierarchy, there is an overrepresentation of black women who head households. Many such women with young children face circumstances that make their lives miserable and des-perate. They are continually at risk and find themselves more often in-carcerated compared to their white counterparts.[7]

In another vein, the black male's economic and social position af-fects the status of all black women. The past and present precarious status of the black male sets the stage for our race-class connections. There is a configuration of forces that have produced black male roles that have served to shape the economic, social, and psychological out-look of black women.

The knowledge that black men are not good economic bets is im-parted intergenerationally and reinforced by experiences derived from objective circumstances. In one form or another, the black female, whatever her specific class status, is told that she better be prepared to take care of herself, support herself, fend for herself, survive on her own terms. Because significantly larger numbers of black men live mar-ginal lives relative to whites, opportunities for stable family formations among black women are significantly less than those had by their white cohorts. And social segregation along racial lines, even in the absence of economic differences between the sexes, makes it unlikely for black women to meet in normal ways, if the desire so prevailed, an "appropriate" pool of white men.

The interface between class and race and its consequences has, from my perspective, one profound implication: the necessary conditions for the elimination of racial disparities and racist practices affecting even blacks with impeccable middle-class credentials must begin with the elimination of the overcrowding of blacks in the lower class. Unfortunately, the black lower class does not beget much social sympathy in the larger American public. At the bottom of the hierarchical economic structure, race and class fuse to define a single pariah group. To the extent that black middle-class leaders cannot cultivate an orientation essential to allocating the necessary resources capable of eliminating the overcrowding effect that casts racial shadows beyond its borders, racism in its various guises will rear its ugly head. The black poor will be periodically sensationalized in vulgar images by the mass media and manipulated through references by demagogic white politicians.

Permanent Ghetto Thesis

The black ghetto is a permanent cluster that is not going to be readily changed or dispersed by piecemeal reforms such as marginal housing or job programs. One consequence of social segregation in our ten largest metropolitan areas is that it breeds (for understandable reasons) extremely balkanized and provincial politics. This self-defeating tendency must be resisted. While issues vary with cities (New York is not Birmingham), the black population of each will need to work at its own method of transcending group particularism by an orientation that embraces social issues more generally. While schools, for example, in black neighborhoods are no doubt the worst in the metropolitan areas, schools are profoundly inadequate in form and content in all working-class neighborhoods. Insofar as all Americans believe the school system can serve as a great social equalizer, as a source of economic advance, and as a means to induce intelligent participation in the civic affairs of society, blacks, in the course of articulating their own school agenda, must speak in a voice that ideologically and programmatically communicates to workers as a whole. If racist fears and sentiments are to be overcome, white workers need to be made part of the solution. Here is an opportunity for unions to use their educational funds to advance everything from literacy campaigns to college-bound scholarships by emphasizing the need for lifelong learning opportunities in adult education programs. Moving in this direction on a consequential scale takes union interests out of the work sphere where more narrowly defined interests are guarded.

Too Large, Too Small

The black population is caught in a dilemma in that it is too large to be integrated into the American mainstream—that would involve unacceptable costs to influential portions of the white majority, especially the middle layers—and too small to achieve power by its own efforts. Success requires that blacks forge strong coalitions, but coalitions often falter for a variety of reasons, such as the perception that blacks are making excessive demands or are advocating primarily race-specific programs. This problem partly explains shifting black involvements from class (integrationist) alignments to black power (separatist) ones. The main political implication of this predicament is that both integrationist and separatist tactics and strategies are incapable of achieving their respective goals. In this sense, both orientations are limited. Neither adequately deals with the problem of cultivating viable means to realize economic and social goals currently blocked by those with more power and capacities to adapt to the profound secular economic forces affecting the direction of American society.

There is no easy way out of this dilemma. Politics is an art and not a science. How blacks will pursue their own interests in a social and political environment that has a high potential for apathy—not to exclude outright hostility—toward black causes and simultaneously retain politically sound contacts with organized portions of the white population (not excluding other nonwhite ethnic groups) is no simple matter. In principle, blacks might serve as the leading edge in the unification of all racial minority groups. In fact, there is often considerable distrust and animosity among racial and ethnic minority groups that are forced to compete with blacks for limited resources, social space, and political influence. The potential for white demagogic backlashes and for fractionalization within the black population and between blacks and other poor minority groups needs continuous attention if they are to be avoided. This is more easily said than done; coalitions cannot be established by catchy slogans in a noncataclysmic, democratic environment like our own. They require the building of a shared *moral* framework that can bind long-run concerns in order to prevent short-run divisive economic and social interests from becoming excessive. Moral imperatives, it needs to be emphasized, are not decreed, but mainly developed and nurtured by noble and nondemagogic leaders who build symbolic trust in the course of battle to overcome barriers that divide people. A moral framework capable of stimulating critical num- bers of people to rise above the grinding, nitty-gritty aggravations in daily life must touch deeply felt—if not always understood—needs. The exercise of compassion for the needy and the willingness to ex- tend hands to others who are outside of the "group" are potential, not inevitable, strains in the human species.

Changing Character of Inner Cities

The convergence of a number of factors has raised serious questions about the very viability of our central cities. The story has been told many times. The migration pattern between regions and within metropolitan ar- eas has led to concentrations of blacks in many of our major central cities and the concentration of whites in outlying suburban areas. The meta- phor describing Detroit—a white-walled tire with a black center—has its relevance for many American urban areas. In place of the urban/rural- North/South division we have substituted a permanent city/suburban- black/white division. Accompanying the exodus of middle-income whites is the exodus of wealth, which has meant the deterioration of the central city's capital, as well as a decline in its spirit of enterprise. Schools, streets, transit systems, water supply sources, sewage, and terminals are over- worked or not properly maintained. Insofar as middle-class blacks have sought to escape the core of the black ghetto, black role models and sta- ble social support groups have disappeared.[8] The correction of this dete- rioration by raising local revenues or expanding the boundaries of the central city is unlikely. The central city's tax base is forever caught between rising expenditure needs and limited sources of revenues. Central city governments display an urge to get quick money for this or that program without regard to the longer-run consequences on people and neighbor- hoods. Many downtown renewal projects that offer short-run employ- ment gains, especially in the construction industry, turn into disasters in- debting the city to banks and real estate interests for the indefinite future. "Solutions" in the form of productivity, layoffs, and taxes to meet periodic crises only tend to worsen the city's main problems. What blacks are therefore inheriting is the management of local governments that are on the edge of perennial bankruptcy.[9] The process is not new in the history of the black population's relative subordination. Just as blacks have often attained entry into industries as they were declining (too little, too late), they now appear to be in sight of political control of a level of government that is on its last legs. This is leading to the development of a black polit- ical elite that is accumulating administrative experience without the cor- responding acquisition of economic power. As black mayors across the nation are learning, it is easier to get hold of a big city's political apparatus than its economic base.[10] Political power does not mean power to forge long-run economic development or control the external reaches of market forces far beyond the city's borders. Without well-conceived economic development prospects and protection by resilient, stable communities from the ravages of unfettered markets, the political promises made to win office will not work well to hold it, or at least to hold it with the optimism that was associated with the initial political victory.

This reality warrants two comments. On the one hand, it has led to a relatively large pool of experienced and talented black leaders who are now available to escalate their political efforts and demands. On the other, it is rife for the corruption and crass opportunism pioneered by white politicians. This second matter relates to our focus on the overcrowding of blacks into the lower class. In the words of one black political scientist:

> [Black political leaders] sustain political capital [from] the suffering of the [black masses through] advocating policies couched in terms that remind the American polity of its historic debt . . . to . . . the poorest blacks, [but] the evidence suggests that, for many of the public policies advocated by black spokesmen, not much of the benefit "trickles down" to the truly poor.[11]

Thus, a "race relations industry," powered by blacks who have succeeded, is constructed on the class conditions of black ghetto dwellers. This constitutes another variant of the race-class nexus. Using poverty to maintain political power is not the same thing as trying to eliminate it. This, of course, is not new. Unfortunately, leaders who want to reform and change society, and not simply get into the act of the going routines, cannot afford to imitate their oppressors too soon and simultaneously be effective, especially since they must confront a racially conscious society that tacitly evaluates their performance by a double standard.

White Freedom versus Black Social Justice

In our society discrimination against blacks takes place under the banner of freedom of choice. Milton Friedman's ideological success is not without reason. Freedom of choice for a white consumer means the freedom to avoid living next door to blacks. The employer's freedom to combine labor and capital in production means freedom not to hire or promote black labor rather than white labor, or freedom to avoid the social costs connected with the movement of a plant from the central city.

To the black population these white market freedoms have meant the negation of their own freedom—if not to exist, at least to live decently. Thus, salvation to blacks, employed and unemployed, has too often existed outside the private market. But once the solution to the black condition is viewed as existing outside the market, it is automatically seen to fall inside the domain of political action that takes the form of demands for equity entitlements of a redistributive nature as citizens of the state; it takes the form of asking the state to interfere with white market choices. In this sense, the exercise of white market freedoms becomes pitted against black demands for social justice. The resolution of this conflict between two kinds of moral imperatives— freedom versus social justice—does not lend itself readily to compromise under the best of circumstances. In a "slow growth" or "no growth" economy, the conflict (especially when compounded by racial stratification and animosities) can only worsen in the absence of a strong, compensating moral and social consensus encompassing the general needs of society.

The Welfare State

I argued earlier that the unfettered market has not proved to be a viable instrument for large portions of the black population. As a result, black leaders have frequently looked to the federal government to provide jobs, eliminate discrimination, and enforce rules to enhance social justice. For reasons unrelated specifically to black-white differences, the federal government and the welfare system it oversees are unable to develop coherent urban and related policies. The national instruments of political economy are currently saddled with the perceived need to decrease their role in urban centers when such centers are in dire need of resources and stability. Inflationary fears, even in the absence of inflation, and the excessive federal debt associated with larger than desired annual deficits tend to make the federal government's demand management policies ineffective in stimulating employment opportunities for the bottom third of the black labor force that is unemployed, casually employed, or employed at dead-end jobs in our central cities. It is evident at this juncture that the welfare state is unable to achieve the kind of market conditions that are necessary for sustained black employment gains and, at the same time, bring about the mitigation of discrimination within the context of black-white competition for jobs and places to live.

Beyond the feared "stagflation" rhythm, the welfare state, as we have come to understand it in the post-World War II period, is undergoing a fundamental reevaluation and overhaul. The reasons, which are complex and subject to a variety of interpretations, need not detain us. What is relevant for our purposes is that "solutions" to the deepening crisis of the welfare state bypass black politics. Even Democratic mayors of our cities—sensitive to the political ineffectiveness of asking the federal government for help—are forced to endorse policies for trimming spending on health and the aged.[12] This is often matched by liberal think tanks, once bastions for more spending on welfare programs; they now yield to the exigencies of the global economy and call for lower taxes and more private investment.[13] Black leaders, adjusting to the realities before them, are returning to an emphasis on a conservative brand of self-help ideas. While it is not my intention to prejudge the kinds of projects derived from a self-help vision, in the present context of a growing disinterest and even hostility to black needs, it can only be interpreted as a strategy of retreat, and that is what it should be called.

Looking beyond the immediate cutbacks, welfare state crisis, and the defensive black self-help response to a shrinking universe, one urban economist, discussing the single "new" idea to emerge from the Democratic party in the 1980s—its industrial policy—points out:

> For many urban [white] professionals, industrial policy implies faster adaptation and change, with economic activity centered in [well-paid] service and high-tech sectors. For most blacks, equity issues remain paramount. Most blacks were never fully included in the postwar prosperity. . . . [Many found themselves] in low-paying service and [less skilled portions of] high-tech manufacturing jobs, where the pay, stability and benefits are lower than jobs in older primary industries.[14]

In essence, the composition of job growth that is projected in the decade ahead is likely to worsen the mismatch between the skill profile of the black labor force and the profile of forthcoming opportunities. This projection is similar, it should be noted, to the one made by Charles Killingsworth about the late fifties and early sixties that culminated a few years later in a chain of race riots throughout the land.[15]

New Directions

Any black movement aimed at changing American society needs to face these structural realities. The sine qua non of a viable black struggle in the future requires the development of a broad social consensus, which is different, I might add, from a collage of interest groups seeking to establish coalition strategies. The latter works when the separate groups, even when they are unequal in power, have some mutual respect for each other and overlapping short-run interests. But in black-white relations, the centrifugal forces within the class-ethnic structure and the political system are awesome. Overcoming them is no easy matter to contemplate under the most advantageous circumstances. Waiting for a crisis that might bring people together, as some are prone to do, involves a very limited understanding of both American society generally and black-white relations specifically. Aside from the fact that a crisis may not come to a head in anticipated ways, the worsening of objective conditions does not necessarily affect all strata of the working and middle classes uniformly; people confronting adversity do not automatically "discover" economic common grounds. If such were the case, the poor of all races and ethnic backgrounds would have had their heads together long ago. Unshared anxieties and suffering can divide people further rather than bring them together. Thus, seeking a moral consensus and working out general principles cannot be postponed in the course of pursuing immediate goals.

My approach is not programmatic. I am not concerned with devising a shopping list of things that the black community—or any poor community—needs. I am not concerned with devising new or novel tax and subsidizing schemes to finance and fund ghetto projects; nor am I interested in examining the costs and benefits of proposals aimed at "helping" the black community in this or that endeavor. There is, in my opinion, an existing surplus of programs and studies. More to the point, detailed agendas of "what to do now" are important when they coincide with a broad, energetic movement that is about to alter successfully the use of resources. This is not on the immediate horizon. At this juncture, we are once again reevaluating basic directions.

While I do not believe that the black prospect for the future is hopeless, I am not easily moved to optimism. Yet I see little meaning in declaring the inevitability of taxes and death. Writing a book of this nature involves, at a very minimum, a consciousness-raising exercise and must imply some hope. I, of course, cannot speak for any organized group, black or white. Nevertheless, I shall venture to suggest guidelines for an orientation accompanied by some commentary. My recommendations, no doubt, will appear utopian to some readers. I make no apologies for this fact. Allegedly realistic policy recommendations are often uninteresting, if not trivial, since they usually tend to accept or work within the very conditions that need changing. A very small change within the existing framework always makes sense, appears possible, and begets little resistance. It also has little impact on what needs to be changed. As for the realities I have identified, more than marginal changes must be considered. Insofar as we choose to overcome such realities, it behooves us to make a quantum leap and establish another vision of how black-white social and economic life might be arranged.

Implicit in my argument is that the urbanized realities in which the shadows of race and class are cast need to be viewed in a larger American context. The economics of dominant-subordinate relations and the race-class nexus cannot be changed without rethinking dimensions of our social system more generally. The racial pattern with which I am concerned is not a small blemish on an otherwise smooth skin; it is a growth that affects the functioning of body parts sometimes far removed from the immediate disease. It is for this reason that I conclude with concerns of a more general nature, but which must be incorporated into the reverberating boundaries that define the race-class debate.

Role of Government

Insofar as most black leaders see salvation — the establishment of social and economic parity — through the political process, through government intervention and support, then we as a nation must reverse the indifferent, bureaucratic inefficiencies taking place in the public sector. The debate about the role of the government cannot be whether we should have more or less of it, but rather about the role and quality of government we as a people desire in the course of its growth and influence.[16] The majority of the American people, in my judgment, would not object to spending more to acquire better public transportation that was safe, to spending more on cleaner streets and air even if it means fewer private automobiles, and to spending more on improved schools that delivered intellectual empowerment in the area of skill acquisition and nurtured social responsibility for enlightened civic participation. What angers people about the government's growth and role (which fed into neoconservative rhetoric in the past decade) was the fact that they were receiving less and paying more. To this perception must be added the tedious, impersonal, and callous runarounds by government agencies that have become common complaints among large numbers of people.

Dealing with government activity — which we need and distrust, which is paradoxically viewed as part of the solution and part of the problem — has dimensions significantly beyond technical and administrative organizational charts. We need to find social and political ways to achieve a greater commitment to civility in public discourse rather than appealing to individualistic plans and self-interests. It means envisioning government as a source of innovation and not simply as an obstacle to overcome or as a vehicle to sustain those who have failed. It means thinking about the public sector in terms of an opportunity to contribute service rather than using government to achieve private ends.[17] It means endeavoring to view government less as an instrument to enhance private benefits and more as a public means to establish social justice and social meanings capable of bringing diverse groups into a dialogue within a shared or universal moral framework.

Developing Values

Since public life, at least for our major metropolitan areas where problems in one portion of the city rapidly spill over into other sections, is city life, we need to reconstruct the sinews that bind people together. This cannot be accomplished without cultivating an ethos of social regard, an appeal to compassion for others who are less fortunate. Whites must learn to see their interests in a larger framework, in a less protective one that too often reads "my" schools, parks, and neighborhoods. Blacks, who are seeking power parity and equal status as a subordinate minority for whom there is little sympathy from the public at large, will have to move from demands for ghetto-based programs to ones that envision the rebuilding of the whole urban complex. Such an orientation involves more than an employment plan for blacks and other minorities embracing road repairs, cleaning and beautifying parks, building public housing and more transportation facilities. These are, of course, vital necessities and their significance should not be underestimated. But more often than not, the benefits and costs of such projects are defined in terms that are too provincial. The post-World War II ecstasy expectations from a suburban life have declined considerably. The problems of the city have traveled to the suburbs without the latter providing any of the enriching opportunities that genuine city life offers. The city still advances a hope if it is able to overcome its tarnished and frightening image. Reforming and rebuilding city life require projecting a more "holistic" vision that encompasses the social, as well as the physical, promises. There is, in my judgment, a desire on the part of many individuals to find fulfillment through civic participation in the social and political life of the city. If white affluence has taught us anything, we know that it can and does exist in the midst of an alarming amount of emptiness of heart and loneliness of soul. The more affluent treadmill no doubt is different from that which runs poor people's lives, but it is nevertheless anxiety-ridden and often meaningless. This suggests that the better-off middle layers (blue-collar, white-collar, and professional workers) must also be part of the solution to the problem of restoring the public sector and city existence. Exit must cease as the only viable option for those who can afford it.[18] Stressing change primarily for poor black neighborhoods is not sufficient. Health facilities, for example, demanded just for black areas where the need is, no doubt, profound, end up being overused and underfinanced and, therefore, "prove" that public health stations are destined to fail. Health is the kind of problem that can very well destroy middle-class families as well as poor ones. By universalizing health facilities without class distinctions, not only is proper funding assured but also their common and nonsegregated use in ways that are self-evidently needed by everyone. The same reasoning should be applied to child care, education, recreation, and a host of other communal services that cities require.

Environment

Allied to the infrastructural and related social needs of our cities is the necessity for more environmental amenities. We not only need to learn how to extend a moral outreach to the less fortunate in our midst, but how to care more about the physical spaces in which we build and reproduce our community and family life. This involves extending our time horizons and concerning ourselves with how activities that fall within our own particular places affect those living in other places — our neighbors on the other side of the river or those across town. Sooner or later, "their" industrial wastes are going to affect "our" drinking water. If "we" want "them" to care about "us," then "we" must begin to support "them" in their environmental concerns that momentarily seem distant from "ours."

Equity and Security

The next general direction that we need to pursue is greater equity in the distribution of income. Equal opportunity to have unequal results is too limited a goal for the simple reason that de facto unequal outcomes affect the distribution of opportunities in the next generation of competition between individuals and groups. The difference between the average income of the top 10 percent and the bottom 20 percent can be narrowed considerably without concern for disincentives.

Greater equality in results needs to be perceived as fair and just if backlashes are to be avoided. Fair and just principles cannot be derived from the calculus; they need to be continually injected into the way ordinary people interpret the meaning of their lives. Doing this constitutes a heroic task for reform-minded leaders. The two evident routes to increased equity are altering unequal outcomes after the fact through taxes and subsidies or making certain that there is social equality in the forms of schools and immediate environments that affect the developmental process at early stages in life. Moving toward equality on both fronts is viable if a consensus about fairness is established. This latter endeavor is possible if work, menial and otherwise, constitutes our common fate. The belief that a large number of undeserving blacks are receiving resources without seeking work prevents the development of common criteria to limit wealth accumulation and seek the redistribution of income.[19]

In addition to seeking a more equal distribution of income and wealth, we also must embrace income security through guaranteed employment. Greater equality and security will induce a shift in our incentive system from materialistic drives to moral or noneconomic ones; at the least, it will bring about a better balance between economic and noneconomic motives and trade-offs in the allocation of people and resources. Becoming a physician will be less a commercial interest and more a calling to heal the ill and lame. People who primarily wish to make money should go into business and not medicine. Income security will undermine the fear of falling off the edge; if it is accompanied by a reformed and humane universal entitlement program, the general economic struggle will be less fraught with anxieties; perhaps some of the pressures, associated with the perceived need to "make it" while the going is good because tomorrow may be too late, will be removed.

Two comments about the value-laden underpinnings of the above deliberations are in order before I continue. First, emphasizing the need for an explicit moral framework that encompasses the whole population is not intended as a substitute for organizing protests and making demands for change; it is not a substitute for a concrete legislative agenda concerning drugs, crime, slum housing, and other problems that plague the black poor. Second, a moral crusade to revitalize the city, to rebuild the city in the name of rebuilding America, rather than simply deal with specific, individual problems and neighborhoods, is not a call to eliminate the role of markets; it is an endeavor to restore a lost balance. Modern capitalism has commodified, although modified by the welfare state, too much of everyday life. It is not a question of markets per se, but one of excessive commercialization of domains of life that should not be reduced to an economic calculus. As Lewis Hyde has so pointedly spelled out:

> Where, on the one hand, there is no way to assert identity against the mass, and no opportunity for private gain, we lose the well-advertised benefit of a market society—its particular kind of innovation, its industrial and material variety, and so on. But where, on the other hand, the market rules alone . . . the fruits of gift exchange are lost. At that point commerce becomes correctly associated with fragmentation of community and the suppression of liveliness, fertility, and social feeling. For where we maintain no institutions of positive reciprocity, we find ourselves unable to participate in those "wider spirits" . . . unable to enter gracefully out of the mass, and, finally, unable to receive, contribute toward and pass along the collective treasures we refer to as culture and tradition.[20]

Education

A genuine politics of reform in a postindustrial society—one where human capital, symbols, and instantaneous communication are an integral part of everyday life—must be aimed at helping people see life beyond their immediate appetites and limited experiences. Education is the modern cathedral in which to accomplish this task. The need here is to develop an educational system and a concept of learning that stretches over the individual's whole life span. The notion of periodic sabbaticals—rather than layoffs, unemployment, and under-employment—should be extended from tenured members of university faculties to the whole labor force.[21] This involves changing the role and meaning of education, especially in the postsecondary area. Credentialism has reached its useful limits for reasons I have elaborated earlier, that is, credentials are becoming void of substance for a larger number of students. Once 50 percent of high school graduates achieve higher degrees, postsecondary degrees are no more useful than high school degrees were a decade or so earlier. Society has employed excessive resources to keep people unproductive. For this and other reasons, education as an instrument to upward mobility must be radically reconsidered.

Keeping up with the world should increasingly mean training or retraining to adapt to a changing world and workplace, not to achieve a higher-paying job. Learning must be more about the art of living rather than making a living. This suggests a break in the current trend of bringing business interests into educational establishments. Our citadels of learning should educate; businesses should train. Both will reap benefits by this division of labor, since educators are inadequate trainers and businesspersons are weak at educating. A lifelong continuing educational system geared to all ages and aimed at achieving an enlightened participation in society, rather than acquiring a certificate for employment and job upgrading, may induce a more creative and less commercial involvement in sport, science and technology, and cultural events (traditional, classical, and popular). People need loyalty and causes. Lifelong learning may facilitate more humane ones, and, at the same time, reduce the hate of "foreigners" in our midst, excessive flag-waving nationalism, ethnochauvinism, self-indulgent cult rituals, various arcane forms of religious experience, and imperial fundamentalist exhortations. Conceiving educational institutions as a place for continual renewal can enhance civic participation and understanding in two areas that are of vital relevance to the black and the larger white population: the community and the family.

Community and Family

Just as work is separated from consumption, with the former "valued" primarily as an instrument of the latter, community interests have become separated from family needs, many of which are currently met by the state welfare bureaucracy.[22] Community is supposed to be a locus where close networks are built, where trust and comfort in relationships are established, where traditions based on rootedness link the past with the present, and where neighbors can be relied upon for support in the event of an unforeseen mishap. But these experiences that we hope to get from community rarely occur because they are perennially undermined by a specific kind of disjunction between family and community.

The organization of space on which community life centers is continually transformed into quicksand by industry and real estate developers. Land on which homes are built, like goods and services, is bought and sold for reasons other than possessing the security of living in a stable community for an extended period of time. The commodifiers, so to speak, keep breaking up the foundations on which social life is constructed. For defensive and offensive reasons, the large bulk of the population internalizes the commodifier's impulses. The local and national government, it should be noted, participate in this process in order to keep the economy growing without sufficient attention to whether the growth actually adds to our sense of well-being.[23] The process undermines the ability of families to integrate with each other in stable social places. Thus, families are forever being *forced* to pick up and find other places in which to establish themselves, either because their present community is being changed by the market or because nearby ones are being destroyed, causing a large number of adjacent dwellers to "invade" surrounding communities. As noted in the preceding chapter, the black "horde" becomes the white fear, which in turn prevents middle-class blacks from rooting themselves in communities commensurate to their class credentials.

Since space is so rapidly changed, altered, defaced, or devoured by larger, industrial real estate and building trade interests, communities have a most difficult time sustaining themselves. Families are induced to think about their purchased home, not in terms of a place to establish rootedness and bondedness with neighbors, but as a source of status, an instrument to capitalize in event of a move, a means to provide retirement, as an opportunity to send their children to better schools to enhance their chances of success. Families are quick to "protect" their investment interest or to abandon it for better investment opportunities. The latter propensity often leaves abandoned communities in a state of decay or disarray. As we observed in an earlier chapter, older and less well-off families are often caught in the rapid crosswinds of what is perceived as destructive change. In any event, the need for exit or for the development of protective and defensive mechanisms divides people, especially white workers from black ones, when the former believe that their property values are being threatened by "invading" blacks who are also victims of disruption. American cultural values, the politics of housing, and unstable communities often converge around issues of race. As two authorities on the housing market have summarily noted:

> [Fending off blacks] reside[s] in two fundamental traits of American culture: aggressive, achievement-oriented mobility and protective, home-related territoriality. Earnings must be spent on the best possible homes and material possessions in the best possible neighborhoods. Any increase in job or financial status must be matched by a move to a better neighborhood. "Downgrading" of the neighborhood through entry of those of lower status must be fought, and if it cannot be contained, one must flee to avoid the inevitably resulting loss of status.[24]

Once a community becomes a concentration of mainly poverty-stricken families and individuals, as William Julius Wilson has argued, decline is likely to take on a self-generating momentum.[25] Many black communities, for structural and related reasons, have lost much of their resiliency. The fact that there are large numbers of working poor blacks struggling beyond endurance in such communities does not prevent the projection of social images in the media that whites consume with contempt. The media provides justification, along with some frightening, albeit limited, experiences for rejecting blacks as undeserving. It undermines the kind of commitment necessary to launch programs to rebuild a city life that embraces a multiplicity of interests.

Conclusion

I have argued persistently that equality in income and job allocations that break down dominant-subordinate patterns are the necessary conditions for the elimination of racism in its various guises. The overrepresentation of blacks in lower-income jobs and low-income neighborhoods casts shadows that affect the status and capacities of all blacks, not excluding those who have "made it."

Since black life is now primarily city life, many of the major cities across the nation are on the verge of another wave of abandonment. This, I suggest, is a tragedy, not only for blacks who are struggling in their communities to build and save our cities, but for all U.S. citizens. City life offers a promise that alternative living arrangements cannot make. It may be too late. In my judgment, a vision of rebuilding our major cities is the only hope for an all-around valuable and purposeful life in a postindustrial society. If the black leaders who have become central to city life can create a national movement to revive the city's vitality, they will once again help America close the gap between its reality and its promise.

NOTES

Introduction

1. I endeavor in this chapter to extend the debate stimulated by William Julius Wilson in *The Declining Significance of Race: Blacks and Changing American Institutions* (Chicago and London: University of Chicago Press, 1978).

2. This characterization was made at a Queens College administrative meeting dealing with student demonstrations on campus, Spring 1971.

3. Gary S. Becker, *The Economics of Discrimination* (Chicago: University of Chicago Press, 1957).

4. Ibid., p. 5.

5. William Darity, Jr., "What's Left of the Economic Theory of Discrimination," in *The Question of Discrimination: Racial Inequality in the U.S. Labor Market*, ed. Steven Shulman and William Darity, Jr. (Middletown, Conn.: Wesleyan University Press, 1989), p. 336.

6. Ibid., p. 337; see also Thomas Sowell, *Ethnic America* (New York: Basic Books, 1981).

7. Raymond S. Franklin, "A Framework for the Analysis of Interurban Negro-White Economic Differentials," *Industrial and Labor Relations Review* 21, no. 3 (April 1968): 368.

8. Shulman and Darity, Jr., "Introduction," in *Question of Discrimination*, p. 3.

9. Ibid., p. 2.

10. Hylan Lewis, *Blackways of Kent* (Chapel Hill: University of North Carolina Press, 1955); Oscar Lewis, *La Vida: A Puerto Rican Family in the Culture of Poverty* (New York: Random House, 1966); Lee Rainwater, *Behind Ghetto Walls: Black Life in a Federal Slum* (Chicago: Aldine, 1970).

11. James P. Smith, "Career Wage Mobility," in Shulman and Darity, Jr., *Question of Discrimination*, pp. 112–13.

12. Charles Murray, *Losing Ground: American Social Policy, 1950–1980* (New York: Basic Books, 1984).

13. John E. Roemer, "Divide and Conquer: Micro-Foundations of a Marxian Theory of Wage Discrimination," *Bell Journal of Economics* 10, no. 2 (Autumn 1979): 695–96.

14. Ibid., p. 704.

15. Ibid.

16. Paul Baran and Paul Sweezy, *Monopoly Capital* (New York: Monthly Review Press, 1966), pp. 263–64.

17. Robert A. Gorman, "Black Neo-Marxism in Liberal America," *Rethinking Marxism* 2, no. 4 (Winter 1982): 119.

18. Erik Olin Wright, *Classes* (London and New York: Verso, 1985), pp. 31–32.

19. Erik Olin Wright, *Class Structure and Income Determination* (New York: Academic, 1979), p. 197.

20. Ibid.

21. Wright, *Classes*, p. 31.

22. Ira Katznelson, *City Trenches: Urban Politics and the Patterning of Class in the United States* (New York: Pantheon, 1981), chaps. 2, 8.

23. Herbert Hill, "Black Labor and Affirmative Action: An Historical Perspective," in Shulman and Darity, Jr., *Question of Discrimination*, pp. 190–267.

24. Molef Asante, *The Afrocentric Idea* (Philadelphia: Temple University Press, 1987).

25. Cornel West, *Toward a Democratic Socialist Theory of Racism* (New York: Institute for Democratic Socialism, 1988, pamphlet), p. 3.

26. Michael Omi and Howard Winant, *Racial Formation in the United States: From 1960 to the 1980s* (New York and London: Routledge, 1986), p. 106.

27. Ibid., p. 107.

28. Ibid., pp. 66–67.

29. West, *Theory of Racism*, p. 3.

30. Ibid., p. 4.

31. Ibid.

32. Ibid.

33. Ibid.

34. Ibid.

35. Omi and Winant, *Racial Formation*, p. 138.

36. Stephen Steinberg, "The Underclass: A Case of Color Blindness," *New Politics* 11, no. 3 (Summer 1989): 42–60.

37. Thomas Vietorisz and Bennett Harrison, *The Economics of the Development of Harlem* (New York: Praeger, 1970); see esp. chap. 4.

38. Barbara Jeanne Fields, "Slavery, Race, and Ideology in the United States of America," *New Left Review* 181 (1990): 110.

39. Ibid., pp. 97–100. See also Omi and Winant, *Racial Formation*, pp. 58–64.

40. A line from the movie *Raintree Country*, quoted by Edward D. C. Campbell, Jr., *The Celluloid South: Hollywood and the Southern Myth* (Knoxville: University of Tennessee Press, 1981), pp. 168–70.

41. Fields, "Slavery, Race, and Ideology," p. 98.

42. David E. Sanger, "Japanese Offers Apology for Slur," *New York Times*, October 18, 1990, sec. A.

43. This comment was made by a Haitian graduate student at City University of New York in 1984.

44. Raymond S. Franklin, "Race and Class Attitudes among Adult Workers at UAW District-65" (a pilot survey of some UAW District-65 adult evening students conducted in New York, 1978).

45. Fields, "Slavery, Race and Ideology," p. 98.

46. Quote cited by John McGurl in a review by Drew Gilpin Faust, "Unpolluted Passion," *New York Times Book Review*, June 3, 1990, p. 13.

47. W. E. B. Du Bois, *Souls of Black Folk: Essays and Sketches* (Greenwich, Conn.: Fawcett, 1961), pp. 16–17.

Chapter 1. From Civil Rights to Civic Disgrace

1. For an extended discussion of the backlash, see Seymour M. Lipset and Earl Raab, *The Politics of Unreason: Right-Wing Extremism in America, 1790–1970* (New York: Harper and Row, 1970); Oscar Handlin, *Firebell in the Night* (Boston: Little, Brown, 1964); Jonathan Rieder, *Canarsie: The Jews and Italians of Brooklyn against Liberalism* (Cambridge, Mass.: Harvard University Press, 1985); Lawrence Mead, *Beyond Entitlement: The Social Obligations of Citizenship* (New York: Free Press, 1986); James Q. Wilson, *Thinking about Crime* (New York: Basic Books, 1975); Nathan Glazer, *Affirmative Discrimination: Ethnic Inequality and Public Policy* (New York: Basic Books, 1975); Fred Block, Richard Cloward, Barbara Ehrenreich, and Frances Fox Piven, *The Mean Season: The Attack on the Welfare State* (New York: Pantheon, 1987).

2. Gerald Horne, "The Impact to Soviet Nationalities Policy on Afro-American Liberation," in *Nations and People: The Soviet Experience*, ed. M. Bechtel and D. Rosenberg (New York: NWR, 1984), p. 197.

3. Ibid., pp. 198–99.

4. Ibid., pp. 197, 199, 200.

5. For other sources leading to the 1954 decision and beyond see Aldon D. Morris, *The Origins of the Civil Rights Movement: Black Communities Organizing for Change* (New York: Free Press, 1984); David J. Garrow, *Bearing the Cross: Martin Luther King, Jr., and the Southern Christian Leadership Conference* (New York: William Morrow, 1986); Clayborne Carson, *In Struggle: SNCC and the Black Awakening of the 1960s* (Cambridge, Mass.: Harvard University Press, 1981); James Farmer, *Lay Bare the Heart: An Autobiography of the Civil Rights Movement* (New York: Arbor House, 1985).

6. John D. Hicks, *The Federal Union* (Boston: Houghton Mifflin, 1975), pp. 452–54. Cited by Lewis H. Carlson and George H. Colburn, eds., in *In Their Place: When America Defines Her Minorities, 1850–1950* (New York: Wiley and Sons, 1972), pp. 113–14.

7. Garrow, *Bearing the Cross*, chap. 1.

8. I am indebted for this point to a discussion with Hylan Lewis.

9. Milton D. Morris, *The Politics of Black America* (New York: Harper and Row, 1975), p. 19.

10. Manning Marable, *Race, Reform, and Rebellion: The Second Reconstruction in Black America, 1945–1982* (Jackson: University Press of Mississippi, 1984).

11. Jack M. Bloom, *Class, Race, and the Civil Rights Movement* (Bloomington: Indiana University Press, 1987), pp. 122–54.

12. Ibid., pp. 146–47.

13. Arthur I. Waskow, *From Race Riot to Sit-Ins: 1919 and the 1960s* (Gloucester, Mass.: Peter Smith, 1975).

14. Bloom, *Civil Rights Movement*, p. 175.

15. Ibid., p. 176.

16. Garrow, *Bearing the Cross*, pp. 282–88. The bill was passed after Kennedy's assassination.

17. Bloom, *Civil Rights Movement*, pp. 183–84.

18. Ibid., p. 184.

19. Sara Evans, *Personal Politics: The Roots of Women's Liberation in the Civil Rights Movement and the New Left* (New York: Vintage, 1980).

20. Frances Fox Piven and Richard Cloward, *The New Class War: Reagan's Attack on the Welfare State and Its Consequences* (New York: Pantheon, 1982); Michael B. Katz, *The Undeserving Poor: From the War on Poverty to the War on Welfare* (New York: Pantheon, 1989); Michael Harrington, *The New American Poverty* (New York: Penguin, 1984).

21. Carson, *In Struggle*, pp. 215–28.

22. Bloom, *Civil Rights Movement*, chap. 6, pp. 154–85.

23. I am omitting a discussion of the older and more established Black Muslim movement, which could, along with others, be classified as religious nationalism. It became a secular force through the work and oratory of Malcolm X, less in my view for its religious meaning and more for the way Malcolm X made it consistent with the general black power struggle. For an excellent, brief historical sketch of black nationalist thought, see Morris, *Politics of Black America*, chap. 6.

24. Raymond S. Franklin and Solomon Resnik, *The Political Economy of Racism* (New York: Holt, Rinehart and Winston, 1973), chap. 8; Thomas Vietorisz and Bennett Harrison, *The Economic Development of Harlem* (New York: Praeger, 1970).

25. In economic deterministic terms, Richard Nixon stated the case for black capitalism: "To have human rights, people need property rights. [Blacks must have] economic power that comes from ownership. . . . [This can come about] by an expansion of black ownership, of black capitalism. We need black employers, more black businesses." (W. F. Haddad and D. Pugh, eds., "Black Ownership and National Politics," in *Black Economic Development* [Princeton: Prentice Hall, 1969], pp. 38–39).

26. Bobby Rush, a former leader of the Black Panther party and a convert to the capitalist spirit, recently stated: "Government is not going to be able to solve all of the problems that afflict the African-American community. We have suffered from over-reliance on government. And it has zapped the creativeness and spirit that was so much a part of life for our grandparents. We must look within ourselves, and find a place within the capitalist system" (Dirk Johns, "A Politician's Life, from Militant to Mainstream," *New York Times*, June 3, 1990, p. 22).

27. See John H. Bracey, August Meier, and Elliott Rudwick, eds., *Black Nationalism in America* (New York: Bobbs-Merrill, 1970), p. 428.

28. W. E. B. Du Bois, "The Talented Tenth," reprinted in *Negro Protest in the Twentieth Century*, ed. Francis L. Broderick and August Meier (New York: Bobbs-Merrill, 1965), pp. 40–48.

29. James Boggs, "The Final Confrontation," *Liberator* 8 (March 1968): 4–8; Bracey, Meier, and Rudwick, *Black Nationalism in America*, p. 521.

30. Todd Gitlin, *The Whole World Is Watching: Mass Media in the Making and Unmaking of the New Left* (Berkeley: University of California Press, 1980), chap. 5.

31. "Text of the Moynihan Memorandum on the Status of Negroes," *New York Times*, March 1, 1970, p. 69. This article includes the text of a "Memorandum for the President" by Daniel P. Moynihan, then counselor to President Nixon, on January 16, 1970.

32. Arthur Jensen, "How Much Can We Boost IQ and Scholastic Achievement?" *Harvard Educational Review* 31, no. 1 (Winter 1969): 1–123.

33. Cornel West, "Black-Jewish Dialogue: Beyond Rootless Universalism and Ethnic Chauvinism," *Tikkun* 4, no. 3 (July-August 1989): 195–97; Carson, "In Struggle"; Paul Berman, "Jackson and the Jewish Left," *Tikkun* 3, no. 4 (July-August 1988): 53–55.

34. Jesse M. Vazquez, "Ethnic-Studies Programs Are in Danger of Being Lost in the Current Rush to 'Universalize' the College Curriculum," *Chronicle of Higher Education*, November 16, 1988, p. A48.

35. Lillian Rubin, *Busing and Backlash: White against White in a California District (Berkeley: University of California Press, 1972)*, chap. 3; Anthony J. Lukas, *Common Ground: A Turbulent Decade in the Lives of Three American Families* (New York: Knopf, distributed by Random House, 1985).

36. Herbert Gans, "We Won't End the Urban Crisis Until We End Majority Rule," *New York Times Magazine*, August 3, 1969, pp. 13–14.

37. James Farmer claims that the push for affirmative action emerged earlier with the actions of the Congress for Racial Equality (CORE). See Farmer's autobiography, *Lay Bare the Heart*; and Glazer, *Affirmative Discrimination*.

38. Charles Murray, *Losing Ground: American Social Policy, 1950–1980* (New York: Basic Books, 1984).

39. William Schneider, "An Insider's View of the Election," *Atlantic* 262, no. 1 (July 1988): 38.

40. "Reverse Exodus: Middle-Class Blacks Quit Northern Cities and Settle in the South," *Wall Street Journal*, May 22, 1990, p. 1.

41. William J. Wilson, *The Truly Disadvantaged: The Inner City, the Underclass, and Public Policy* (Chicago: University of Chicago Press, 1987).

42. "Black Intellectuals Divided over Ideological Direction," *New York Times*, July 28, 1975, p. 57.

43. Ibid.

44. Ibid.

45. Ibid.

46. Ibid.

47. Ibid.

48. For evidence of its success, especially with regard to the recruiting of blacks by business, see Herman Schwartz, "Affirmative Action," in *Minority Report*, ed. Leslie W. Dunbar (New York: Pantheon, 1984), pp. 58–74; "A Report of the Citizen's Commission on Civil Rights," cited by Stephen Steinberg in *The Ethnic Myth: Race, Ethnicity, and Class in America*, 2d ed. (Boston: Beacon Press, 1989), p. 294. See also Jonathan S. Leonard, "The Impact of Affirmative Action Regulation and Equal Employment Law on Black Employment," *Journal of Economic Perspective* 4, no. 4 (Fall 1990): 47–63.

49. See Joel Dreyfuss and Charles Lawrence III, *The Bakke Case: The Politics of Inequality* (New York: Harcourt Brace Jovanovich, 1979).

50. See Herbert Hill, "Black Labor and Affirmative Action: An Historical Perspective," in *The Question of Discrimination: Racial Inequality in the U.S. Labor Market*, ed. Steven Shulman and William Darity, Jr. (Middletown, Conn.: Wesleyan University Press, 1989), pp. 190–268.

51. Wilson, *The Truly Disadvantaged*, pp. 110–18.

52. Shelby Steele, "A Negative Vote on Affirmative Action," *New York Times Magazine*, May 13, 1990, p. 49.

53. Ibid. For a more extensive critique of affirmative action, see Thomas Sowell, *Preferential Policies: An International Perspective* (New York: William Morrow, 1990).

54. William Julius Wilson, *The Declining Significance of Race* (Chicago: University of Chicago Press, 1978).

55. See Joseph R. Washington, Jr., *The Declining Significance of Race: A Dialogue Among Black and White Social Scientists* (Philadelphia: University of Pennsylvania, 1979); Charles Verty Willie, Caste and *Class Controversy* (New York: General Hall, 1979).

56. Wilson has subsequently elaborated his position more carefully. His "neutrality" thesis is partly a tactical adaptation to the political scene and partly, I believe, a matter of principle. See "Race-Neutral Programs and the Democratic Coalition," *American Prospect* (Spring 1990): 74–81.

57. Katz, *Undeserving Poor*, pp. 236–39.

58. Thomas Sowell, *Civil Rights: Rhetoric or Reality?* (New York: William Morrow, 1984), p. 8.

59. I use Sowell's book regularly in my classes at Queens College and the Graduate Center of the City University of New York and am invariably questioned, and sometimes castigated, by both white and black students representing a wide range of persuasions about why I use a racist reactionary book like this by a white author.

60. Sowell, *Rhetoric or Reality?*, p. 32.

61. Ibid., p. 25.

62. Ibid., p. 26.

63. Ibid., pp. 61–72.

64. The demand for preferential treatment by blacks is only one among a number of ways to seek social justice. While one might legitimately argue on tactical grounds that the struggle for preferential treatment may be nearing the limits of its usefulness, it does not follow, as many critics suggest, that terminating the affirmative action strategy will necessarily improve the opportunities of the black middle class or axiomatically make programs for the black underclass more palatable to the larger public. In my view, it symbolizes a retreat from the struggle for generalized social justice.

65. Derrick Bell, *And We Are Not Saved* (New York: Basic Books, 1987), p. 14.

66. Ibid.

67. Sowell, *Rhetoric or Reality?*, p. 73.

68. Ibid.

69. Steinberg, *The Ethnic Myth*. This is one of the main themes of Steinberg's book.

70. Peter Applebome, "Louisiana Tally Is Seen as a Sign of Voter Unrest," *New York Times*, October 8, 1990, p. 1.

71. Peter Riddell, "Bush Presidency under a Cloud," *Financial Times*, October 19, 1990, p. 18.

72. Winthrop Jordan, *White over Black: American Attitudes Toward the Negro, 1550–1812* (Chapel Hill: University of North Carolina Press, 1968).

73. Jacqueline Jones, *Labor of Love, Labor of Sorrow: Black Women, Work, and the Family from Slavery to the Present* (New York: Vintage, 1986); Herbert G. Gutman, *The Black Family in Slavery and Freedom, 1750–1925* (New York: Pantheon, 1976); Carol Stack, *All Our Kin: Strategies for Survival in a Black Community* (New York: Harper and Row, 1974).

74. Martin Luther King, Jr., "Martin Luther King Defines Black Power," *New York Times Magazine*, June 11, 1967, pp. 27, 99.

75. A. B. Spellman, "Interview with Malcolm X," *Monthly Review* 16 (May 1964): 24.

76. Wilson, *The Declining Significance of Race*, pp. 22–23, 144-54.

77. This, I believe, is a limited interpretation. Wilson was primarily focused on the work sphere and, in particular, the relative success of recent college graduates. He never suggested that discrimination was seriously abating in the social domains of American society. This issue is further discussed in chapter 6.

78. Roger Wilkins, "In Ivory Towers," *Mother Jones* (July-August 1990): 10.

79. See chap. 6.

80. "Excerpts From Jackson Appeal to Convention Delegates for Unity in Party," *New York Times*, July 18, 1984, p. A18; for a more extensive interpretation of Jackson, see Sheila Collins, *The Rainbow Challenge* (New York: Monthly Review Press, 1986); Adolph L. Reed, *The Jesse Jackson Phenomenon* (New Haven: Yale University Press, 1986).

81. See Schneider, "An Insider's View," p. 38.

82. Robert Kuttner, *The Life of the Party: Democratic Prospects in 1988 and Beyond* (New York: Viking, 1987), chap. 1.

83. Orlando Patterson, "Toward a Study of Black America," *Dissent* (Fall 1989): 477.

Chapter 2. American Slavery: Contemporary Meanings and Uses

1. Willie Lee Rose, *Slavery and Freedom* (New York: Oxford University Press, 1982), p. 165.

2. David Brion Davis, "The Great Slavery Boom," *New York Times Book Review*, April 3, 1978, p. 20.

3. Rose, *Slavery and Freedom*, p. 176.

4. Harold Sheppard, "Poverty and the Negro," in *Poverty as a Public Issue*, ed. Benjamin B. Seligman (New York: Free Press, 1965), p. 124.

5. This social holocaust portion is based on Nathan Irwin Huggin's work, *Black Odyssey* (New York: Vintage, 1979).

6. Ibid., p. 27.

7. Orlando Patterson, "On Slavery and Slave Formation," *New Left Review* 117 (September-October 1979): 32–33.

8. Orlando Patterson, *Slavery and Social Death* (Cambridge, Mass.: Harvard University Press, 1982), pp. 5, 7.

9. Patterson, "On Slavery," p. 34.

10. Ibid., pp. 35–36.

11. Ibid., p. 37.

12. The development of the thematic portions of the slave debate and its implications is modeled after two articles: Stanley M. Elkins, "The Slavery Debate," *Commentary* 60 (December 1975): 40–64; and George M. Fredrickson, "The Gutman Report," *New York Review of Books*, September 30, 1976, pp. 11–12.

13. Ulrich B. Phillips, *American Negro Slavery* (New York, 1918), pp. 342–43; cited by Kenneth Stampp, *The Peculiar Institution* (New York: Vintage, 1964), pp. 11–12.

14. Phillips, *American Negro Slavery*, pp. 291–92; cited by Stampp, *The Peculiar Institution*, pp. 8–9.

15. See Charles E. Silberman, *Criminal Violence, Criminal Justice* (New York: Random House, 1978), especially chaps. 2, 5.

16. Henry S. Commager and Samuel E. Morison, *Growth of the American Republic*, 2d ed. (New York: Oxford University Press, 1942), p. 537.

17. James Q. Wilson, "The Rediscovery of Character: Private Virtue and Public Policy," *Public Interest* 81 (Fall 1985): 3, 5.

18. Kenneth M. Stampp, *The Peculiar Institution*.

19. Ibid., p. 430.

20. Stanley M. Elkins, *Slavery: A Problem in American Institutional and Intellectual Life*, Universal Library edition (New York: Grosset and Dunlap, 1963). Originally published by the University of Chicago Press in 1959.

21. Bruno Bettelheim, "Individual and Mass Behavior in Extreme Situations," *Journal of Abnormal Psychology* 38, no. 4 (October 1943): 444–47.

22. The black-Jewish dialogue to which I refer stretches over a period of years (1967–1987) in the teaching of a course on the economics of race and class to Queens College undergraduates; see also Stephen Steinberg, *The Ethnic Myth: Race, Ethnicity, and Class in America*, 2d ed. (Boston: Beacon Press, 1989), p. 270.

23. Elkins, *Slavery*, pp. 82, 84.

24. Lee Rainwater and William L. Yancy, *Moynihan and the Politics of Controversy: A Trans-action Social Science and Public Policy Report* (Cambridge, Mass.: MIT Press, 1967), pp. 75–92; see also the special issue of *The Nation*, "Conscience of a Neoconservative," September 22, 1979.

25. William Styron, *The Confessions of Nat Turner* (New York: Random House, 1967).

26. See John Henrik Clarke, ed., *William Styron's Nat Turner: Ten Black Writers Respond* (Boston: Beacon Press, 1968). For an excellent discussion of the issues involved in the black writers' response to Styron's book, see Harvard Sitkoff and Michael Wreszin, "Whose Nat Turner? William Styron vs. the Black Intellectuals," *Midstream* (November 1968): 10–20.

27. John W. Blassingame, *The Slave Community: Plantation Life in the Antebellum South* (New York: Oxford University Press, 1972).

28. Ibid., rev. and enl. ed. (New York: Oxford University Press, 1979), pp. 147–48.

29. Herbert G. Gutman, *The Black Family in Slavery and Freedom, 1750–1925* (New York: Pantheon, 1976).

30. Herbert G. Gutman, "Black History: Seduced and Abandoned," *The Nation*, September 22, 1979, p. 234.

3l. Gutman, *The Black Family*, chaps. 1–3, pp. 3–143.

32. Robert W. Fogel and Stanley L. Engerman, *Time on the Cross* (Boston: Little, Brown, 1974); Eugene D. Genovese, *Roll, Jordan, Roll: The World the Slaves Made* (New York: Vintage, 1976).

33. Fogel and Engerman, *Time on the Cross*, p. 5.

34. Ibid., p. 5.

35. Ibid., pp. 126–44.

36. Ibid., esp. pp. 117–26.

37. This is a puzzling point, since the senior author, Fogel, is a strong advocate of the free market.

38. See Paul A. David et al., *Reckoning with Slavery* (New York: Oxford University Press, 1976).

39. To the extent that this idea is viewed as "common" knowledge, see the casual reference made by David Wellman, "The New Political Linguistics of Race," *Socialist Review* 88/89 (1986): 46.

40. See Thomas Sowell, *Race and Economics* (New York: David McKay, 1975), esp. chap. 6; E. Olfari, *Black Capitalism* (New York: Monthly Review Press, 1970); Joseph Berger, "What Do They Mean by 'Black' Learning Style?" *New York Times*, July 6, 1988, p. 84.

4l. Dirk Johns, "A Politician's Life, from Militant to Mainstream," *New York Times*, June 3, 1990, p. 22.

42. Stampp, *The Peculiar Institution*, pp. 21–22.

43. Ibid., p. 22.

44. Eric Williams, *Capitalism and Slavery* (New York: Capricorn, 1966); originally published in 1954 by the University of North Carolina Press.

45. Stampp, *The Peculiar Institution*, p. 23.

46. George K. Fredrickson, "Why Blacks Were Left Out," *New York Review of Books*, February 7, 1974, p. 23. This was a review of Winthrop D. Jordan, *The White Man's Bur-*

den: Historical Origins of Racism in the United States (New York: Oxford University Press, 1974).

47. Stampp, *The Peculiar Institution*, p. 22.

48. Edmund S. Morgan, *American Slavery/American Freedom: Ordeal of Colonial Virginia* (New York: Norton, 1975), p. 386.

49. Rose, *Slavery and Freedom*, p. 25.

50. Ibid.

51. Ibid., p. 34.

52. Carl N. Degler, *Neither Black nor White: Slavery and Race Relations in Brazil and the United States* (New York: Macmillan, 1971).

53. Rose, *Slavery and Freedom*, p. 152.

54. For an excellent summary of the Marxian view of the slave mode of production, see John Anthony Scott, "Review of *Roll, Jordan, Roll: The World the Slaves Made*," *Challenge* (May–June 1975): 65–71.

55. Edward C. Banfield, *The Unheavenly City Revisited* (Boston: Little, Brown, 1974).

56. See the discussion by William Darity, Jr., "What's Left of the Economic Theory of Discrimination?" in *The Question of Discrimination*, ed. Steven Shulman and William Darity, Jr. (Middletown, Conn.: Wesleyan University Press, 1989), pp. 341–43.

57. Orlando Patterson, "Toward a Study of Black America," *Dissent* (Fall 1989): 476–86.

Chapter 3. Scientific Racism and Social Class

1. *American Telephone and Telegraph Company, Notice of the 1988 Annual Meeting and Proxy Statement*, p. 31. The psychological study referred to by the AT&T stockholder also linked IQ to crime, a view that has a long history of twisted and misspecified data. Colleen Cordes (American Psychological Association), *Monitor* (February 1987): 20–21. For a more influential work connecting IQ with black criminality, see James Q. Wilson and Richard J. Herrnstein, *Crime and Human Nature: The Definitive Study of the Causes of Crime* (New York: Simon and Schuster, 1985).

2. Joseph Berger, "Professors' Theories on Race Stir Turmoil at City College," *New York Times*, April 20, 1990, p. B1. It is possible that the IQ debate may again emerge in the 1990s if the conservative social scientist Charles Murray successfully launches his newly acquired interest. See "An Architect of the Reagan Vision Plunges into Inquiry on Race and I.Q.," *New York Times*, November 30, 1990, p. A22.

3. See the reference to the memoirs of Louis Agassiz in R. C. Lewontin, Steven Rose, and Leon J. Kamin, *Not in Our Genes* (New York: Pantheon, 1984), p. 28.

4. George M. Fredrickson, *The Black Image in the White Mind: The Debate of Afro-American Character and Destiny, 1817–1914* (Middletown, Conn.: Wesleyan University Press, 1987), p. 2. This historical section mainly dealing with the nineteenth century relies primarily on Fredrickson.

5. Ibid., p. 20.

6. Ibid., pp. 27, 41.

7. Ibid., p. 74.

8. Ibid., p. 84.

9. Ibid.

10. Ibid., p. 156.

11. Ibid., p. 83.

12. Richard Hofstadter, *Social Darwinism in American Thought*, rev. ed. (Boston: Beacon Press, 1955), chap. 9.

13. Ibid., p. 46.
14. Fredrickson, *The Black Image*, p. 235.
15. Ibid., p. 251.
16. Ibid.
17. Arthur Jensen, "How Much Can We Boost IQ and Scholastic Achievement?" *Harvard Educational Review* 39, no. 1 (Winter 1969): 2.
18. Fredrickson, *The Black Image*, pp. 254–55.
19. Ibid., p. 255.
20. Ibid., p. 314.
21. Ibid.
22. Ibid., p. 315.
23. Ibid., p. 255.
24. Ibid.
25. Leon J. Kamin, *The Science and Politics of IQ* (Potomac, Md.: Erlbaum, 1974), p. 16.
26. Lewontin, Rose, and Kamin, *Not in Our Genes*, p. 86.
27. Ruth Benedict and Gene Wetfish, *Race: Science and Politics* (New York: Viking, 1945). This book includes Benedict's essay "The Races of Mankind," which was widely circulated as a pamphlet. See also Theodore M. Newcomb and Eugene L. Hartley, eds., *Readings in Social Psychology* (New York: Henry Holt, 1947); Thomas F. Gosset, *Race: The History of an Idea in America* (New York: Schocken, 1965), chap. 16.
28. Jerry Hirsch, "To 'Unfrock' the Charlatans," *Sage Race Relations Abstract* 6, no. 2 (May 1981): 1.
29. Ibid., p. 2.
30. Daniel Bell, *The Coming of Post-Industrial Society* (New York: Basic Books, 1973).
31. The word meritocracy was used by Michael Young in his satirical book about the British elite and the possibility of England becoming a two-class society. Michael Young, *The Rise of the Meritocracy* (Harmondworth: Penguin, 1961).
32. Fred Hirsch, *Social Limits to Growth* (Cambridge, Mass.: Harvard University Press, 1976), pp. 27–31.
33. Paul Blumberg, *Inequality in an Age of Decline* (New York: Oxford University Press, 1980), pp. 76–84.
34. Hirsch, *Social Limits to Growth*, pp. 162-63, n. 2.
35. Mark Baldassare, *Trouble in Paradise: The Suburban Transformation in America* (New York: Columbia University Press, 1986).
36. Ira Katznelson and Margaret Wier, *School for All: Class, Race, and the Decline of the Democratic Idea* (New York: Basic Books, 1985); Christopher Jencks, *Inequality: A Reassessment of the Effects of Family and Schooling in America* (New York: Basic Books, 1972).
37. Miriam Slater, "Let Them Eat Shit" (paper presented at the Conference on Cultural Change of the Center for the Study of Democratic Institutions, Claremont, Calif., May 3, 1972).
38. Everett Carll Ladd, Jr., and Seymour M. Lipset, *The Divided Academy: Professors and Politics* (New York: McGraw-Hill, 1975), pp. 221–22.
39. For a negative evaluation of intellectuals, especially as their opinions relate to the "lower orders," see Richard F. Hamilton, *Class and Politics in the United States* (New York and London: John Wiley, 1972), pp. 523, 527, 552–53.
40. Charles Kadushin, *The American Intellectual Elite* (Boston: Little, Brown, 1974), chap. 12.
41. Ibid.

42. For a radical treatment of this issue, see Samuel Bowles and Herbert Gintis, *Schooling in Capitalist America: Educational Reform and the Contradictions of Economic Life* (New York: Basic Books, 1976).

43. Benjamin Ward, *What's Wrong with Economics?* (New York: Basic Books, 1972), pp. 9–11.

44. Daniel Goleman, "An Emerging Theory on Blacks' IQ Scores," *New York Times*, April 10, 1988, education sec., p. 22.

45. Anthony Giddens, *New Rules of Sociological Method* (New York: Basic Books, 1976), p. 15.

46. Ibid.

47. Lester Thurow, *Dangerous Currents: The State of Economics* (New York: Random House, 1983), p. 21.

48. For a number of recent books that focus on the centrality of the ethical or moral dimension, see Alan Wolfe, *Whose Keeper? Social Science and Moral Obligation* (Berkeley: University of California Press, 1989); Amitai Etzioni, *The Moral Dimension: Toward a New Economics* (New York: Free Press, 1988); Amartya Sen, *On Ethics and Economics* (Oxford: Basil Blackwell, 1987); Robert N. Bellah et al., "Social Science as a Public Philosophy," appendix to *Habits of the Heart: Individualism and Commitment in American Life* (Berkeley and Los Angeles: University of California Press, 1985).

49. Marvin Harris, *The Rise of Anthropological Theory* (New York: Crowell 1968), pp. 100–101.

50. Richard Herrnstein, "IQ," *Atlantic Monthly* 228 (1971): 62–63.

51. Ibid., p. 63. For a succinct summary and discussion of Herrnstein's view, see Wallace A. Kennedy, *Intelligence and Economics: A Confounded Relationship* (Morristown, N.J.: General Learning Press, 1973), p. 12; for a critique, see Karl W. Deutsch and Thomas Edsall, "The Meritocracy Scare," *Society* (September-October 1972): 71–79.

52. Ibid., p. 12.

53. Ibid., p. 13.

54. Gary S. Becker, "A Theory of Marriage," *Journal of Political Economy* 8, no. 4 (July-August 1973): 832, 834.

55. One kind of anxiety among human capital-genetic advocates is that bright, well-educated, better-off Americans are having fewer children, a phenomenon that may affect productivity and the gene pool. The suggested fear is that the birthrate of the poor, namely blacks and Hispanics, is much greater than that of the white middle classes. See Richard J. Herrnstein, "IQ and Falling Birth Rates," *Atlantic Monthly* (May 1989): 73–79.

56. Stuart A. Hoenig, *Business Week*, October 24, 1988, p. 12.

57. Lewontin, Rose, and Kamin, *Not in Our Genes*, p. 9.

58. Nicholas Pastore, *The Nature-Nurture Controversy* (New York: King's Crown Press, 1949), pp. 1–19.

59. The category system was developed by Margery B. Franklin, professor of psychology at Sarah Lawrence College.

60. Kennedy, *Intelligence and Economics*, p. 12; see also Lewontin, Rose, and Kamin, *Not in Our Genes*, p. 84.

61. Lewontin, Rose, and Kamin, *Not in Our Genes*, p. 266.

62. Ibid.

63. Ibid., pp. 251, 269.

64. R. C. Lewontin, "The Fallacy of Biological Determinism," *The Sciences* (March-April 1976): 8.

65. Lewontin, Rose, and Kamin, *Not in Our Genes*, pp. 268–69.

66. Herbert G. Birch and Joan Dye Gussow, *Disadvantaged Children: Health, Nutrition, and School Failure* (New York: Harcourt, Brace and World, 1970), pp. 267–68.

67. Kennedy, *Intelligence and Economics*, p. 15.

68. William Labov, "Academic Ignorance and Black Intelligence," *Atlantic Monthly* 229, no. 6 (1972): 60.

69. Joseph Berger, "What Do They Mean by Black Learning Style?" *New York Times*, July 6, 1988, p. 84.

70. Jacqueline Fleming and Louise DuBois, "The Role of Suppressed and Perceived Hostility in Academic Performance: An Exploratory Study of Black Students," *United Negro College Fund Report to the Spencer Foundation*, August 31, 1981 (unpublished).

71. Samuel Bowles and Valerie Nelson, "The Inheritance of IQ and the Intergenerational Transmission of Economic Inequality," *Review of Economic Statistics* 56 (February 1974): 39–51.

72. Ibid.

73. Zena Smith Blau, "The Social Structure, Socialization Process, and School Competence of Black and White Children," in *The Question of Discrimination*, ed. Steven Shulman and William Darity, Jr. (Middletown, Conn.: Wesleyan University Press, 1989), pp. 319–26.

74. Lewontin, Rose, and Kamin, *Not in Our Genes*, p. 8.

75. Ibid.

76. R. C. Lewontin, "The Inferiority Complex," *New York Review of Books*, October 22, 1981, pp. 12, 15.

77. R. C. Lewontin, "Is Intelligence for Real? An Exchange," *New York Review of Books*, February 4, 1982, p. 41.

78. Lewontin, Rose, and Kamin, *Not in Our Genes*, p. 98.

79. Ibid., pp. 98–99.

80. Ibid., p. 117.

81. Ibid., p. 118.

82. See ibid., pp. 110–17, for an extended discussion of this line of reasoning.

83. For the first exposé of Sir Cyril Burt's falsification of his twin studies, see Kamin, *Science and Politics of IQ*, p. 153.

84. Lewontin, Rose, and Kamin, *Not in Our Genes*, pp. 106–10.

85. Ibid., pp. 113–14.

86. Ibid., p. 113.

87. Alan Gartner and Frank Riessman, "The Lingering Infatuation with IQ," *Social Policy*, special pamphlet series (1974): 2.

88. Arthur R. Jensen, "Environment, Heredity, and Intelligence," reprint, no. 2, compiled for *Harvard Educational Review* (1969): 73. Cited by Gartner and Riessman, "Lingering Infatuation with IQ."

89. Gartner and Riessman, "Lingering Infatuation with IQ," p. 2.

90. Ibid., p. 7.

91. Lewontin, Rose, and Kamin, *Not in Our Genes*, chap. 10. The ontological argument is developed as part of their general criticism of the biological reductionist approach.

92. Stephen Jay Gould, *The Mismeasure of Man* (New York: Norton, 1981).

Chapter 4. Economics of Dominant-Subordinate Relations

1. This paradox was revealed in a pilot survey among Queens College students. One questionnaire, consisting of statements or questions, was presented to a random sample

of about two hundred students with instructions that the respondents express their own personal views. The same questionnaire was presented to a random sample with instructions to state only what they understood were the beliefs of others. The statements or questions involved an array of descriptions primarily, but not exclusively, about African-Americans. Many of these statements concerned stereotypes or ambiguous situations. For example: Most blacks are on welfare because they really do not wish to work:

a: most people believe this
b: many people believe this
c: few people believe this
d: no one believes this
e: no opinion

On the questionnaire in which students were instructed to respond with their personal judgment, about 30 percent checked either a or b. In contrast, on the questionnaire in which the respondents were instructed to make a judgment about how others believed, about 70 percent checked a or b. The survey was conducted in the spring of 1988.

2. It is for this reason that blacks cannot be conveyors of institutional racism. No doubt slurs against whites or against particular ethnic groups occur; but however offensive such statements are, they are for the most part defensive. The reason is not difficult to understand. Since whites do not seek what blacks possess, since blacks have little power to exclude whites, it makes no sense to speak of black racism in the same vein as its white counterpart.

3. Robert Higgs, "Black Progress and the Persistence of Racial Economic Inequalities, 1865–1940," in The Question of Discrimination: Racial Inequality in the U.S. Labor Market, eds. Steven Shulman and William Darity, Jr. (Middletown, Conn.: Wesleyan University Press, 1989), p. 25, n. 3.

4. Edward C. Banfield, The Unheavenly City: The Nature of Our Urban Crisis (Boston: Little, Brown, 1970), p. 284. It should be pointed out that insofar as the service industry is on the rise and is generating the kinds of jobs (finance, insurance, trade) in which "aesthetics" matter, blacks are likely to run into further barriers to employment. If machinery can serve as the interface between the service performed and the individual, barriers may lessen.

5. Frederick Douglass, "A Letter of Harriet Beecher Stowe," in Black Viewpoints, ed. A. C. Little and M. M. Burger (New York: Mentor, 1971), p. 28.

6. Brent Bowers, "Black Owners Fight Obstacles to Get Orders," Wall Street Journal, November 16, 1990, p. B2.

7. This conversation was reported to me by a white contractor in June 1982. I was told that this was not an uncommon experience.

8. Alice Walker, The Color Purple (New York: Washington Square, 1982), p. 246.

9. Roy Wilkins, "Equal Employment Opportunity Hearings on Manpower before the Subcommittee of Employment and Manpower of the Committee on Labor and Public Affairs" (U.S. Senate, 88th Congress, First Session, 1963).

10. This was reported to me by a foreman who worked in a General Motors plant in Flint, Michigan, 1973.

11. Herbert Hill, "Black Labor and Affirmative Action: A Historical Perspective," in Shulman and Darity, Jr., eds., Question of Discrimination, pp. 190–267.

12. For an excellent critical survey of this approach to discrimination in the labor market, see William Darity, Jr., "What's Left of the Economic Theory of Discrimination?" in Shulman and Darity, Jr., eds., Question of Discrimination, pp. 335–74.

13. Gary S. Becker, *The Economics of Discrimination*, 2d ed. (Chicago: University of Chicago Press, 1971).

14. Michael Tanzer, *Racial Discrimination in Southern Manufacturing Employment* (Cambridge, Mass.: Harvard College, 1957); Raymond S. Franklin and Michael Tanzer, "Traditional Microeconomic Analysis of Racial Discrimination: A Critical Review and Alternative Approach," in *Economics: Mainstream Readings and Radical Critiques*, ed. David Mermelstein (New York: Random House, 1970).

15. This point was made at a meeting sponsored by the National Industrial Conference Board in June 1968. The focus of the meeting was on the education, training, and employment of "hard-to-employ" minority workers, a euphemism in the New York area for blacks and Puerto Ricans. The view is repeated often by managers of supermarkets and small textile firms.

16. Sterling D. Spero and A. L. Harris, *The Black Worker* (New York: Atheneum, 1969), p. 169.

17. Quoted by Harold M. Baron, "The Demand for Black Labor: Historical Notes on the Political Economy of Racism," *Radical America* 5, no. 2 (1971): 23.

18. William Kornblum, *Blue-Collar Community* (Chicago: University of Chicago Press, 1974), pp. 39, 48–51.

19. "Many Hurdles, 'Old and New,' Keep Black Managers Out of Top Jobs," *Wall Street Journal*, July 10, 1986, p. 27.

20. John W. Blassingame, *The Slave Community: Plantation Life in the Antebellum South*, rev. and enl. ed. (New York: Oxford University Press, 1979), pp. 293–94.

21. This is a composite quote from four workers I spoke with in a computer company in Poughkeepsie, New York, in 1966.

22. Women, it should be noted, are often cornered into similar positions. When they appear too aggressive, they are derided for not acting like women. When they are not aggressive (i.e., appear gentle or passive), an explanation is at hand as to why they do less well in some lines of work compared to their male counterparts.

23. Michael Reich, *Racial Inequality: A Political-Economic Analysis* (Princeton, N.J.: Princeton University Press, 1981), p. 312.

24. See "Of History and Politics: Bitter Feminist Debate," *New York Times*, June 6, 1986, p. B1, for an example of this. The Equal Employment Opportunity Commission, charging that Sears had discriminated against women, spent months compiling statistics for their case. They could not find a witness to testify against Sears and Sears won.

25. Economists call this statistical discrimination. For an earlier development of this construct under another designation, see Raymond S. Franklin, "A Framework for Analysis of Negro-White and Inter-Urban Economic Differentials," *Industrial and Labor Relations Review* 21, no. 3 (April 1968): 367–74; see also Kenneth J. Arrow, "Models of Discrimination," in *Racial Discrimination in Economic Life*, ed. Anthony H. Pascal (Lexington, Mass.: Lexington Books, 1972).

26. Edna Bonacich, "Advanced Capitalism and Black-White Relations in the United States: A Split Labor Market Interpretation," *American Sociological Review* 41 (February 1976): 34–51.

27. For an elegant application of traditional economic theory to this kind of problem, see Glenn C. Loury, "Why Should We Care about Group Inequality?" Shulman and Darity, Jr., eds., *Question of Discrimination*, pp. 268–90.

28. See William Julius Wilson, *The Truly Disadvantaged: The Inner City, the Underclass, and Public Policy* (Chicago: University of Chicago Press, 1987).

Chapter 5. White Uses of the Black Underclass

1. For a discussion of the origin and uses of the term underclass, see Herbert J. Gans, "Deconstructing the Underclass: The Term's Dangers as a Planning Concept," *APA Journal* (Summer 1990): 271–77.

2. William Julius Wilson, who revised the term in his book *The Truly Disadvantaged* in order to break the silence about the poorest of the black poor, is having second thoughts. In a presidential address at the American Sociological Association meetings (August 1990), he suggested that the term has such pejorative connotations that it may not serve to arouse public compassion. On the contrary, it may conjure "an image of people unwilling to help themselves." Jason DeParle, "Underclass Reconsidered: What to Call the Poorest Poor," *New York Times*, August 26, 1990, p. E4.

3. See Frank Bonilla, "Idle Classes, Underclasses" (a talk presented at the Department of Urban Studies and Planning, MIT, April 8, 1988); Ken Auletta, *The Underclass* (New York: Random House, 1982), pp. 20–30.

4. William Julius Wilson, "The Crisis of the Ghetto Underclass and the Liberal Retreat, *Democratic Left* (May-August 1987): 5; Katherine McFate, "Defining the Underclass," *Focus* 15 (June 1987): 8.

5. Nicholas Lemann, "The Origins of the Underclass," parts 1 and 2, *The Atlantic*, (June 1986): 31–55 and (July 1986): 54–68.

6. Douglas G. Glasgow, *The Black Underclass: Poverty, Unemployment, and Entrapment of Ghetto Youth*, 2d ed. (New York: Vintage, 1981), chap. 6 and pp. 87–104.

7. Auletta, *The Underclass*, pp. 31–43.

8. Loïc J. D. Wacquant and William Julius Wilson, "The Cost of Racial and Class Exclusion in the Inner City," special issue on "The Ghetto Underclass: Social Science Perspectives," *Annals of the American Academy of Political and Social Science* (January 1989); Norman Fainstein, "The Underclass/Mismatch Hypothesis as an Explanation for Black Economic Deprivation," *Politics and Society* 15, no. 4 (1986/1987): 403–52.

9. Auletta, *The Underclass*, p. xvi.

10. Christopher Jencks, "What Is the Underclass—and Is It Growing?" *Focus* 12, no. 1 (Spring-Summer 1989): 15.

11. Ibid., pp. 19–25. More recently, Jencks has not only demonstrated the decline of the underclass but has even gone so far as to question its very existence. "There Is No Underclass," *Wall Street Journal* (April 17, 1991), p. 14A.

12. Martha A. Gephart and Robert W. Pearson, "Contemporary Research on the Urban Underclass," *Items*, Social Science Research Council Bulletin 4, nos. 1 and 2 (June 1988): 2–3.

13. Erol Rickets and Isabel Sawhill, "Defining and Measuring the Underclass," *Journal of Policy Analysis and Management* (Winter 1988): 316–25; Gephart and Pearson, "Urban Underclass," pp. 1–9.

14. In a review of the explanations of the underclass summarized in a publication of the Social Science Research Council, only one of the eleven basic explanations referred to was race—"Continued racial discrimination in jobs and housing." The others were in the direction of impersonal forces: international competition, changes in the nature of jobs, industry location, production methods, composition of commodities, development of the illicit economy, increases in immigration, public policies, culture, and the misfit between "minority" skills and industry skills among our inner city youth. Robert W. Pearson, "Economy, Culture, Public Policy, and the Urban Underclass," *Items* 43, no. 2 (June 1989): 24.

15. Paul Blumberg, *Inequality in an Age of Decline* (New York: Oxford University Press, 1980), pp. 76–83; Jonathan Rieder, *Canarsie: The Jews and Italians of Brooklyn Against Liberalism (Cambridge, Mass.: Harvard University Press, 1985)*.

16. Lawrence Michelle, *State of Working America*, (Armonk, N.Y.: Sharpe, 1991).

17. "The Squeeze on the Middle Class," *Business Week* (March 10, 1975): 52–60.

18. Wacquant and Wilson, "Racial and Class Exclusion," p. 9.

19. See Kevin Phillips, *The Politics of Rich and Poor* (New York: Random House, 1990).

20. John F. Kain, "Housing Segregation, Negro Employment, and Metropolitan Decentralization," *Quarterly Journal of Economics* 82, no. 2 (February 1968): 176–77.

21. Paul Wilkes, "As the Blacks Move in, the Ethnics Move Out," *New York Times Magazine*, January 24, 1971, p. 10.

22. Ibid., p. 10.

23. Ibid., p. 11.

24. Ibid.

25. Ibid., p. 57.

26. Robert Staples, "Black Male Genocide: A Final Solution to the Race Problem in America," *Black Scholar* 18, no. 3 (May-June 1987): 3.

27. Andrew Hacker, "Black Crime, White Racism," *New York Review of Books*, March 3, 1988, p. 36.

28. See Jay MacLeod, *Ain't No Makin' It* (Boulder, Colo.: Westview Press, 1987). It is the slightly hopeful segment of the black poor, struggling against odds, that is the focus of MacLeod's case study.

29. Arthur Kempton, "Native Sons," *New York Review of Books*, April 11, 1991, p. 57, quoting Gibbs, *Young, Black, and Male in America: An Endangered Species* (New York: Auburn House, 1988).

30. Anders Stephanson, "Interview with Cornel West," in *Universal Abandon? The Politics of Postmodernism*, ed. Andrew Ross (Minneapolis: University of Minnesota Press, 1988), p. 276.

31. A. Schucter, *White Power/Black Freedom* (Boston: Beacon Press, 1968), p. 100.

32. Winthrop D. Jordan, *The White Man's Burden: Historical Origins of Racism in the United States* (New York: Oxford University Press, 1974), pp. 196–97.

33. George M. Fredrickson, *The Black Image in the White Mind* (New York: Harper and Row, 1971), chap. 9.

34. Ibid., p. 260.

35. Ibid., pp. 274, 276.

36. Sydney H. Schanberg, "Covering the Wrong Wounds," *New York Times*, November 10, 1981, p. A23.

37. Hofstra University, UAW District-65 Program.

38. Gans, "Deconstructing the Underclass," p. 274.

39. Arne Duncan, "The Values, Aspirations, and Opportunities of the Urban Underclass" (B.A. honor thesis, Harvard University, 1987), pp. 18ff., in Wacquant and Wilson, "Racial and Class Exclusion," p. 14.

40. C. Krans, "Forty-Two Catholic Churches without a Prayer," *New York Times*, August 14, 1988, p. A35.

41. "The American Underclass," *Time*, August 29, 1977, p. 18.

42. Robert Staples, "Bound Manhood in the 1970s: A Critical Look Back," *Black Scholar* 12, no. 3 (May-June 1981): 4.

43. An undated newsletter appealing for funds circulated by PUSH for Excellence, Inc., and addressed, "Dear Fellow Americans." Received by the author in the mail in 1980.

44. "In Slums, Fields and a Hall of Graduates, Jackson Strives to Turn on Hope," *New York Times*, May 7, 1984, p. B8.

45. "Jackson Advises Class in Brooklyn," *New York Times*, June 15, 1986, p. 28. This wave of critical self-examination, with the intention of generating self-help values, is taking place across the political spectrum; see, for example, Glenn C. Loury, "The Moral Quandary of the Black Community," *Public Interest* 79 (Spring 1985): 9–22.

46. CBS, "Six O'clock News," June 14, 1986.

47. Sara Rimer, "Yonkers Anguish: Family in Two Worlds," *New York Times*, December 22, 1987, p. B7.

48. Auletta, *The Underclass*, p. 3.

49. Rimer, "Yonkers Anguish," p. 7.

50. Quoted in Auletta, *The Underclass*, p. 40. A major criticism of Assistant Secretary of Labor Daniel Patrick Moynihan's 1965 White House report on the Negro family was that "it did not take into account the emergence, partly as an adaptive response to slavery, of the black extended family—aunts, uncles, grandparents, and friends who don't always show up in statistics but nevertheless often provide role models and parental guidance." Census Bureau estimates that about 11 percent of black children are raised in extended families (ibid., p. 41).

51. Ibid., p. 46.

52. Ibid., p. 97.

53. Ibid., p. 108.

54. Ibid., p. 96.

55. Ibid., p. 90.

56. Ibid.

57. Ibid., p. 97.

58. Christina Milner and Richard Milner, *Black Players* (Boston: Little, Brown, 1972), pp. 170–71; cited by Charles E. Silberman, *Criminal Violence, Criminal Justice* (New York: Random House, 1978), p. 149.

59. Troy Duster, "Social Implications of the 'New' Black Urban Underclass," *Black Scholar* 19, no. 3 (May-June 1988): 5.

60. Christopher Muldor, "Do Black Crime Victims Matter?" *Wall Street Journal*, May 9, 1988, p. 22.

61. Auletta, *The Underclass*, p. 109.

62. My paraphrase from Elliot Liebow, *Tally's Corner* (Boston: Little, Brown, 1967); Auletta, *The Underclass*, p. 47.

63. Sylvester Monroe, "Brothers," *Newsweek*, March 23, 1987, p. 76.

64. Andrew Hacker, "The Lower Depths," *New York Review of Books*, August 12, 1982, p. 16.

65. Jacquelyne J. Jackson, "Aging Black Women and Public Policies," *Black Scholar* (May-June, 1988): 33.

66. Lemann, "Origins of the Underclass," part 2 (July 1986): 67.

67. Hacker, "The Lower Depths," p. 16.

68. Lemann, "Origins of the Underclass," part 2 (July 1986): 67.

69. Auletta, *The Underclass*, pp. 52–53.

70. Hacker, "The Lower Depths," p. 16.

71. Monroe, "Brothers," p. 76.

72. Piven and Cloward, cited by Auletta, *The Underclass*, p. 43.

73. Ibid., p. 53.

74. See Charles Murray, "New Welfare Bill, New Welfare Cheats," *Wall Street Journal*, August 29, 1988, p. A22.

75. See Thomas Byrne Edsall, *The New Politics of Inequality* (New York: Norton, 1984); William Schneider, "An Insider's View of the Election," *The Atlantic* 262, no. 1 (July 1988): 29–57.

76. Michael Harrington, *The New American Poverty* (New York and London: Penguin, 1984), pp. 29–30, 42.

77. Auletta, *The Underclass*, p. 274.

78. Andrew Hacker, "Black Crime, White Racism," *New York Review of Books*, March 3, 1988, pp. 36–41.

79. See Jencks, "What Is the Underclass."

80. Hacker, "The Lower Depths," p. 19. It should be pointed out that this is not Hacker's view; he is underscoring the "solution" provided by the conservative trend.

81. Mike Davis, "Los Angeles: Civil Liberties between the Hammer and the Rock," *New Left Review* (July-August 1988): 47.

82. Ibid., p. 46. Interview with Harry Edwards was by Ken Kelly and appeared in the San Francisco *Focus* (March 1984): 100.

83. Rimer, "Yonkers Anguish," p. 7.

84. "Harvard Teacher Faces Drug Charges in Boston," *New York Times*, December 3, 1987, p. A20.

85. Brent Staples, "Black Men and Public Spaces," *Harper's*, December 1986, pp. 19–20.

86. Martin Laskin, "The Black Underclass: The Critical Factor in Achieving the Goal of Racial Integration and Equality" (seminar paper, Graduate Center of City University of New York, Spring 1988): 30. Mr. Laskin is a New Jersey resident and public school teacher.

87. See Michael Katz, *The Undeserving Poor: From the War on Poverty to the War on Welfare* (New York: Pantheon, 1989).

88. "The American Underclass," *Time*, August 29, 1977, p. 15.

89. Wilson, "The Ghetto Underclass," p. 7.

90. Ibid.

91. Ibid.

92. Auletta, *The Underclass*, p. 41; and Alan Wolfe, *Whose Keeper? Social Science and Moral Obligation* (Berkeley and Los Angeles: University of California Press, 1989).

93. Herbert Gans, "Deconstructing the Underclass," p. 277.

94. Leslie Inniss and Joe R. Feagin, "The Black 'Underclass' Ideology in Race Relations Analysis," *Social Justice* 16, no. 4 (Winter 1989): 13.

Chapter 6. Race-Class Connections

1. Statistical discrimination could, as I have indicated in the preceding chapter, incorporate reasoning in this direction; but those who argue along these lines rarely specify the factors that influence statistical discrimination. Moreover, it is usually applied primarily in the employment sphere.

2. To understand the role of race in discrimination against African-Americans and how it is fused with culture, see the adoption study by Sherrie A. Kossoudji, "Price and Prejudice: Culture's Role in Markets," in *The Question of Discrimination*, ed. Steven Shulman and William Darity, Jr. (Middletown, Conn.: Wesleyan University Press, 1989). She demonstrates how the "adoption market provides a unique arena for examining the

issues of race and prejudice because, on the supply side, characteristics other than race can be held constant" (p. 295). For an understanding of the differences between the burden of race and that of class, see Richard Sennett and Jonathan Cobb, *The Hidden Injuries of Class* (New York: Vintage, 1973), and Lillian Breslow Rubin, *Worlds of Pain* (New York: Basic Books, 1976).

3. "Martin Luther King Defines Black Power," *New York Times Magazine*, June 11, 1967, pp. 27, 99.

4. A. B. Spellman, "Interview with Malcolm X," *Monthly Review* 16, no. 1 (May 1964): 24.

5. Edward C. Banfield, *The Unheavenly City: The Nature and Future of Our Urban Crises* (Boston: Little, Brown, 1970), pp. 68–70, 73.

6. William Julius Wilson, *The Declining Significance of Race: Blacks and Changing American Institutions* (Chicago: University of Chicago Press, 1978).

7. Erik Olin Wright, *Class Structure and Income Distribution* (New York: Academic Press, 1979), p. 192.

8. Kenneth B. Clark, "The Role of Race," *New York Times Magazine*, October 5, 1980, p. 25.

9. Ibid.

10. Ibid., p. 27.

11. "Report Plays Down Class Division among Blacks," *New York Times*, August 2, 1983, p. A13.

12. "Children and Families in a Changing Society," Sarah Lawrence College, 1979.

13. "Excerpts from Jackson Appeal to Convention Delegates for Unity in Party," *New York Times*, July 18, 1984, p. A18. E.J. Dionne, Jr., *Why Americans Hate Politics* (New York: Simon and Schuster, 1991), p. 306.

14. Harry McPherson, "How Race Destroyed the Democratic Coalition," *New York Times*, October 28, 1988, p. A35.

15. For a critique of this mode of reasoning, see Raymond S. Franklin, "A Framework for the Analysis of Interurban Negro-White Economic Differentials," *Industrial and Labor Relations Review* 21, no. 3 (April 1968): 367–74.

16. Ralph E. Winter, "Productivity Debate Is Clouded by Problem of Measuring Its Lag," *Wall Street Journal*, October 13, 1980, p. 1; Stanley B. Henrici, "How Not to Measure Productivity," *New York Times*, March 7, 1982, p. 29; Harry Magdoff, "Measuring Productivity: The Economists' New Clothes," *The Nation*, May 27, 1982, pp. 359–61.

17. "East Harlem Triangle: A Sociological and Economic Study" (submitted to the Housing and Development Administration of New York City by the Social Dynamics Corporation, May 1968).

18. Leslie Inniss and Joe R. Feagin, "The Black 'Underclass' Ideology in Race Relations Analysis," *Social Justice* 16, no. 4 (Winter 1989): 21.

19. Orland Patterson, "Rethinking Black History," *Harvard Educational Review* 41, no. 3 (August 1971): 304.

20. Daniel Patrick Moynihan, "Memorandum to Nixon on the Status of Negroes, January 16, 1970." Printed in the *New York Times*, March 1, 1970, p. 69.

21. H.S. Terrel, "Wealth Accumulation of Black and White Families: The Empirical Evidence," *Journal of Finance*, proceedings (May 1971): 363. A 1986 study on wealth differences suggests a more extreme gap: Robert T. Kilborn, "Whites Own 10 Times the Assets Blacks Have, Census Study Finds," *New York Times*, July 19, 1986, pp. 1, 46; see also William O'Hare, *Wealth and Economic Status: A Perspective on Racial Inequity* (Washington, D.C.: Joint Center for Political Studies, 1983).

22. O'Hare, *Wealth and Economic Status*.

23. Peter Mieszkowski and Richard F. Syron, "Economic Explanation for Housing Segregation," New England Economic Review (November-December 1979): 33–34.

24. Ibid., p. 35.

25. Nathaniel C. Nash, "Panel Is Told of Race Pattern in Lending," New York Times, May 17, 1990, p. A19; Alan Finder, "Blacks Remain Shut out of Housing in White Areas," New York Times, March 13, 1989, p. B1.

26. Mieszkowski and Syron, "Housing Segregation," p. 36.

27. Larry Long and Diane DeAre, "Suburbanization of Blacks," American Demographics 3, no. 8 (September 1981): 16–24, 44; Philip L. Class, "The Process of Black Suburbanization," Urban Affairs Quarterly 14, no. 4 (June 1979): 405–24.

28. Mieszkowski and Syron, "Housing Segregation," p. 35.

29. This composite statement was derived from a number of white residents of Queens, N.Y., in the spring of 1971.

30. J. S. Fuerst, "Forest Hills, 12 Years Later," New York Times, September 24, 1983, p. 23.

31. "An End to Innocence," WCBS-TV Special Broadcast, Warren Wallace, producer/director, September 17, 1969.

32. Mieszkowski and Syron, "Housing Segregation," p. 35.

33. Ibid.

34. This was told to me by a Wayne State University graduate who was a department manager of a Sears Roebuck store in Detroit, Michigan, in 1981.

35. Raymond S. Franklin, "The Relative Economic Status of the Negro Male: An Econometric Study" (Ph.D. diss., University of California, Berkeley, 1966), pp. 69–113.

36. Gary S. Becker, The Economics of Discrimination, 2d ed. (Chicago: University of Chicago Press, 1971), chap. 3.

37. Frances Fox Piven and Richard H. Cloward, Regulating the Poor: The Future of Public Welfare (New York: Pantheon, 1971), p. 233.

38. See Franklin, "The Negro Male."

39. Elliot Liebow, Tally's Corner (Boston: Little, Brown, 1967).

40. Ntozake Shange, For Colored Girls Who Have Considered Suicide When the Rainbow Is Enuf: A Choreopoem (New York: Macmillan, 1977).

41. See Paula Giddings, When and Where I Enter: The Impact of Black Women on Race and Sex in America (New York: Bantam, 1984), pp. 52–53, 173, 284.

42. This position has been detailed in an extensive empirical study of the black family by William Julius Wilson and Kathryn M. Neckerman, "Poverty and Family Structure: The Widening Gap Between Evidence and Public Issues" (unpublished manuscript, February 1985).

43. Cynthia Fuchs Epstein, "Positive Effects of the Multiple Negative: Explaining the Success of Black Professional Women," in Changing Women in a Changing Society, ed. Joan Huber (Chicago: University of Chicago Press, 1973), p. 163.

44. "East Harlem Triangle: A Sociological and Economic Study." At one of the weekly staff meetings of the Triangle Association in 1967, Roy Innis, who was at that time involved in a Central Harlem research project, informed East Harlem Triangle black women staff members that "good women stay behind their men."

45. William A. Blakey, "Everybody Makes the Revolution," Civil Rights Digest 6, no. 3 (Spring 1974): 19.

46. Robert Staples, "The Myth of Black Macho: A Response to Angry Feminists," Black Scholar (March–April 1979): 24, 28, 29.

47. Michele Wallace, Black Macho and the Myth of the Black Superwoman (New York: Dial, 1979).

48. Calvin C. Hernton, *The Sexual Mountain and Black Women Writers* (New York: Anchor Books, 1990), chap. 1, pp. 1–36.

49. E. Yvonne Moss and Wornie L. Reed, "Stratification and Subordination: Change and Continuity in Race Relations," Trotter Institute Review (Summer 1990): 5; David T. Ellwood and Jonathan Crane, "Family Change among Black Americans: What Do We Know?" *Journal of Economic Perspectives* 4, no. 4 (Fall 1990): 67, 69.

50. Raymond S. Franklin, "Race and Class Attitudes among Adult Workers at UAW District-65" (a pilot survey of some UAW District-65 adult evening students conducted in spring of 1981).

51. Kenneth B. Noble, "One Approach to the Shortage of Men Is Sharing," *New York Times*, September 9, 1983, p. 84.

52. William Julius Wilson, *The Truly Disadvantaged: The Inner City, the Underclass, and Public Policy* (Chicago: University of Chicago Press, 1987), pp. 80–106.

53. For an empirical critique of the mismatch thesis, see Norman Fainstein, "The Underclass/Mismatch Hypothesis as an Explanation for Black Economic Deprivation," *Politics and Society* 15, no. 9 (1986–87): 403–52; for its defense, see Wilson, *The Truly Disadvantaged*, pp. 80–106.

54. Glenn Loury, "Wage Patterns among Blacks," *New York Times*, August 9, 1985, p. 2.

Chapter 7. City as Promise? Shades and Politics of Race, Class, and Gender

1. Thomas Byrne Edsall, *The New Politics of Inequality* (New York: Norton, 1984), chap. 1; also, Frances Fox Piven, "The American Democratic Party" (New York: unpublished paper, 1990); Harry McPherson, "How Race Destroyed the Democrats' Coalition," *New York Times*, October 28, 1990, p. A35.

2. One of Jesse Helms's TV commercials in his 1990 North Carolina senate race against Harvey Gantt, a black challenger, shows a white person crumpling a job rejection letter, accompanied by the following voice-over: "You needed that job and you were the best qualified. But they had to give it to a minority because of a racial quota. Is that really fair? . . . That makes the color of your skin more important than your qualifications"; "Subtle and Otherwise, Race Is Issue in North Carolina," *New York Times*, November 11, 1990, p. A19.

3. For the development of this thesis, see Barbara Ehrenreich, *Fear of Falling: The Inner Life of the Middle Class* (New York: Pantheon, 1989); Katherine S. Newman, *Falling from Grace: The Experience of Downward Mobility in the American Middle Class* (New York: Free Press, 1988).

4. Edsall, *New Politics*, chaps. 4 and 5.

5. Restated from Raymond S. Franklin and Solomon Resnik, *The Political Economy of Racism* (New York: Holt, Rinehart and Winston, 1973), pp. 259–64.

6. Regina Arnold, Paul J. Goldstein, Henry A. Brownstein, and Patrick J. Ryan, "Women, Drugs, and Violence: Female Homicide Victims and Perpetrators" (unpublished paper, New York, 1990).

7. William Julius Wilson, *The Truly Disadvantaged: The Inner City, the Underclass, and Public Policy* (Chicago: University of Chicago Press, 1987), p. 144.

8. William K. Tabb, *The Long Default: New York City and the Urban Fiscal Crisis* (New York: Monthly Review Press, 1982).

9. See "Brawling City: Chicago Political Rift Deepens, Worsening City's Many Problems," *Wall Street Journal*, August 6, 1984, pp. 1, 13.

10. Glenn C. Loury, "The Moral Quandary of the Black Community," *Public Interest*, no. 79 (Spring 1985): 19, 20, 21; see also Lena Williams, "Blacks Debating a Greater Stress on Self-Reliance Instead of Aid," *New York Times*, June 22, 1986, p. 24.

11. "Can Democrats Defy Decline?" *The Economist*, July 21, 1984, p. 11; see also John Hebers, "Shift in Strategy Is Sought on Cities," *New York Times*, June 22, 1986, p. 24.

12. "Can Democrats Defy Decline?" p. 11.

13. Richard McGahey, "Industrial Policy's Problem," *New York Times*, July 6, 1984, p. A23.

14. "Hearings before Subcommittee on Employment and Manpower," U.S. Senate, 88th Congress, 1st Session, September 20, 1963, part 5, pp. 1475–79.

15. "Resolved: Government Not the Solution; It Is the Problem," Channel 13, New York Public Television, September 10, 1990, 9-11 p.m.

16. William F. Buckley, Jr., *Gratitude: Reflections on What We Owe Our Country* (New York: Random House, 1990); also Albert O. Hirschman, *Shifting Involvements: Private Interest and Public Action* (Princeton, N.J.: Princeton University Press, 1982.)

17. For a theoretical discussion of the exit option to cope with disappointment, see Albert O. Hirschman, *Exit, Voice, and Loyalty* (Cambridge, Mass.: Harvard University Press, 1970).

18. See Lester Thurow, "A General Tendency toward Inequality" (Paper prepared for the American Economic Association meetings, December 1985). For a theoretical discussion of motivation and its relation to economic interests, see Amartya Sen, *On Ethics and Economics* (Oxford: Basil Blackwell, 1987).

19. For a broader discussion of attitudes toward the "undeserving" poor, see Michael B. Katz, *The Undeserving Poor: From the War on Poverty to the War on Welfare* (New York: Pantheon, 1989).

20. Lewis Hyde, *The Gift: Imagination and the Erotic Life of Property* (New York: Vintage Books, 1979), pp. 38–39.

21. A proposition developed some years ago by Otto Feinstein, professor of sociology, Wayne State University, Detroit.

22. For a more elaborate statement discussing fuller implications of the fragmentation and instrumentalization of community and family life that includes the work sphere, see Bertram Silverman and Raymond S. Franklin, "Workers and Affluence: The Limits of Liberalism" (paper presented at the Applied Social Science Association meetings, December 1986). The paper is part of a larger project by the same authors.

23. See Michael N. Danielson, *The Politics of Exclusion* (New York: Columbia University Press, 1976).

24. Brian J. L. Berry amd Katherine B. Smith, "A Closer Look: Chicago," *City* (January-February 1971): 38. Danielson, *Politics of Exclusion*, pp. 6–7.

25. Wilson, *The Truly Disadvantaged*. This, it should be pointed out, is not Wilson's main thesis; yet, scattered throughout his book is the suggestion that such a process occurs as a result of the structural dislocations taking place in central cities.

INDEX

Compiled by Eileen Quam and Theresa Wolner

Academy: disciplines in, 53; hierarchy in, 53; hiring blacks in, 82; and middle class, 51; post-WWII, 48; social sciences in, 53-56; specialists in, 52
Accommodation: of slaves, 23, 27, 29. *See also* Sambo personality type
Acheson, Dean: on discrimination and foreign relations, 2
Adoption: and IQ inheritance, 66; and racial prejudice, 174-75n
Affirmative action, xix, 5, 10, 11, 161n; AT&T and, 42-43; and black middle class, 12, 162n; contradictions of, 12; and inferiority, 12, 15; and minorities, 12, 15; as reverse discrimination, 12; success of, 12, 161n; and underclass growth, 114
Africa: black roots in, 18, 19, 65; racism in, xx; segregation in, 2
African-American studies programs, xiv, 9, 23
African-Americans: compared to other ethnic groups, 17, 66; discrimination against, 174n; on evolution, 97; population size dilemma of, 142-43; on race, xxiv; subordinate position of, ix, xiii, xxii, 64; in work sphere, 16
Aged: as minority, 15

Aggressiveness: of middle-management blacks, 83-84
AIDS: and black women, 104; and exploitation of blacks, 96
American Historical Association, xxvi
American Sociological Association, 171n
American Telephone and Telegraph Company, 165n; and affirmative action, 42-43
Ancestry: common, 45; multiple, 44
Anthropology and environmentalism, 47
Applied Social Science Association, 178n
Arrests: racial, 107, 108, 110
Asia: racism in, xx; segregation in, 2
Asian-Americans: economic success of, 14-15; as minority, 12; as oppressed, xxi, xxiv
Assailants: by race, 108, 110
AT&T. *See* American Telephone and Telegraph Company
Auletta, Ken: on underclass, 90
Authority: and personal empowerment, 70; reversing, 71
Automobile industry: employment policies in, 76-77
Autonomists, black, 59, 60, 63; on race, 67-68

Autonomy: and dependency, 34; in preslave black culture, 29
Awareness: of racial biases, 69

Backlash, 5, 8-18, 51, 52, 91, 111, 136, 159n
Banfield, Edward: on class/race, 119
Banks: and discrimination, 124
Baraka, Imamu Amiri: and Marxism-Leninism, 11
Becker, Gary S.: on economics of discrimination, xv-xvi, xviii, 78; on human capital, 57-58; on population ratios, 128
Bell, Derrick: on Sowell as spokesperson for white neoconservatives, 16
Bellow, Saul, xxv
Benedict, Ruth: on race, 47
Biological determinism, 48, 54
Biological racism, 56
Biological reductionism, 67
Biological scientism: misuse of, 68
Biology: and class subordination, 45, 55-56, 59; vs. environment, 44; and intelligence, 53, 54, 59, 68; and racism, 17, 41; vs. social science, 19, 68. See also Genetics; Heredity
Birmingham: desegregation in, 4-5
Birthrate: of poor vs. white middle class, 167n; and productivity, 167n
Black Family in Slavery and Freedom, The (Gutman), 29-30
Black-Jewish alliance, 9, 164n
Black Macho and the Myth of the Black Superwoman (Wallace), 131
Black movement: new directions for, 146-48
Black Muslim movement, 160n
Black Panther party, 111, 160n
Black population. See African-Americans
Black power, 4, 6-8; on black family, 19; emergence of, 5; on equal opportunity, 50; vs. integrationism, 142; on slave mentality, 29; Third World and, 9
Black studies programs. See African-American studies programs
Blacks. See African-Americans
Blakey, William: on black men vs. women, 130-31

Blassingame, John: on slave resistance, 29
Blassman, Bill, 93
Blue-collar workers: as threatened, 9, 94
Brazil: blackness in, 39
Brotherhood of Man (film): anthropological ideas in, 47
Brown v. Board of Education of Topeka (1954), 2, 3, 14, 47-48, 159n
Buckeye Neighborhood Nationalities Civic Association, 93-94
Burt, Cyril, 66
Bush, George: and civil rights, 18; as presidential candidate, xxvi
Busing: and backlash, 9, 15

Cab drivers: avoiding black customers, xiv
Cancer: as metaphor for underclass neighborhood, 100
Capitalism: black, 160n; and black power, 6, 7; vs. slavery, 31
Career ladders: and black/white workers, 73, 74
Caribbeaners: as oppressed, xxiv
Carmichael, Stokely, 6
Carter, Landon: on blacks, 38
Cashiers, black: perceptions of, 87
CBS news, 99
Center for the Study of Democratic Institutions (Claremont, Calif.), 166n
Character, black: assumptions about, 26-28, 39, 86
Chauvinism, xxiv, 17
Cities, 136-55; and integration, 9-10; poor in, 10, 11, 13; rebuilding, x, xxvii; structural dislocation in, 178n. See also Inner cities
City University of New York, xi, 158n, 162n
Civil Rights Act (1964), 5, 14
Civil rights bill (1990): Bush veto of, 18
Civil rights movement, ix, xxvii, 1-21, 84, 136; and bias of history, 23; legal basis of, 48
Civil Rights: Rhetoric or Reality? (Sowell), 14
Clark, Kenneth: on racism, 119-20
Class: commonality, 20; and cultural characteristics, 18; defined, xxiv; and

economics, xiii, xiv, 6, 13, 61; and environment, 61; as oppression, xix; politics of, 136-55; and scientific racism, 42-68. *See also* Race; Race-class relations

Class determinism, xiv, xvii-xx, xxii, 117; and environmentalists, 68. *See also* Class reductionism

Class interest: vs. self-interest, xviii

Class reductionism, ix, xix, 121; biological, 67, 168n; vs. culturalism, xx. *See also* Class determinism

Class subordination: and biology, 45, 55, 56, 59. *See also* Dominant-subordinate relations; Subordination

Cleveland, Ohio: Slovak neighborhood reaction to blacks, 92-94

Cognitive tests: and immigrants, 47, 67

Cold war, 2

Collective bargaining power: weakening of, xviii

College education: blacks acquiring, 10, 12

Color: as pejorative, 70

Color-blind policies, 13

Color Purple, The (Walker), 76, 131

Communism: international, 2

Community, 153-55; defined, 153

Community development, black: and black power, 6, 7

Compensatory education, 9, 46

Competition: and discrimination, 78; global, 137; and species survival, 45

Competitive logic, 78

Concentration camps: as infantilizing, 28

Conference on Cultural Change, 166n

Confessions of Nat Turner, The (Styron), 29

Congress for Racial Equality: and affirmative action, 161n

Congressional Liaison for the U.S. Commission on Civil Rights, 130

Connor, Eugene ("Bull"), 5

Conservatives: on civil rights movement, 1; on punishment of criminals, 111, 174n; on underclass, 113-14

Consumer: discrimination, 71-76, 86; market, xv, xxiv

Consumption capacities: communicating, xxiv-xxv, xxvii

CORE. *See* Congress for Racial Equality

Cosby Show, The (TV series), 88

Criminality, 100-103; and assumptions about blacks, 27; as "innate," 47, 111; and IQ, 111, 165n; punishment of, 111-13, 174n; statistics, 107-11

Cultural nationalism: and black power, 6, 7

Culturalism: and black autonomy, 63-64; vs. class reductionism, xx. *See also* Multiculturalism; Non-Eurocentric culturalism

Culture, black: as protection, 40

Darwin, Charles, 45

Darwinism, 97; and emancipation, 45; and race endowment, 46; social, 45; West Indian blacks and, 97

Dawson, Pearl: on criminality, 102

Declining Significance of Race, The (Wilson), 13, 127

Degeneracy, 46

Degler, Carl: on blackness in Brazil, 39

Democratic party: and black demands, 137; as divided, 136; and liberal welfare state, 136; 1984 convention, 120; and race-class tension, 20

Demonstrations: in South, 3-5

Denton, Herb: on black families, 101

Dependency: and autonomy, 34

Desegregation: de facto, 5; in southern cities, 4-5; of southern schools, 48

Determinism: biological, 48, 54. *See also* Class determinism

Developmental geneticists, 59, 60, 61-62, 68

Disabled: as minority, 15

Discrimination: and competition, 78; international, 2; nature of, xiii; and race, 20, 174n; and race-class interplay, xxiv; statistical, 170n, 174n; structure of, 69, 84; and tastes, xv-xvi, xviii; and underclass, 76-84, 171n; in work sphere, 162n. *See also* Economic discrimination

Dissociationism: among blacks, 123

Dominant class: and economics, xviii; and oppression, xix; racism determined by, xviii. *See also* Oppression; Subordination

Dominant-subordinate relations, x, xiv, xxiv, xxvi, xxvii; breaking down, 155; economics of, 21, 69-88, 117; and exceptionalism, 83; and policymaking, 13; and reverse authority, 71; structure of, 70. *See also* Subordination
Domination. *See* Dominant class; Dominant-subordinate relations
Double standard, 70, 84
Douglass, Frederick: on prejudice, 74
Downtown renewal, 143
Du Bois, W. E. B.: on black intelligentsia, 7; on black self, xxvi
Dukakis, Michael: as presidential candidate, xxvi, 89, 121
Duke, David, 17

Economic discrimination, xv-xvi, xviii-xix, xx, 50-51
Economics: and class, xiii, xiv, xviii, 6, 13, 61; and politics, 14
Economics of Discrimination, The (Becker), xv
Education, 152-53; remedial, 34
Edwards, Harry: on punishment of young drug peddlers, 111-12
Elizabethan attitude toward blacks, 37
Elkins, Stanley M.: influence of, 29; on slavery as evil, 28-29, 31
Ellison, Ralph, xxv
Emancipation: blacks' achievements since, 33-34; and Darwinism, 45
Employee: discrimination against, 76-78; harmony, 77
Employer discrimination, 78-84
Employment: guaranteed, 151; practices in large industries, 86, 87; rights, 138
Engerman, Stanley: on slavery, 30-32
Enslavement. *See* Slavery
Environmental issues, 150
Environmentalists, 43-44, 47; vs. biology, 44; and class, 61, 68; external, 59, 60-61; vs. hereditarians, 49; internal physiological, 59, 60, 62-63
Equal Employment Opportunity Commission: on discrimination, 170n
Equal opportunity, 50, 70, 81
Ethnic rivalry: on campuses, 9
Ethnic studies, 9

Eurocentrism, xxii
Europe: racism in, xx
Evolution. *See* Darwinism; Lamarckian evolutionism
Expertise: and respect, 75
Extended families: children in, 173n
Extinction: black, 45, 46

Family, black, 1, 8, 11, 19, 100-102, 153-55, 173n, 176n; diversity of, 120; pathology of, 28-29; problems in, 27; in slavery, 31; strength of, 29, 31
Farmer, James: on affirmative action, 161n
Fascism: racialist theories of, 47; war against, 2
Federal Reserve System; on segregation, 125
Feinstein, Otto, 178n
Feminism, black, 5. *See also* Women, black
Filipinos: as oppressed, xxiv
Fogel, Robert W.: on free market, 164n; on slavery, 30-32
Folklore, black: as protection, 40
For Colored Girls Who Have Considered Suicide When the Rainbow Is Enuf (Shange), 129-30
Foreign blacks, xxiii-xxiv
Foremen: vs. black workers, 81-82
Franklin, John Hope: on race and history, xxvi
Franklin, Margery B.: on IQ category system, 167n
Frazier, E. Franklin: on black families, 101
Free blacks: status of, 38
Free choice, 144-45; absence of in slavery, 25, 31
Free market, 164n
Friedman, Milton: and free choice, 144

Gans, Herbert: on black underclass, 115; on urban poor, 10
Gantt, Harvey: as Senate candidate, 177n
Gender: differences, xxvii; politics of, 136-55
General Motors, 169n
Geneticism, racial, 43
Geneticists: developmental, 59, 60, 61-62, 68

Genetics, xvii; and human capital, 58, 167n; and social influences, 46. *See also* Biology; Heredity

Genovese, Eugene: Marxism of, 32; on slavery, 30, 32-33

Ghettoization, xiv, 18, 137, 143; and community development, 7; as permanent, 141-42

Gibbs, Jewelle T.: on young black males, 95

Giddens, Anthony: on nature and man, 55

Government: role of in race-class relations, 148-49

Gutman, Herbert: on black family, 29, 31; on slavery, 29-30

Hacker, Andrew: on black crime, 107, 110

Haitians, xxiv

Helms, Jesse: and race as issue in senate campaign, 177n

Hereditarians, 56-58; biological, 43, 59; class, 56; vs. environmentalists, 49; IQ, 59-60, 64-67; on race, 46, 56, 67-68; racial biases of, 68

Heredity, 19; and intelligence, 42, 58-60. *See also* Biology; Genetics

Herrnstein, Richard: on inherited differences and social standing, 56-57, 64

Hiring: of black academics, 82; information denied to blacks, 81

Hirsch, Fred: on equal opportunity, 50; on positional goods, 49

Hispanics: birthrate of, 167n; as minority, 12, 15; as oppressed, xxi; race categorizing of, xxiii-xxiv

Historicism, xxi

History: justification of, 22; racist bias of, 23; reconstructing, 22, 23-24, 40; as social construction, 22

Horton, Willie, 89

Housing, 124-27, 134, 138, 154; access to, 124; appreciation with black owner, 125

Human capital, 57-58, 167n; and community development, 7; and genetics, 58, 167n; of individual, xvii, xviii

Huxley, Thomas: on Darwinism and emancipation, 45

Hyde, Lewis: on market and nonmarket spheres, 152

Immigrants: cognitive testing of, 47, 67

Income: of black women, 130; equity, 150-52, 155; of ethnic groups, 108; and productivity, 57-58; and SAT scores, 109, 110; status of black middle class, 127-28, 134, 140; and subordination, 80

Indentured servants. *See* Servants

Individualism: emphasis on, 88. *See also* Human capital; Rational individualism

Inferiority, black: and affirmative action, 12, 15; as "innate," 12, 44, 45, 68; and preferential treatment, 12; and white supremacy, 39

Inflation, 145

Inner cities: black poor in, 11, 13, 90, 97, 114-15; changing character of, 143-44; deterioration of, 143; revitalizing, 151

Innis, Roy: on black women, 176n

Insurance companies: and discrimination, 124

Integration, 9-11; black power vs., 142; and busing, 9, 15; disutility to whites, xv; in economic sphere, 13; in schools, 6; as threat, 100

Intellectuals: negative evaluation of, 166n

Intelligence: and biology, 53, 54, 59, 68; black, 42-43, 56; and environment, 42, 68; as hereditary, 42, 58, 60. *See also* IQ

Internal physiological environmentalists, 59, 60, 62-63

IQ, ix, xi, xxvii, 1; and biological determinism, 48, 54; category system, 167n; and class, 57; and crime, 111, 165n; differences between blacks/whites, 8-9, 35, 48, 49, 52, 54, 56, 59, 64, 69, 110; research, 43, 52; tests, 60, 66-67

IQ hereditarians. *See* Hereditarians; IQ

Jackson, Jesse, 99; political rise of, 20; as presidential candidate, xxvi, 121; on race and class, 120-21

Jacksonian era, 44

Japanese: racism of, xxiv
Jasko, Michael, 92-93
Jefferson, Thomas: on intellectual
    inferiority of blacks, 110
Jencks, Christopher: on underclass, 91
Jensen, Arthur: on compensatory use of
    resources, 46; on IQ differences, 8-9,
    66, 110
Jews: infantilizing of, 28
Jim Crow laws, 17, 96
Johnson, Lyndon Baines, 5
Jones, LeRoi. See Baraka, Imamu Amiri
Jordan, Winthrop D.: on origin of
    racism, 96
Jordon, Vernon: on black delinquents,
    101
Judeo-Christian discourse, xxi

Kennedy, John F.: and civil rights, 5, 160n
Kenya: African-Americans in, xxiv
Killingsworth, Charles: on race riots, 146
King, Martin Luther, Jr., 4, 5; on class, 19,
    118
Koreans: and racial slurs, xxiv

Labor market, xvi, xvii, xxiv, xxvii
Labov, William: on psycholinguistics, 63
Lamarckian evolutionism, 46
Language: and learning, 63
Laskin, Martin: on black underclass, 174n
Latin America: racism in, xx; slavery in,
    36
Latinos: as oppressed, xxiv; as
    underclass, 89
Layoffs: and inner-city problems, 143; of
    white/black workers, 81, 86
Learning styles: of black/white children,
    34, 63
Leisure: and slavery, 32
Lewis, Hylan G., xii
Lewis, John, 6
Liberals: on civil rights movement, 1; vs.
    conservatives, 138
Liebow, Elliot: on poor black men/
    women, 129
Literature, black: as protection, 40
Liverpool, England: inner-city problems
    in, 115
Looting: by blacks, xiv

Loury, Glenn C.: on black underclass,
    112
Lower class, black, xxvii;
    overrepresentation in, 87, 117-35, 139.
    See also Underclass, black
Lynchings: in South, 96

MacLeod, Jay: on black poor, 172n
Malcolm X, 5, 11, 160n; on race, 19, 118
Males, black, 94-95, 99, 102-4; vs. black
    female leaders, 130; class position of,
    128, 140; machismo of, 129; as
    "savage," 27, 96; white women and, 5
Management: and employee
    discrimination, 76-78
Managers, black: and promotion, 82
March on Washington (1963), 4, 5
Market capacity. See Consumer, market
Market choices. See Consumer, market
Market system: and discrimination, 34,
    80; virtues of, 10, 35
Marriage: black women and, 130, 131,
    132; market, 58
Marxism: black, xviii-xix; on class, xix,
    40, 61, 119; criticism of, xx; on race,
    40, 119; and racial discrimination, xvii-
    xviii; on slavery and productivity, 32,
    165n
Marxism-Leninism: on ownership vs.
    capitalism, 8, 11
Mass media: race-class dialogue in, xiii;
    on underclass, 98, 107
Master race: opposition to idea of, 2
Mayors: black, 143-44; Democratic, 146
Mechanisms: of racism, 69, 84-85
Medgar Evars College (Brooklyn), 99
Meritocracy: of middle class, 48-53, 56;
    syllogistic legitimization of, 56-57; use
    of word, 119, 166n
Microeconomics: and economic
    discrimination, xv
Microstimuli: of environment, 60
Middle class: and affirmative action, 12,
    162n; black, ix, x, xxvi, xxvii, 1, 6, 127-
    28, 139-40; discrimination in, 117-18;
    income status of, 127-28; meritocracy
    of, 48-53, 56; move from inner cities,
    11, 112-13; perceptions of, 91-98;
    post-WWII, 48; squeeze of, 137;

status anxiety of, 49, 51, 92; success
    of, 16; in work sphere, 13
Militants: blacks vs. white radicals, xiv.
    See also Supermilitant rhetoric
Minorities: and affirmative action, 12, 15;
    employment of, 170n; and identity, 9;
    international discrimination against, 2;
    and racial employment quotas, 177n
Mismatch thesis, 177n
Mississippi Summer Project (1964), 5
Montgomery bus boycott (1955), 3; effect
    in southern cities, 4
Moore, Alex, 101
Moral Majority: vs. scientific
    evolutionism, 97
Morrison, Toni, xxv
Moynihan, Daniel Patrick, 160n; on
    benign neglect, 8; on black family, 8,
    19, 28-29, 173n; influence of, 29
Muldor, Christopher: on black crime
    victims, 103
Multiculturalism, 17
Murray, Charles: on IQ, 165n
Music, black: as protection, 40

NAACP, 2, 3
Natal alienation: as element of slavery, 25
National Academy of the Sciences (U.S.),
    48
National Committee Against
    Discrimination in Housing, 124
National Industrial Conference Board,
    170n
National Urban League conference
    (1983), 120
Nationalism: black, 160n; cultural, 6, 7;
    religious, 160n; revolutionary, 6, 7-8;
    Third World, 2, 3
Native Americans: as minority, 15; as
    oppressed, xxi
Nativism: and cultural nationalism, 7
Natural selection, 45-46
Nature: vs. nurture, 58-68; vs. society, 55
Neighborhoods: downgraded, 154-55;
    images of black underclass in, 98-99
Neoconservatives, 10, 14, 16
Neutral class policies: vs. race-specific
    policies, 13
New Deal, 136
New racism, 120

Newby, Idus A.: on desegregation, 48
Nixon administration: academics support
    of, 52; on black capitalism, 160n; and
    white backlash, 8
Non-Eurocentric culturalism, ix, xiv,
    xx-xxii, 117
North Carolina: Senate campaign in,
    177n
Nurture: vs. nature, 58-68

Oppression, xxi, xxiv; and civil rights,
    14; class as, xix; and independence,
    64; and subordination, 46-47. See also
    Dominant class; Dominant-
    subordinate relations; Subordination
Organization of American Historians, xxvi
Ownership: and domination, xviii, 25;
    and economic power, 8, 11, 160n; and
    slavery, 25

Pan-African Congress, Sixth, 11
Parenting, black: problems of, 27
Parks, Rosa, 3
Passivity: of middle-management blacks,
    83
Paternalism: slavery and, 32-33
Patronage: and socialization, 75
Patterson, Orlando: on elements of
    slavery, 25-26
Peculiar Institution, The (Stampp), 28
Phillips, Ulrich: on slavery as benign, 26
Physical characteristics: and slavery, 26
Physioenvironmentalists. See
    Environmentalists; Internal
    physiological environmentalists
Plantation system: as training institution,
    26, 28. See also Slavery
Plessy v. Ferguson (1896), 3
Poetry, black: as protection, 40
Political Economy of Racism, The
    (Franklin and Resnik), xi
Polygenesis, 44; Darwin and, 45
Poor: as disadvantaged, 171n; hopeful
    struggle of, 172n; in inner cities, 11,
    13, 90, 97, 114-15; opportunities of,
    117; status of, 117; "undeserving,"
    178n; urban, 10. See also Lower class,
    black; Underclass, black
Positional goods: defined, 49; of middle
    class, 50; threat to, 51

Postindustrial society, 49, 56
Post-World War II, 2-6, 48, 84, 145
Poverty: slavery as, 25
Power: political vs. economic, 144
Powerlessness: as element of slavery, 25
Pragmatism: and black-white
    collaboration, 11
Preferential treatment, 5; of blacks as
    social justice, 162n; and inferiority/
    victimization, 12
Primacy, xiii; of class, xix; as race, xx
Prison populations, 109, 110
Privilege, 51
Productivity, xv, xvi, 85, 121; and
    birthrate, 167n; of black/white
    salespersons, 74; and income, 57-58;
    and inner-city problems, 143; and
    slavery, 32, 165n
Professional class: black, xiv, 73, 82, 86;
    black women in, 131; services of, 73;
    white, xiv, 73. See also Middle class
Profit: and discrimination, 78-79; and
    layoffs, 80-81; and subordination, 80
Promotion: and black managers, 82;
    denied to blacks, 81; in large
    industries, 86, 87
Psycholinguists: and black autonomy, 63
Psychologists: on environment, 47
Psychosexual discourse, xxi
Puerto Ricans: employment of, 170n; as
    oppressed, xxi
Puritanism, 34
PUSH for Excellence, Inc., 99, 173n

Queens College, 157n, 162n, 168n-69n
Queens, N.Y.: white residents of, 176n
Quotas: as racist, 119

Race: categorizing, xxi, xxiii; defined, xx;
    discrimination based on, 20, 174n;
    endowment, 46; and environment,
    44; ideology and African-Americans,
    xxiii, 38; politics of, 136-55;
    reductionism, 121; and
    socioeconomics, 18; and underclass,
    171n. See also Class; Race-class nexus
Race and History: Selected Essays, 1938-
    1988 (J. H. Franklin), xxvi
Race-class interactionism, 121-24

Race-class relations, xiii, xiv, xxvi, xxvii,
    1-2, 6, 11, 12, 18, 19-21, 58-68, 112,
    116, 121-35, 138-41, 144, 148-49, 175n
Races of Mankind (Benedict), 47
Racial geneticism. See Geneticism, racial
Racism: biological, 56; black, 169n;
    institutional, 69, 70, 169n; manifest
    forms of, 69, 84, 86; new, 120;
    perception of, 69-70; preslavery, 37;
    social, 20, 84. See also Scientific
    racism
Racist rhetoric, 96-97
Raintree Country (movie), 158n
Rational individualism, ix, xiv, xv-xvii,
    xviii, xx, xxii, 79, 117
Reagan, Ronald, 10, 13
Reconstruction, black, 46
Reductionism. See Biological
    reductionism; Class reductionism
Religious nationalism: Black Muslim
    movement as, 160n
Residential segregation, 124-27, 139. See
    also Housing
Resistance: by slaves, 23, 26, 29-30, 32,
    33, 34, 35; white, 1
Resnik, Solomon, xi
Respect: and expertise, 875
Reuther, Walter: on segregation, 2
Reverse discrimination, 119, 177n
Revolutionary nationalism: and black
    power, 6, 7-8
Roemer, John E.: on Marxist theory and
    racial discrimination, xvii-xviii
Roll, Jordan, Roll (Genovese), 30, 32-33
Rush, Bobby: on capitalism, 160n
Russians: intelligence of, 47

Sales: blacks in, 73-74
Sambo personality type, 28, 29
SAT scores, 56; and income, 109, 110
Savage: black male as, 27, 96
Scholars, black, xxvi; on individualism,
    88
Schooling: and job success, 49;
    problems of blacks, 27
Scientific discourse, xxi
Scientific IQism. See IQ
Scientific racism: in post-WWII period,
    48-53; and social class, 42-68
Scientists: as racially biased, 68

Segregation: de facto, 3, 4; as illegal, 4; international, 2; legal foundation of, 3; residential, 124-27, 139; social, 139
Self-help, 7, 99, 173n
Self-interest: vs. class interest, xviii; of employers, xviii
Separatists, 11
Servants: black vs. white, 36, 37
Service industries, 71-76, 87-88, 137, 169n
Shange, Ntozake: on black women, 129-30
Shockley, William: on race and genes, 57
Skills: and paying jobs, 122
Slave Community, The (Blassingame), 29
Slavery, 18, 19, 22-41; adaptive themes of, 30-33; as "benign," 23, 26-27, 30, 34, 35, 39; vs. capitalism, 31; coercion in, 30, 33; damage by, 30, 33, 34, 35; debate about, ix, 24, 26-28, 33, 34-39, 163n; defined, 25-26; economic origins of, 36; English attitude toward, 37; as evil, 23, 26, 28-29; as infantilizing, 28; in Latin America, 36; legacy of, x, xxvii, 1, 17, 21, 22, 23, 24, 31, 39, 69, 117; move to rural tenancy, 137; origins of, 36; vs. other exploitive systems, 25; as poverty, 25; and productivity, 32, 165n; as social holocaust, 24-25. See also Plantation system
Slavery: A Problem in American Institutional and Intellectual Life (Elkins), 28
Slaves: acommodation by, 23, 33; division among, 33; resistance of, 23, 26, 29-30, 32, 33, 34, 35
Small Business Administration, 7
Small businesses: and cheap labor, 80
SNCC. See Student Nonviolent Coordinating Committee
Social change: and business, 78
Social institutions: discriminatory practices by, 15
Social justice, 14, 162n; and equality, 59
Social racism, 20, 84
Social Science Research Council: on underclass, 171n
Social scientists, 19, 52, 56, 68, 167n; on IQ, 54; research of, 54-55; on underclass, 90, 91

Socialization: and patronage, 75
Society: vs. nature, 55
Sociobiology, 44
Sources: of racism, 69, 84, 85
South: demonstrations in, 3-5; desegregation in, 4-5, 48; industrialization of, 84; justification of slavery by, 38-39; lynching in, 96; Republicanization of, 136
Southern Christian Leadership Conference, 4, 6
Southern Historical Association, xxvi
Soviet Union: cold war with, 2
Sowell, Thomas: on civil rights movement, 14-17, 162n
Species: and ancestry, 44; survival of, 45
Stagflation: defined, 10
Stampp, Kenneth B.: on black/white servants, 36; on slavery, 28, 36
Stanford-Binet intelligence test, 47
Staples, Brent: on race-class entanglement, 112
Staples, Robert: on black males, 99, 131
Statistical discrimination, 170n, 174n
Stereotypes, 90, 98, 100, 169n
Stokes, Carl, 93, 94
Student Nonviolent Coordinating Committee, 4, 5; leadership, 6
Students: white radical, xiv
Styron, William: black writers' response to, 164n; influence of, 29; on slavery as evil, 28, 29
Subordinate-dominant relations. See Dominant-subordinate relations
Subordination, 3, 18, 71; and biology, 45, 55-56, 59; in jobs, 80, 81; in industries, 80; nature of, xxii; and oppression, 46-47; and profit, 80. See also Dominant class; Dominant-subordinate relations; Oppression
Suburbs: blacks in, 124-25; flight to, 124-25, 136; whites in, 143
Supermilitant rhetoric, 8
Supremacy. See White supremacy
Supreme Court, 3, 4, 47
Survival of the fittest, 45

Tally's Corner (Liebow), 129
Tanzer, Michael: on competitive logic, 79
Taxes: and inner-city problems, 143

Teenage pregnancy, 20, 96, 104-5
Terman, Lewis: on dullness as racial, 47
Territorial invasion: of southern
   demonstrations, 4; in white
   neighborhoods, 9
Tests. *See* Cognitive tests; IQ; SAT
   scores; Stanford-Binet intelligence
   test
Third World: and black power, 9;
   nationalism, 2, 3
Thurow, Lester, 55
Time magazine: on black underclass,
   98-99
Time on the Cross (Fogel and Engerman),
   30-32
Triangle Association, 176n
Truly Disadvantaged, The (Wilson), 11,
   132, 171n, 178n
Twins: mental ability studies of, 66

Underclass, black, x, xiv, xxvii, 1, 11,
   174n; and affirmative action, 162n; as
   class issue, 88; explanations of, 88,
   171n; and generalizations as racism,
   90; in inner cities, 11, 13, 90, 97, 114-
   15; overrepresentation in, 87; and
   population statistics, 91; problems in,
   27; and racial discrimination, 171n;
   threat of, ix; use of word, 171n; white
   images of, 89-116
Underclass: economic, 91; educational,
   91; moral, 91
Unemployment: and class, 64;
   differences for blacks/whites, 80, 86;
   and intelligence, 57; rates for blacks,
   80; rise of, 137
Unions, 118, 130, 141
University. *See* Academy
Updike, John, xxv
Upper class: discrimination in, 117-18
U.S. Commission on Civil Rights, 130

Values: developing, 149-50; master/slave
   shared, 26
Vazquez, Jesse M.: on black studies
   programs, 9
Victimization: and affirmative action, 12;
   of black men and women, 102-4
Victims of crimes: by race, 108, 110
Voting Rights Act (1965), 5

Walker, Alice: on black men/women,
   131; on dominance-subordination, 76,
   82
Wallace, Michele: on black men/women,
   131
War on Poverty, 5, 8, 136
Washington, Booker T.: and self-help
   motives, 99
Wealth, accumulation of, 124-27, 134
Welfare state, 136, 138, 145-46
Welfare system: dependency on, xvii, 10,
   18, 87, 92, 96, 98, 104-7, 113-14
West, Cornel: on black underclass, 95;
   on history of racism, xx-xxi
West Indian blacks: vs. African-
   Americans, 66; on class bias, xxiv;
   and Darwinism, 97
White Citizens Councils, 4
White-collar workers. *See* Middle class
White supremacy: as "biological
   destiny," 46; as biosocially
   determined, xxi; and black
   "inferiority," 39; liberation from, 7;
   and scientific racism, 43; and slavery
   as benign, 39; war against, 2
Williams, Eric: on origin of slavery, 36
Wilson, James Q.: on black character,
   27-28
Wilson, William Julius: on black family,
   176n; on class, 20, 119; on
   disadvantaged, 11, 171n; on
   discrimination, 20, 162n; on
   downgraded neighborhoods, 154-55;
   on equal incomes, 127; on
   marriageable black men, 132;
   neutrality thesis of, 13, 162n; on
   progress of blacks, 119; on race, 13,
   20; on structural dislocation in cities,
   178n
Women: and aggressiveness, 170n;
   discrimination against, 170n; as
   minority, 12, 15; and passivity, 170n
Women, black, 95-96, 104, 128-34, 140-41,
   196n; distribution of, 79; expectations
   of, 129, 140; historic legacy of, 130;
   income of, 130; and marriage, 130,
   131, 132; profile of, 131; and white
   men, 140-41
Women, white: and black men, 5

Workers: exploitation of, xviii-xix, xx;
and family life, 178n; minority, 170n;
racial discord among, xviii, xix
World War II. *See* Post-World War II
Wright, Erik Olin: on class reductionism,
xix

Young, Michael: on meritocracy of
British elite, 166n
Youth, black, 95, 101-2

Raymond Franklin is professor of economics and labor studies at Queens College—CUNY, professor of sociology at CUNY Graduate Center, and also the director of The Michael Harrington Center for Democratic Values and Social Change in New York City. He is the co-author (with Solomon Resnik) of *The Political Economy of Racism* (1973) and the author of *American Capitalism: Two Visions* (1977) and several articles on socialism and economics.